EXPLORING THE MA
FOR

CW01661621

Murder is often regarded as both the eas
courts are normally given discretion he
sentence is mandatory – indeterminat Since the crime and the punishment come as a 'package deal' this book looks at both the legal nature of the offence and at the current operation of the mandatory life sentence. Not only does the book adopt a critical approach, by assessing the strengths and weaknesses of the status quo, it also draws upon comparative material from both common and civil law jurisdictions in an attempt to provide a comprehensive exploration of these issues. The need for public confidence in the criminal justice system is particularly acute in the way it deals with the most serious homicides. In this book the authors report findings from the first systematic exploration of public attitudes to sentencing murder in this or any other common law jurisdiction. The picture of public opinion emerging from this recent large-scale nationwide qualitative and quantitative survey, funded by the Nuffield Foundation, is likely to surprise many, and will be of interest to all jurisdictions where the mandatory life sentence for murder has been questioned.

Exploring the Mandatory Life Sentence for Murder

Barry Mitchell
and
Julian V Roberts

·HART·
PUBLISHING

OXFORD AND PORTLAND, OREGON
2012

Published in the United Kingdom by Hart Publishing Ltd
16C Worcester Place, Oxford, OX1 2JW
Telephone: +44 (0)1865 517530
Fax: +44 (0)1865 510710
E-mail: mail@hartpub.co.uk
Website: http://www.hartpub.co.uk

Published in North America (US and Canada) by
Hart Publishing
c/o International Specialized Book Services
920 NE 58th Avenue, Suite 300
Portland, OR 97213-3786
USA
Tel: +1 503 287 3093 or toll-free: (1) 800 944 6190
Fax: +1 503 280 8832
E-mail: orders@isbs.com
Website: http://www.isbs.com

British Library Cataloguing in Publication Data
Data Available

ISBN: 978-1-84946-228-0

Typeset by Hope Services, Abingdon
Printed and bound in Great Britain by
MPG Books Ltd

FOREWORD

Ever since the abolition in 1965 of the death penalty for murder, the judiciary has persistently, but decorously urged Government and Parliament to reform both the law of murder and its mandatory penalty of life imprisonment. After pronouncements in numerous appellate cases, in which judges uniformally declared that reform could not properly be entertained in ad hoc decisions of courts in fact-specific appeals, the judicial disinclination to create a modernised law on culpable homicide has indicated the limits of the courts to reform the common law (as opposed to statutory criminal offences). Executive government is deafeningly silent. Thus there is a stalemate over reforming the law of murder, entrapped by the writings of Sir Edward Coke, four hundred years ago.

In 2004, the Law Commission, when reporting on the two partial defences of provocation and diminished responsibility referred to it, invited the Home Secretary (then the Minister responsible for criminal justice) to refer to it the whole subject of murder. Unfortunately, the ministerial response was hopelessly partial. The terms of reference to the Law Commission specifically precluded any review of the mandatory penalty, and furthermore restricted the remit by stating that there was to be no dismantling of the murder/manslaughter dichotomy. Given the straitjacket of the limited review, the Law Commission, in November 2006, produced a brave, but ultimately unavailing, attempt at clearing up what it aptly described as 'a mess'. It produced a three-tier classification, stripping off some cases from murder I into a lesser category of murder II (with an adjustment of the penalty from a mandatory life sentence to a maximum term of life imprisonment) and manslaughter in its present form. The Government rejected this solution of a three-tier substitute, and proceeded to amend, in the Coroners and Justice Act 2009, the law of provocation (introducing a stricter partial defence under the rubric of 'loss of self-control') and brought up-to-date psychiatric thinking in amending the partial defence of diminished responsibility. The new loss of self-control provision is itself a tortuous piece of legislation that puzzles judges, never mind confusing jurors.

As recently as 24 January 2011 (confirmed in the House of Lords on 9 March 2012) the Coalition Government announced in the House of Lords that it had no present plans to review the law of murder. And, apart from some minor adjustments to the provisions of Schedule 21 to the Criminal Justice Act 2003 (which set out the starting points for normal, mitigating and aggravating categories for the purpose of fixing the tariff for individual murderers before there can be any consideration of discharge from custody) no change in the law of murder, or, more emphatically, its penalty, is envisaged. All this official bumbledom and patchwork activity by the legislature is neatly analysed by the authors. If none of it is strictly new, it is painfully true. What is pleasantly new is the authors' empirical evidence of what the public really wants.

The second half of the book turns to new material about the state of knowledge and opinion about murder – which the media maddeningly and indiscriminately use as a label when reporting any violent and unnatural killing. Helpfully, the authors demonstrate how opinion polls over recent years have predictably failed to provide an adequate test of levels of public support for the mandatory life sentence. This experimental study, however restricted in its scope, is the more welcome if only for replacing the crude instrument of opinion polls. When it comes to their handling of key methodological issues, the authors would seem to put aside their role as social scientists, when turning their attention to what politicians believe, and how they act upon public opinion.

The authors do not stop at demonstrating, from their invaluable empirical evidence, the real complexity about the present, inflexible sentencing of murderers to the mandatory life sentence, and, moreover, the significant difference between general and considered opinion. They seek to provide the answer to the ensuing questions: 'So what?' and 'What next?' Hence, their prescription for the future penalty for murder is a ternary classification – first (rarely imposed, 'in the most serious cases') of life imprisonment without the benefit of parole (which is 'whole life', currently under judicial challenge on the basis that it contravenes the ECHR); second, life imprisonment with reviewable discharge from custody at the end of the minimum term (being the tariff fixed by the court of trial); and third, fixed terms of imprisonment, the last portion of which would be served on licence in the community. Faced with a more complete picture of public opinion on these matters and the consequential intellectual acrobatics needed to fit a sentencing classification to it, legislators might reasonably consider the rather more straightforward alternative of dropping the mandatory element altogether. The authors believe, however, that their ternary classification would avoid the current potential for injustice and, at the same time, properly accommodate well-established principles of the courts in sentencing all offenders. They claim merit for their solution on the grounds that it stands 'some chance of adoption by Parliament and acceptance by legal practitioners'; although neither of these attitudes is subjected to substantiation by way of evidence or reasoned argument.

But to return to the key empirical findings from this novel and penetrating research: support for the existing law in terms of public opinion is nowhere as strong or consistent as many politicians believe. And where there are grounds for claiming public support, it turns out to be grounded on a misconception and ignorance of current practice and outcomes. The public, in evaluating time spent in custody by prisoners, is almost invariably unaware of the effects of the licensing system. The sentence is generally thought, misconceptually, to end when the minimum term has been spent. More significantly, for an eventual parsimonious solution to the present muddle, there is evidence of strong public support for judicial discretion, even among those interviewed who believe that 'in general' judges are too lenient in passing sentence.

What happens next depends on whether politicians choose to react to a scientifically-derived description of public opinion, or one generalised by the media. Politicians should instinctively place reliance on the views of the judiciary, which is most closely involved in the administration of criminal justice, apart from having the practical experience of sentencing in cases of culpable homicide. In this extraordinarily taxing field of penal law, reliance on the wisdom of judges should not be seen by legislators as either a sign of weakness or of their incapacity to formulate sound systems of legal principle. Trial judges are effectively answerable to the appellate system for the sentencing of the individual offender for the instant criminal offence, as they do for every other criminal offence, including manslaughter and attempted murder.

Whenever it comes to bold and long-needed reform, Governments (of whatever political complexion) nowadays go in trepidation of the power of popular newspapers. Is it too much to ask of our policy-makers that they should hereafter pay less attention to the promptings of an unthinking media and rather more to the empirical evidence elicited by serious social science researchers, such as Professors Mitchell and Roberts?

Louis Blom-Cooper

ACKNOWLEDGEMENTS

The idea for this volume arose from a survey carried out in the summer of 2010 in England and Wales which examined public knowledge of, and attitudes towards, the mandatory sentence of life imprisonment for murder. The survey – the first of its sort either in this country or (as far as we are aware) elsewhere – cast serious doubts about the assumption that there is overwhelming public support for the current law. We would like to reiterate our thanks to various people who assisted and supported us in conducting that survey – to Nick Moon and colleagues at GfK/NOP and to the three-man Advisory Group – Professors Jeremy Horder (former Law Commissioner and now at King's College London) and Mike Hough (Birkbeck College London), and Mr Paul Mendelle QC – for their advice on methodological issues; to the armies of researchers who asked the survey questions and to the respondents who gave their time and goodwill by participating; and to the Nuffield Foundation for their generous funding of the survey.

In writing this volume we have been assisted by Mr George Mawhinney, postgraduate student in the Faculty of Law at the University of Oxford, in obtaining material relating to the sentencing of the most serious forms of homicide in other jurisdictions. In this regard, our thanks are also due to Ian Leader-Elliott, Emeritus Fellow, Faculty of Law, University of Adelaide, and to Professor Arieberg, Faculty of Law, Monash University. We have been assisted in obtaining useful statistical data by the National Offender Management Service at the Ministry of Justice.

Finally, we would like to offer our thanks to staff at Hart Publishing, especially Tom Adams, Mel Hamill and Rachel Turner, for their help and patience in preparing the manuscript.

CONTENTS

TABLE OF CASES

ENGLAND AND WALES

AUSTRALIA

CANADA

TABLE OF STATUTORY PROVISIONS

STATUTORY PROVISIONS

STATUTORY INSTRUMENTS

OTHER CODES

INTRODUCTION

Consider these four following criminal cases:

In 2008, a woman slipped into a hospital room where her severely disabled son lay comatose. She locked herself in the room for long enough to take his life. He had been hospitalised since suffering a tragic accident several years earlier.

Years earlier, a man finally acceded to the repeated wishes of his very seriously ill spouse, and took her life. She had been suffering for years from a terminal illness and was unable to take her own life.

The third case involved a man with a young daughter who suffered from a variety of debilitating illnesses which medical treatment had been unable to alleviate. Her father took her life in order to end her suffering.

Finally, Jim and Pete, two 16-year-old schoolboys, were walking home when they met Steve, also 16. Jim didn't like Steve, and they argued. A fight began, during which Jim pulled out a knife and stabbed Steve to death. Pete shouted to Jim 'Go on mate', but otherwise simply stood and watched, making no attempt to intervene. Jim and Pete were subsequently convicted of the murder of Steve.

Most people would probably regard these four people – the killers in the first three cases together with Pete in the fourth – as having performed an illegal act worthy of condemnation.[1] The first three were convicted of murder and sentenced to imprisonment for life,[2] and the fourth (Pete) could well be. But how many people would regard them as murderers? How many people would impose a sentence of life imprisonment which will end only at the death of the offender? All these cases arise because the law of murder in England and Wales defines these actions as murder and then imposes the same mandatory life sentence on all four offenders. These individuals will serve different periods in prison – reflecting their minimum terms – but all will carry the label of 'murderer' and the sentence of imprisonment for life for the remainder of their days. Are the interests of justice best served by these sentencing arrangements?

This book explores the mandatory life sentence in England and Wales, and its consequences for the offenders on whom this sentence is imposed.

[1] It is important to note that these three cases were not 'mercy killings' in the conventional or popular sense. The mother who took her own son's life did so despite medical opinion that he might recover at least some of his mental functions, and the daughter in the third case was not mortally ill – although she was subject to multiple disabilities and had been suffering from these for years.

[2] The first two cases occurred in England and Wales, the third in Canada, though the case would not be treated differently here. However, on these facts – taken from the Court of Appeal judgments in these three cases – the offenders would probably be sentenced to life imprisonment in all common law jurisdictions with the exception of the few where murder does not carry a mandatory life sentence.

OVERVIEW

What sentence is appropriate for offenders convicted of the most serious crime in the criminal calendar ? All offenders convicted of murder in this country are sentenced to life imprisonment, and the mandatory life sentence (hereafter MLS) is the focus of our research. We begin by describing the existing law, placing the sentencing provisions within a limited international context. This accomplished, we discuss findings from the first systematic empirical investigation of public knowledge of, and attitudes to sentencing murder.

THE ARGUMENT

Over the course of this volume we will advance the following arguments:

- The mandatory sentence of life imprisonment violates consensual and important sentencing principles of restraint and proportionality.
- Imposing the same sentence on all offenders convicted of murder results in mislabelling of crimes and offenders, and a loss of justice with respect to the most serious crimes.
- Sentencing arrangements should reflect the informed views of the community.[3]
- Retention of the mandatory life sentence has been justified by reference to the views of the public who, it has always been assumed, strongly support the MLS and oppose the use of any fixed-term alternatives but this representation of public opinion has never been tested empirically.
- Politicians and policy-makers have neglected to consider reform of the MLS out of concern for a public backlash if they are seen to propose alternatives to the MLS, or even to question the current sentencing arrangements.
- The public surveys to date which have posed questions about sentencing offenders convicted of murder have used an inappropriate methodology which misrepresents the true state of public opinion.
- Analysis of scientific public opinion evidence using a representative sample of the public and actual murder scenarios demonstrates that the public endorses a quite different sentencing model than that reflected in the current law of murder.
- The British public supports a model which would retain a life imprisonment sentence for the most serious cases of murder but which would replace the current MLS with long-term, definite sentences of custody for many less serious cases.

[3] By the word 'informed' we mean public opinion measured in an adequate manner – for example by asking the public to sentence in specific scenarios rather than asking them to punish categories of crime in the abstract (see Chapter 5 of this volume).

- The public appears to be less punitive than the law in relation to sentencing cases of murder where important mitigation exists – for example, when a parent takes the life of their child in order to terminate his or her suffering.
- There is very little public support for the imposition of an MLS in cases of 'joint enterprise' murder – where offenders who are convicted of murder despite their relatively peripheral involvement in the killing. The law with respect to joint enterprise murder is clearly at odds with community views.
- The current sentencing arrangements for murder create injustice and undermine public confidence – with no offsetting benefits in terms of crime control.
- A thorough review of the current arrangements is clearly necessary to devise a sentencing scheme which reflects proportionality in sentencing.
- Schedule 21 – which contains the statutory starting-points for murder laid down by Parliament – should be repealed and replaced by a regime which permits the imposition of natural life terms; discretionary life sentences (with periodic reviews by the Parole Board) and definite terms of custody which include the possibility of release on parole.
- Statutory reforms of murder sentencing provisions should be accompanied by a definitive sentencing guideline from the Sentencing Council of England and Wales. This guideline would follow the new guidelines format[4] created in 2011 with nine steps for courts to follow.

OVERVIEW OF THE VOLUME

Chapter one explores the current definition of murder in this country. Chapter two describes the origins of the mandatory life sentence for murder. In Chapter three we discuss the MLS in practice, addressing the question 'What does it mean to serve[5] a sentence of life imprisonment?' Having described the status quo in England and Wales we provide some brief comparative examples from other jurisdictions, including Canada and Australia. Chapter four summarises the arguments for and against the use of a mandatory life sentence.

The next three chapters (Chapters five to seven) report on our empirical findings relating to public opinion. We conducted quantitative and qualitative research in order to determine where the public stands on sentencing for murder. Chapter five begins by highlighting the relevance of public opinion for the debate over the punishment for murder and then describes the methodology. This chapter documents the misperceptions about sentencing for murder to which many people subscribe. Public levels of knowledge are compared to the reality as emerging from official sources. Chapter six presents the findings on public attitudes to sentencing based upon reactions to actual murder cases. Chapter seven discusses

[4] See Roberts and Rafferty (2011) and Ashworth (2011) for discussion and www.sentencingcouncil.org for examples of existing sentencing guidelines.

[5] A number of organisations have called for reform of the definition of murder and the sentencing provisions relating to this offence – see, most recently, the report of the HOMRAG (2011).

the relationship between public knowledge of murder trends and sentencing patterns, and attitudes towards punishing offenders convicted of murder. In the final chapter (Chapter eight) we draw together our arguments to propose a new sentencing regime for murder, one which is more principled, humane and closer to the views of the informed community.

Ultimately, our goal is to contribute to the on-going debate about the reform of homicide law in this and other common law jurisdictions.

1

Defining Murder and Other Forms of Criminal Homicide

In England and Wales whenever a person is convicted of murder the judge has no choice but to impose a sentence of life imprisonment (or equivalent).[1] We may therefore think of murder and the mandatory life sentence as a package deal; the one automatically goes with the other. Thus, although this book is primarily about the mandatory life sentence, it is necessary to begin by saying something about murder, about the acts that are regarded as not simply warranting but actually requiring a sentence of life imprisonment.[2] Murder is one of two principal conventional homicide offences recognised by the criminal law in England and Wales – the other being manslaughter – and the intention is that murder should encompass what are regarded as the most serious cases of unlawful killing, leaving manslaughter to capture those that are not quite so heinous.

OVERVIEW

This chapter examines how the law, both here and (briefly) in other jurisdictions, defines the most serious forms of criminal homicide and distinguishes them from less serious instances. We then consider some of the main criticisms of the current homicide law in England and Wales. Before embarking upon these tasks there are two preliminary issues to be addressed. These are: (a) how many crimes of homicide should be recognised by the law and how widely they should be defined; and (b) the related question of whether, assuming the law should recognise more than one offence, the crimes should reflect fundamentally different forms of wrongdoing or simply different grades of homicide.

[1] Those convicted of murder who are under 21 years of age at the date of conviction must be sentenced to 'custody for life' under s 93, *Powers of Criminal Courts (Sentencing) Act 2000*, whilst murderers under the age of 18 years when the murder was committed must be ordered to be 'detained at Her Majesty's pleasure', under s 90 of the 2000 Act. In either case, like life imprisonment the sentence is indeterminate.

[2] Readers who are familiar with the criminal law may like to pass over chapter 1 and proceed directly to chapter 2.

I. SOME PRELIMINARY CONSIDERATIONS

A. The Number and Scope of Offences

Whilst the very concept of 'the most serious homicides' suggests there must be other, less serious forms of unlawful killing, we might nevertheless conclude that, compared to other crimes, all criminal homicides are so serious that it would be undesirable to distinguish between them.[3] Two commentators have argued precisely that – that the law should replace murder and manslaughter with a single offence carrying a maximum (ie discretionary) penalty (see Morris and Blom-Cooper, 2011; Blom-Cooper and Morris, 2004).[4] But the view taken in the vast majority of (if not all) other jurisdictions is that criminal homicides vary so considerably in the degree of moral blameworthiness that the law should recognise two or more separate offences, usually with separate sentencing provisions for each crime.

Indeed, it is worth noting at this early stage that senior members of the judiciary in England and Wales have publically commented that the range of circumstances that fall within the legal definition of murder is vast and that some cases are markedly more heinous than others. Thus, for example:

> It is no longer true, if it was ever true, to say that murder as we now define it is necessarily the most heinous example of unlawful homicide; [5]

and

> Murder, as every practitioner of the law knows, though often described as one of the utmost heinousness, is not in fact necessarily so, but consists in a whole bundle of offences of vastly differing degrees of culpability, ranging from brutal, cynical and repeated offences like the so-called Moors murders to the almost venial, if objectively immoral, 'mercy killing' of a beloved partner.[6]

We have written this book on the basis that the better approach is for the law to adopt more than a single homicide offence. Nevertheless, the debate about whether creating a single homicide offence is preferable to legislating for multiple offences also draws our attention to an important issue about the definition of offences, namely their scope. A single offence encompassing all criminal homicides would clearly have to be so defined as to cover an enormously wide range of situations and circumstances. Traditionally, English law has been characterised by creating fairly broad definitions of crimes and then leaving it to the courts to determine just how they apply to different sets of facts. In this way the precise meaning and limits of the definitions are gradually revealed. Recently though,

[3] Although presumably the sentence might vary from one homicide to another.
[4] A similar view was expressed by Lord Kilbrandon in *DPP v Hyam* [1975] AC 55, 98.
[5] ibid, 98 (Lord Kilbrandon).
[6] *R v Howe et al* [1987] 2 WLR 568, 581 (Lord Hailsham).

there have been signs of a change in this respect, with the creation of narrower definitions of crimes which are clearly targeted at specific kinds of behaviour.

An example of this recent fashion in the context of homicide is the offence of causing or allowing the death of a child or vulnerable adult.[7] This offence was designed to address situations in which a child was being cared for by two or more adults (either or both of whom were probably the parents) and the child dies in circumstances in which it is unclear which of the carers was responsible for causing the death. The obvious danger of choosing narrower rather than broader definitions is that a situation might arise which we would want to fall within the scope of the offence but which fails to fulfil one element of the definition and thus falls outside its scope.

If a legal system adopts a general policy in favour of broadly defined crimes it is more likely that any given set of circumstances will fall within at least one of them. On the other hand, the more broadly offences are defined the more they tend to become vague, lacking a core definable character. The danger of this approach is that it undermines one of the basic principles of English criminal law, the principle of fair labelling, which implies that the nature and gravity of any crime should be reflected in its name and definition (eg Ashworth, 2010: 78–80).[8] This is clearly of particular significance to the current task – defining the most serious homicides; broader definitions are, for example, likely to permit a wide range of circumstances and contexts and of moral blameworthiness. The result is that sentences imposed in cases which lie at the lower end of this range will probably undermine the seriousness with which the crime is perceived by society. Indeed, as will be demonstrated later in this chapter, one of the long-standing criticisms of English homicide law is that the crime of murder, which is supposed to encompass the most serious forms of homicide, is in some respects defined too widely. Some defendants who are convicted of murder do not deserve anything like the same degree of moral censure and level of punishment as others. This, of course, frustrates the essential purpose of recognising separate crimes, and emphasises the importance of getting the offence definitions right in the first instance.

B. The Labelling Versus Grading Debate

In any jurisdiction criminal offences may be structured in either of two quite distinct ways. On the one hand, the law may decide to recognise a basic wrongdoing together with one or more aggravated forms of it. In England and Wales, for example, we could define the basic offence as 'murder' in which the essential wrongdoing is the deliberate killing of another human being. This could then be supplemented with 'aggravated murder' which would include more serious forms of the crime – for example, where the victim was especially vulnerable or where

[7] *Domestic Violence, Crime and Victims Act 2004*, s 5.

[8] Note that, as Ashworth reminds us, fair labelling is a principle, not an absolute imperative.

the killing was premeditated. In addition, a third offence – call it 'manslaughter' – might encompass cases where all the elements of murder were present but the killing had been provoked or where the defendant suffered from a mental illness or disorder at the time of the offence. In this way the law would be recognising a basic form of criminality (murder) along with more or less serious variations or *grades* of that basic crime.

On the other hand, the law might distinguish separate offences on the basis that each one represents a fundamentally different form of wrongdoing, so that the separate offences (wrongdoings) are *labelled* differently. The essential wrongfulness of the current crime of murder is that it is wrong to kill another human being. Antony Duff argues that what matters in murder is not simply the harm caused but also the way in which it is caused – it involves an 'attack on another's life' (Duff, 1990: 112–13). By contrast, although it appears to be simply a lesser form of murder, what is often described in English law as 'involuntary manslaughter' (outlined later in this chapter) is really concerned with a different kind of wrongdoing – ie, wrongfully *endangering* the life of another. In other words, it is not merely right to assert that murder is a more serious crime than manslaughter: rather it is that murder reflects a fundamentally different form of wrongdoing from manslaughter. William Wilson's contention that this latter structure is to be preferred on the ground that offences and offence labels should be linked to the 'social obligations that underscore them' (Wilson, 2000: 23) is persuasive.

II. THE LAW'S REFLECTION OF THE SERIOUSNESS OF HOMICIDES

Unsurprisingly, different jurisdictions – even different common law or different civil law jurisdictions – define offences of criminal homicide in different ways.[9] The way in which the more serious offences are distinguished from the lesser homicides varies from one jurisdiction to the next. In recent years there has been a good deal of debate about whether the basic structure of the substantive law in England and Wales – including offence definitions – should be revised (see, eg Law Commission, 2006). Reference has already been made to the debate about whether we should abandon the current distinction between the two principal offences, murder and manslaughter, and replace them with a single all-embracing crime carrying a single maximum penalty (presumably of life imprisonment) (Blom-Cooper and Morris, 2004).

Alternatively, we could retain the existing offences or replace them with a different set, the most serious of which may or may not attract a mandatory life sentence. Any change from the status quo would represent a significant departure from the approach that has been taken over more than 300 years, but it is worth acknowledging that the recognition of multiple offences dealing with unlawful

[9] Although equally unsurprisingly, there are some obvious similarities in the offences (and defences) of common law systems.

killing is atypical of the criminal law generally. Elsewhere in the criminal law of England and Wales separate crimes are recognised for each different form of harm or combination of harms. Thus, theft deals with dishonestly taking another person's property, whereas robbery criminalises the dishonest taking of another's property through the use or threat of violence.

A. Murder

Although on the face of it the law in England and Wales recognises a distinction between two principal crimes – murder and manslaughter – closer inspection reveals a more complex situation. In both instances, the defendant must have caused the death of another human being – someone who has been born[10] and not yet died.[11] This latter statement of the obvious is in fact quite important because there are further discrete offences such as unlawful abortion[12] and child destruction[13] that penalise harm done at a chronologically earlier stage than murder and manslaughter.[14]

Murder is meant to encapsulate the most serious kinds of criminal homicide and the law does this through a combination of two elements. First, it requires the prosecution to show that at the time of inflicting the fatal blow the defendant acted 'with malice aforethought'.[15] Although it seems that this phrase was originally construed according to the ordinary meaning of these words, the courts have subsequently interpreted it in a very technical, legal sense. Put simply, the defendant must have intended either to kill another human being or at the very least to cause serious injury to someone. There is now no need for the prosecution to show any 'malice' as we would normally interpret it, or evil or wicked intent; nor is there any requirement that the killing be premeditated.

B. Clarifying Intent

Given its significance to crimes such as murder, it is helpful at this point to briefly outline English law's interpretation of the concept of intent. There are essentially two quite distinct meanings. On the one hand, a person may be said in law to have intended a consequence if he desired that consequence to come about or if it was

[10] In essence, the victim is treated as capable of being murdered if s/he has 'an existence independent of its mother'; the child must have been wholly expelled from the mother's body and be alive; *R v Poulton* (1832) 5 C & P 329.

[11] The test of death is brain stem death: *Airedale NHS Trust v Bland* [1993] 1 AC 789; the civil case *Re A (a minor)* [1992] 3 Med LR 303; and Royal College of Physicians (1995).

[12] *Abortion Act 1967*, s 1 and the *Offences Against the Person Act 1861*, ss 58 and 59.

[13] *Infant Life (Preservation) Act 1929*, s 1.

[14] The commission of what might otherwise be a potentially fatal assault on a corpse might be evidence of an attempted murder.

[15] This term is derived from the definition of murder according to Sir Edward Coke; 3 *Inst* 47.

his aim or purpose to bring it about, even though he may have thought it very unlikely that the consequence would occur. This is probably a natural interpretation of intent. Alternatively – and perhaps less naturally – the court *may* conclude that the defendant intended a consequence if he foresaw that it was virtually certain or inevitable that it would happen, even though it was not his purpose to bring it about.[16]

This second interpretation of intent may be significant in cases where the defendant acts with a particular purpose but simultaneously recognises that there will be additional side-effects. For example, in *Hyam*[17] the defendant set fire to a house because she wanted to frighten a woman (who was her rival for a man's affections) into leaving the area. Tragically, two children were killed in the blaze, and she was charged with their murder. If those facts arose today this defendant should only be convicted of murder if the court concluded that although her primary purpose was to frighten, she nonetheless realised that it was inevitable that someone would be killed or seriously injured.

Unfortunately, with regard to the latter meaning of intent – intent arising through foresight of the consequences – although the jury should be satisfied that the defendant foresaw that death or serious harm was inevitable before they can infer that he intended to kill or cause serious harm, they are not obliged to make such a reference, and there is no specific advice to be given to them about how they should decide whether or not to make the inference.

C. Serious Injury

'Serious injury', which is the minimum degree of harm that the defendant must intend to be guilty of murder, may but need not amount to life-threatening harm. Thus, suppose X strikes you across the arm with a blunt instrument. Your arm is broken, as X intended, and you are taken to hospital where you undergo surgery to set the bone properly. But complications arise during surgery and you die. In the absence of any recognised defence, X is guilty of murder, even though neither he nor anyone would have expected you to die in those circumstances. Since we are prohibited by the *Contempt of Court Act 1981* from enquiring into the basis of the jury's verdict, we have no idea what proportion of murder convictions are based on an intent to kill as opposed to those based on intent to cause serious injury. The Lane Committee suggested that the majority of murder convictions are based on an intent to cause serious injury, but it is understood that that state-

[16] *R v Woollin* [1999] AC 82 (HL).

[17] The meaning of intent in law has changed since *Hyam*'s case was decided. The House of Lords in *Hyam* said that a person may intend to kill if s/he foresaw death as *highly probable* or *very likely.* But as explained in the text, the courts now say that such an intent may only be inferred if the defendant foresaw death as *virtually certain* or *inevitable.* In other words, a greater level of foresight is now required before the court can conclude there was an intent to kill (or cause serious harm).

ment was founded on judicial beliefs and perceptions rather than on scientific research and analysis (Prison Reform Trust, 1993).

D. Manslaughter

i. Involuntary Manslaughter

If the killer did not intend to kill or cause serious injury he is liable instead to be convicted of some form of what is called *involuntary manslaughter*, provided he nonetheless had some lesser degree of moral blameworthiness. There are almost certainly three distinct varieties of involuntary manslaughter,[18] namely:

a. The most common variety is known as killing 'by an unlawful and dangerous act'. The words 'unlawful act' effectively mean that the defendant must be committing some other criminal offence, in the course of which s/he causes the death of a person (who may or may not also be the victim of the other crime). Instead of having an intention to kill or cause serious injury, the defendant has some less morally culpable state of mind – more precisely, he has the knowledge or awareness that makes him guilty of the other (non-homicide) offence that he was committing, and he intended to commit the act which caused the victim's death. In addition, the commission of the other crime must have created a risk, apparent to any reasonable person (though not necessarily to the defendant), that some (albeit not serious) injury would be caused to someone.

   Thus, for example, if D throws a brick through the window of a house and the occupant subsequently dies from a heart attack caused by the shock, D may be guilty of unlawful and dangerous act manslaughter. By throwing the brick through the window and smashing it D has committed the crime of criminal damage to property provided he intended to break it or knowingly risked doing so. The prosecution would have to prove that the act of throwing the brick through the window created a risk which any reasonable person (though not necessarily D) would have recognised of causing some (albeit minor) harm. The only other mental element is that D intended to throw the brick through the window; D need not have appreciated that he was committing a crime or that his act was dangerous.
b. Arguably the most serious cases of involuntary manslaughter occur when the defendant's state of mind comes very close to that which would have made it murder – ie he fell just short of the necessary intent to kill or cause serious injury. These cases are known as 'reckless manslaughter' and seem to be relatively uncommon. The defendant is not certain that s/he will cause death or serious harm but foresees either as being very likely – ie the defendant did not quite foresee death or serious harm with the degree of certainty that is

[18] For an analysis of a sample of recent cases see Mitchell and Mackay (2011).

required for murder. It is also likely that many cases of reckless manslaughter will also constitute unlawful and dangerous act manslaughter.

c. A small number of cases result in conviction for 'gross negligence manslaughter'. These crimes occur where the defendant is committing what is essentially a lawful act but carries it out in an unlawful manner because s/he is grossly negligent. In other words, the standard of care displayed by the defendant fell far short of what could reasonably have been expected. Being negligent in the way that would suffice for a claim in the civil courts is not enough: the defendant must be grossly negligent. As well as falling a long way short of what might reasonably have been expected of him/her, the defendant's negligence must also have created a risk that someone would die as a consequence. Such cases may occur where the defendant is carrying out his trade or profession – for example, a doctor's gross negligence results in a patient's death.

ii. Voluntary Manslaughter

In addition to what has just been said, murder is also distinguished from a second category of manslaughters in a negative way. The court must be satisfied that there is no legally recognised mitigating circumstance or (partial) defence. Currently, the law recognises three such circumstances – (i) loss of self-control – when the defendant committed the fatal attack either the killer was provoked to lose his self-control by something done or said by another (usually the victim) or the killer acted out of fear of serious violence from the victim; (ii) diminished responsibility – the killer was suffering from an abnormality of mental functioning when he killed the victim; or (iii) the existence of a suicide pact – the killer had made an agreement with the victim that they should commit suicide, but the killer survived. If the defendant kills with the intent to kill or cause serious injury but in any one of these circumstances, he is liable to be convicted of *voluntary manslaughter.*

Homicide law in England and Wales thus represents a mixture of 'grading' and 'labelling'. The distinction between murder and involuntary manslaughter reflects a labelling approach – the wrongness in murder is that it is wrong to take the life of another individual, whereas involuntary manslaughter is concerned with the wrongful endangerment of life. On the other hand, the distinction between murder and voluntary manslaughter – the latter being a form of mitigated murder – is based on grading, since in both instances the defendant launches an attack on the victim's life.

E. Other Aggravating (and Mitigating) Factors and How to Reflect Them in the Law

The seriousness of a crime is usually assessed through a combination of the harm that is caused or threatened and the offender's personal moral blameworthiness (eg von Hirsch and Jareborg, 1991). Aside from the factors that constitute the current legal definitions of murder and manslaughter there are of course many other aggravating and mitigating features that may arguably influence our assessment of the seriousness of a homicide. Important but difficult decisions have to be made about how to reflect these factors in the law. All criminal justice systems have to decide whether any individual factor or combination of factors should influence the offence of which the accused is convicted, or instead be taken into account at the sentencing stage.

There is no immediately obvious right or wrong answer to this, and comparison of the laws in different jurisdictions reveals different approaches. Clearly though, it is desirable to identify some form of underlying rationale which would indicate how different factors should be reflected in the law. Offenders convicted of murder in England and Wales will all spend a period of time in prison, and in determining the length of this period judges are given statutory guidance that requires them to identify and assess the various aggravating and mitigating features. The majority of the factors that judges should consider relate to either the harm or the defendant's moral culpability, and in that respect they might have been reflected in the definition of the offence.

III. THE MOST SERIOUS FORMS OF CRIMINAL HOMICIDE AS DEFINED BY OTHER JURISDICTIONS

Other jurisdictions reflect a variety of approaches in the way in which they distinguish between the more and the less serious forms of criminal homicide. Those based on the common law tend to broadly follow the England and Wales model and seek to reflect variations in the seriousness of offences by reference to the killer's moral blameworthiness for causing the victim's death.

A. Homicide in Common Law Jurisdictions

Let us begin by looking at what is regarded as the most heinous forms of criminal homicide in two common law jurisdictions that have been influenced by the system in England and Wales.

i. Canada

The Canadian *Criminal Code* identifies four ways of committing murder which, as in England and Wales, is a more serious form of criminal homicide than manslaughter. Murder occurs where:

(1) The defendant kills another human being either (a) meaning to kill – ie it is the defendant's *purpose* to kill;[19] or (b) meaning to cause bodily harm that he

[19] This includes, for example, mercy killing, because motive is generally irrelevant to liability. It seems that Canadian courts have not addressed the issue whether it is also murder where the defendant

knows is likely to cause death and at the same time knows there is a risk that death may ensue;[20] or

(2) As in (1) but by accident or mistake the defendant causes the death of someone other than the person he meant to kill or harm; or

(3) There is some uncertainty about the third situation in which murder may be committed. The Canadian Code states that it may arise where the defendant kills someone whilst trying to commit some other serious crime. He either knows or ought to know that committing the other serious crime is likely to result in death, even though he may not have desired to kill anyone.[21] In pursuing the other serious crime the defendant must have committed an act that endangered life. However, in *Martineau*[22] the Supreme Court held that the defendant must foresee death to be guilty of murder and that anything less would be unconstitutional. This clearly casts serious doubts about the objective part (viz 'ought to know') of this version of the offence. In *Meiler*[23] the Ontario Court of Appeal stated that only the objective part was unconstitutional and the rest of the definition was valid. Thus, the law now is probably that the defendant must have done something that he knew was likely to cause death (though he may not have desired it). If the defendant lacks the necessary intent for murder he may be convicted of manslaughter.[24]

ii. Australia

In many respects, Australian criminal law seems to define the mental element in murder very similarly to the law in England and Wales, but there are important differences between them.[25] There are important distinctions in the different States (Leader-Elliot, 2007: 149), but as a general statement it may be said that Australian case law indicates that murder occurs where the defendant either intentionally or recklessly caused death or serious injury.[26] However, the concepts of intention and recklessness are not construed in the same way as in England and Wales. Intentional murder in Australian law is confined to cases where it is the defendant's *purpose* or *desire* to kill or cause serious injury. Reckless murder encompasses situations in which the defendant foresees death or serious injury,

foresees death etc as inevitable even though he does not aim to kill. But it has been suggested that if, for example, the defendant plants a bomb on a plane because he wants to collect the insurance whilst hoping not to kill the crew when the bomb explodes mid-flight, he would be convicted of murder. See Holland (2007).

[20] It has been held that once it is established that the defendant intentionally caused bodily harm knowing that death was likely, there is no need to add a requirement of recklessness as to death ensuing; see Cory J in *R v Nygaard* [1989] 2 SCR 1074.

[21] Criminal Code (RSC, 1985, C-46), s 229.

[22] *R v Martineau* [1990] 2 SCR 633, 58 CCC (3d) 353.

[23] *R v Meiler* (1999) 136 CCC (3d) 11 (Ont CA).

[24] Criminal Code, s 234.

[25] Valuable expositions of Australian criminal law relating to homicide can be found in Leader-Elliott (2007) and Yeo (1997).

[26] *R v Crabbe* (1985) 156 CLR 464.

stretching from envisaging the possibility of it arising to thinking that it will arise. So whereas in England and Wales the defendant may be said to have intended to cause death if he foresaw death as *inevitable* – he thought his act *would* result in death (even though he did not desire it) – Australian law recognises a wider definition of murder in that the defendant may be guilty even though he was less sure that he would cause death or serious injury – he merely foresaw that he *might* kill or seriously injure.

In addition, some Australian States also recognise a form of what is commonly called 'constructive murder'. Essentially, this arises where the defendant kills in the course of pursuing a separate form of illegal activity and liability for murder is 'constructed' therefrom. The law in Victoria and South Australia includes what is sometimes called 'escape-murder' or 'resisting arrest murder' – where the defendant kills whilst using violence in trying to resist, prevent or escape from, lawful arrest or custody. It is important to note here that the only elements of moral blame are that (1) the defendant must know that the deceased was some sort of officer in the justice system who was acting in the course of his duties as such; and (2) the defendant must have intended to resist, prevent or escape etc. Thus, this is a very different kind of murder from that described in the previous paragraph, and the fact that the defendant need not have intentionally or recklessly caused death or serious harm has led to calls for the law to be changed (Yeo, 1997: 91–2).

Victoria, South Australia, Queensland and New South Wales also recognise 'felony-murder', namely a murder committed during the commission of another crime. Sometimes the felony must contain an element of violence, but at other times it need not. Similarly, the seriousness of the felony varies between States, often because the range of felonies that suffice for this purpose is determined by reference to the sentences they attract, rather than the extent to which they necessarily involve the endangerment of life. Like 'escape-murder', the recognition of 'felony-murder' has been criticised for its lack of sufficient moral blame for killing. In both instances, this criticism does not ignore the significance of the context in which the deceased is killed; rather it seeks to emphasise that such cases do not deserve to be included amongst the most heinous homicides.

B. Civil Law Jurisdictions

The structure of homicide offences in civil law systems varies much more. In Italy, for example, the law recognises a basic or simple offence of intentional killing and then supplements that with various aggravated forms of it where certain specified factors are present. Predictably, the aggravated form attracts a more severe punishment. French penal law (Code pénal) is similar in that the presence of an aggravating factor can turn simple murder – 'meutre', which consists of intentional killing – into its aggravated counterpart, though in one instance, where the murder is premeditated, the offence is known as 'assassination'.

In Germany, the Strafgesetzbuch (Penal Code) also recognises a basic offence of intentional killing – 'totschlag' – which normally carries a sentence of between five and 15 years' imprisonment, though 'in especially serious' cases it may warrant life imprisonment. There is then a more serious offence – 'mord' – which is committed when the defendant intentionally kills another person for one of a variety of bad motives or in a manner that causes additional harm. 'Mord' carries a mandatory life sentence. Thus, in contrast to English law, the presence of an aggravating factor can not only increase the punishment, but it may also alter the nature of the conviction. There is also a further element of contrast. In England and Wales we put the presence of an intent to kill coupled with an *absence of mitigating factors* at the top of the hierarchy of offences, and then go down the hierarchy for cases where mitigation is present or there is less moral blameworthiness. In France, Germany and Italy on the other hand, intentional killing constitutes the basic offence, but the addition of aggravating factors points to a more serious offence.

Further details of the ways in which other jurisdictions deal with the most serious forms of criminal homicide are set out in Appendix A.

IV. THE OVER-INCLUSIVITY AND UNDER-INCLUSIVITY OF MURDER IN ENGLAND AND WALES

As commentators have often argued, the definition of murder in England and Wales is both under-inclusive because there are some cases which fall outside the definition even though they are widely regarded as particularly serious homicides, and over-inclusive because the law encompasses some cases as murder which are not generally viewed as being amongst the most serious.

A. Aspects of the Law that are Over-inclusive

i. The Meaning of Intent

Earlier in the chapter we explained that in England and Wales the jury may infer that the defendant intended to kill or cause serious injury if they conclude that s/he foresaw that death or serious injury would result, but there is no guidance that can be given to them as to whether they should or should not make such an inference (*Woollin*). The Court of Appeal has acknowledged that this makes life potentially very difficult for juries,[27] but the more crucial point here is that the uncertainty in the law which this ruling creates effectively provides juries with the opportunity to expand or contract the reach of the law of murder, and (of course) the accompanying mandatory life sentence.

[27] *Matthews and Alleyne* [2003] 2 Cr App R 30 (CA) 45 (Rix LJ)

ii. Intent to Cause Serious Harm

Somewhat controversially the law in England and Wales continues to allow an intent to cause serious, but quite possibly non-life-threatening, harm to suffice for murder – this is sometimes referred to as the 'gbh rule'.[28] It is comparatively rare to find other jurisdictions that also take the view that such an intention may provide sufficient moral blameworthiness for what are treated as the most serious forms of criminal homicide. In France and Germany, for example, there must be an intent to kill.[29] Even other common law jurisdictions which are heavily influenced by our own, have usually adopted a stricter approach. In Australia, some States do and some do not take the English approach.[30] In Canada, murder requires some further fault element in addition to an intent to cause serious injury.[31]

In favour of the gbh rule it is argued that when we act we cannot exercise absolute control over the consequences; there is almost inevitably an element of luck involved. Moreover, if we think of a hierarchy of harm, death is just one stage further up that hierarchy from serious injury. From a moral perspective therefore, it is said there is no significant difference between intending to kill and intending to cause serious injury. Conversely, it may be argued that non-life-threatening serious injury is very different from death. In the example given earlier in this chapter in which *X* strikes you across the arm with a blunt instrument, although all surgical operations carry an element of risk, your death during surgery on a broken arm was quite unexpected. Neither *X* nor anyone else would, in those circumstances, foresee that you would die, and it is not surprising that senior members of the judiciary have criticised the gbh rule in murder.[32]

It also clearly breaches the principle of correspondence – that a person should only be held criminally liable for those consequences which were foreseen or at the very least foreseeable (Ashworth, 2010: 245) – and what is supposed to represent the most serious forms of homicide should not be characterised in this way. Murder is meant to be reserved for the very worst kinds of homicide, and criminal homicides that do not fall into that category can be prosecuted as manslaughter, which potentially attracts the same sentence as murder. The fear is that by allowing an intent to cause non-life-threatening serious injury to suffice, the law effectively devalues the crime of murder and becomes self-defeating; the crime ceases to be seen to reflect the most serious cases.

[28] 'gbh' stands for 'grievous bodily harm', which the courts have construed as 'serious injury'. For a résumé of the arguments for and against the current law, see Law Commission (2005: paras 3.60–3.148).

[29] *Code Pénal*, Art 221-1; and *Strafgesetzbuch*, s 212.

[30] See the very useful table setting out the differences between States in Australia in Leader-Elliott (2007: 149)

[31] *Criminal Code*, s 229.

[32] See, for example, *Cunningham* [1982] AC 566, 582–3 (Lord Edmund-Davies); *R v Powell and Daniels; R v English* [1999] 1 AC 1, 11 (Lord Mustill); Lord Steyn in both *Powell* and in *Woollin* (n 16 above) 90.

Following a period of consultation, the Law Commission found that there is a widespread feeling that the gbh rule is an inadequate means of ensuring that the killer has necessarily committed one of the more serious forms of criminal homicide (Law Commission, 2006: para 1.18). That led the Commission to recommend tightening the current law by restricting what they called 'murder in the first degree' (ie what the Commission proposed as the most serious form of murder that would continue to attract a mandatory life sentence) to cases where the only alternative fault element (ie alternative to intent to kill) is intent to cause serious harm and awareness of the serious risk of causing death (ibid: paras 2.50, 9.5). Obviously, the two states of mind are not synonymous, but the Commission thought there is sufficient 'moral equivalence' between them (ibid: para 2.62).[33] This recommendation would keep the principle of correspondence intact and it would exclude cases where the intended serious harm was unlikely to be fatal. As such it appears to address the concern of commentators who have argued that those who intentionally attack others are morally responsible and accountable for the consequences even though those consequences may not have been foreseen, provided they are not out of proportion to the nature of the attack (Wilson, 2006: 475; and Horder, 1997).

Nevertheless, some concern may be expressed about this aspect of the Commission's recommendations. First, the decision not to offer a definition of 'serious injury' has been questioned by Ashworth (2007). Whilst the concept of 'serious harm' does not appear to have been especially problematic in practice, Ashworth rightly points out that as well as the natural desire for precision in such an important area of the law it would be vital, under the Commission's proposals, to distinguish clearly between first- and second-degree murder. Second-degree murder (which the Commission suggested would attract a discretionary life sentence) would include cases where the defendant intended non-serious injury whilst aware of the serious risk of causing death, so that the difference between serious and non-serious injury would be critical (ibid: 336).

Secondly, the use of the words 'serious risk' – as in the need for awareness of a serious risk of causing death – is ambiguous. Ashworth has suggested that it may be unwise to use the adjective a second time in the same phrase – intending *serious* injury whilst aware of a *serious* risk etc (ibid). The Commission were clear that 'serious' in this context should not be construed simply by reference to the degree of probability with which the risk might materialise;[34] rather it means the risk 'ought to be taken seriously' (Law Commission, 2006: para 3.36). But, as Ashworth comments, this might well be taken to imply that 'juries should be free to evaluate whether taking this degree of risk with someone's life might render the offence

[33] The Commission did not believe that 'people would see any significant moral difference between someone who repeatedly shoots or stabs another in the chest intending to kill and someone who does these self-same actions both intending to cause serious injury and aware of a serious risk of causing death' (Law Commission, 2006: para 2.61).

[34] Although they did say that it should be 'more than insignificant or remote' (Law Commission, 2006: para 3.40).

unworthy of the second-degree murder label and sufficient only for manslaughter'. In that case, some further guidance would be necessary to assist in the making of such a significant decision (Ashworth, 2010: 337).

Another concern must be the practicality of the Commission's proposal. How confident should we be that jurors could be persuaded so that they are sure the defendant had both the intent (to do one thing) and the awareness (of the risk of causing something different), and that his awareness was of a *serious* risk of death (rather than some lesser risk)? Whilst the Commission's proposal is clearly designed to address problems highlighted with the current law, it is rather lengthy and complicated, compared to many moral fault requirements. In the circumstances therefore, we might wonder whether it constitutes a sufficiently sound basis for distinguishing between the most serious form of criminal homicide (which currently attracts a mandatory life sentence), and one that is not quite so serious.

iii. Mercy Killing

The term 'mercy killing' tends to be used to describe a variety of situations in which the defendant deliberately kills his victim in order to prevent him/her from further suffering and in the belief that there is no prospect that the victim's suffering will end or even moderate. In theory, there is no doubt that in England and Wales those who commit such homicides, however genuine and compassionate their motives, are guilty of murder, because they intend to kill and there is no legally recognised (partial or complete) defence – such as compassionate killing – available to them. In practice, however, there frequently appears to be a strong desire that such people should be convicted of manslaughter rather than murder, partly because they do not deserve to be regarded as amongst the most heinous killers and thus do not merit the label 'murderer', but more importantly because they do not deserve a sentence of life imprisonment.

As Mackay notes, in cases of mercy killing the law relating to diminished responsibility may well be 'stretched' so as to fit the facts of the case. '[I]n order to achieve the desired outcome for the accused . . . there must be something of a benevolent conspiracy between the psychiatrist and the trial judge' (Mackay, 1995: 186, citing Bluglass, 1980: 10–11). The accused is psychiatrically examined in the hope that the medical experts will find some form of mental illness or disorder – for example, depression and/or post-traumatic stress disorder. The psychiatrists then present their reports supporting a plea of diminished responsibility – the defendant was suffering from a mental abnormality that substantially reduced his or her responsibility for the killing. Thus, the mercy killer is convicted of the lesser crime of manslaughter, and the court is given the discretion to impose what it regards as a much more proportionate sentence (which may not be a custodial one).

But this is a far from satisfactory situation, in which the law has to be stretched in order to avoid what is commonly regarded as an unjust outcome. Moreover, it is highly invidious that experts are placed under such pressure to prevent the law's inadequacies from producing an unfair outcome. Indeed, sometimes it proves impossible to do this – even if the terms of the diminished responsibility plea are stretched to the absolute limit there may be no possible means of assembling a defence on that basis. Predictably, therefore, some 'mercy killers' are convicted of murder and given a life sentence.

Although it is understood that the case was not presented as such at trial, *Cocker*[35] was surely a case that might have been an example of a mercy killing. The defendant had for 11 years been looking after his wife who suffered from an incurable and incapacitating disease. She had frequently told him that her life was not worth living and begged him to kill her. As her condition deteriorated her pleas to him increased. After a largely sleepless night she scratched him and swore at him, and he put his hands around her throat and then suffocated her with a pillow for about 30 seconds. She died from asphyxiation, and the defendant subsequently gave himself up to the police.

At his trial for murder there was no evidence to support diminished responsibility and the judge ruled there was no evidence of provocation. He was convicted of murder and leave to appeal was denied. The Court of Appeal took the view that the facts reflected the very antithesis of a loss of self-control – Cocker had deliberately agreed to carry out his wife's wish. It is interesting to note that one commentator on the case remarked that it was unfortunate that the court did not treat Cocker as having lost his self-restraint in the face of his wife's entreaties and that 'in a very real sense had ceased to be master of his mind when his will was overwhelmed by his wife's insistence on death'.[36] This point is obviously all the more pertinent given that current new law in the *Coroners and Justice Act 2009* (section 54(1)(c)) uses the word 'self-restraint' as synonymous with self-control.

B. Aspects of the Law that are Under-inclusive

Although it has been argued that a simple intent to cause serious injury should not per se suffice as the moral fault for the most serious forms of murder, it is equally arguable that relying solely on an intention to kill would similarly be inadequate. We therefore now turn to consider two kinds of homicide which currently fall outside the English definition of murder but which arguably ought to be brought within it.

i. Indifference to Life or Death

An alternative form of moral culpability to intent to kill that is not recognised in English criminal law but that is sometimes found in other jurisdictions focuses on

[35] *R v Cocker* [1989] Crim LR 740.
[36] ibid, 741.

the defendant's attitude about what happens to the victim. That is to say, it asks: 'was the defendant indifferent to whether the victim lived or died?'. Did he care in the sense that he would have acted differently had he known in advance that the victim would die? In its consultation paper the Law Commission had recommended that second-degree murder should include '[r]ecklessly indifferent killing, where the offender realised that his or her conduct involved an unjustified risk of killing, but pressed on with that conduct without caring whether or not death would result' (Law Commission, 2005: para 1.39). But the concept of 'reckless indifference' – along with the Scottish concept of 'wicked recklessness' – was criticised by consultees for its lack of sufficient precision, and the Commission accepted this and abandoned the recommendation (Law Commission, 2006: paras 2.105–2.116).

An alternative version of the concept is offered in the American Law Institute's *Model Penal Code*, which defines murder as including killing with 'recklessness under circumstances manifesting extreme indifference to the value of human life' (American Law Institute, 1980: s 202.2(1)(b)).[37] As Wilson commented, juries would probably 'characterise the defendant's recklessness as either murderous or not, according to the perceived degree of heinousness' (Wilson, 2007: 170). Against this it may be countered that it would be no bad thing to give juries the authority to decide precisely where in the hierarchy of homicide offences a particular case should sit. Granted there would be the obvious risk that different juries would return inconsistent verdicts, but is there not a case for having some means of correcting the law's imperfections? Yet Wilson is not persuaded by this: 'whether someone has committed murder is not a matter of simple moral judgement. It is a matter of satisfying an offence definition with a sufficiently high degree of specificity to justify the hugely symbolic label and the penalty range attached to it' (ibid).

Nevertheless, we should not abandon all hope of focusing on the defendant's indifference to the consequences: Wilson has suggested we can effectively do this but by more traditional means. His recommendation is that, as an alternative to intent to kill, murder (or the most serious form of criminal homicide) should arise where the defendant intended to expose the victim to the serious risk of death (ibid; Wilson, 2006: 479–80). One benefit of this is that it requires a victim and is thus consistent with the conceptualisation of murder as an attack on a person, emphasising that the essential wrong lies in killing a human being. It is important to be aware, though, that the 'intent' here should be confined to its narrower, everyday meaning of acting with the object or purpose of bringing about a consequence.[38]

[37] It is worth noting that, even at the time of writing their consultation paper, the Law Commission was concerned about the elasticity of such an evaluative concept, that it might give the scope to juries 'to use moral judgement in deciding after the fact whether the element was or was not present'. They might, for example, treat a killing as wickedly reckless or extremely indifferent 'simply because the victim happened to be a child' (Law Commission, 2005: para 3.165).

[38] The Law Commission did not feel that an intent to expose a person to the risk of death is morally distinguishable from foresight of the risk of death (Law Commission, 2005: paras 3.168–3.169). In reply, Wilson relies on the narrowness of the definition of intent.

Suppose, for example, a gunman wantonly shoots at a passing carriage or bus, or into a busy shop. Wilson's crucial point is that the gunman shoots 'for the sake of' the risk of death – if he knew the carriage or bus was empty he would not fire the gun. Contrast this with the dangerous driver who is aware of the risk of killing other road-users; he hopes the risk of death will not materialise, he drives *despite* the risk of death. The other benefit of this formulation is said to be its evidential advantage: instead of relying on the jury's 'gut feeling' that the defendant would not have acted differently had he known the outcome in advance (as would be necessary if the law was based on reckless indifference), Wilson's suggestion would 'require the jury to consider whether the defendant would have acted differently if he had known that there was *no* risk of death, for which the circumstantial evidence available *for or against*, is likely to be correspondingly stronger' (Wilson, 2007: 171).

ii. Murder in the Course of Other Serious Crime

Although a staunch advocate of recognising an intent to expose a person to a risk of mortal danger, alongside intent to kill, as appropriate fault elements for murder, Wilson accepts that that would still (albeit perhaps only occasionally) leave some of the most reprehensible killers guilty of manslaughter only. These are killers whose moral fault falls within the category of recklessness or gross negligence but the killing occurred in the context of committing another serious crime. By way of illustration he cites the Australian case of *Taber*[39] as an instance of a reckless killing attracting greater revulsion and indignation than some intentional killings.

The defendants robbed an elderly lady, bound and gagged her, and left her in her home deprived of food and water. She subsequently died from dehydration and suffocation. Evidence of a telephone call to the emergency services suggested that the defendants intended that she would be rescued. The trial judge directed the jury that they might be guilty of murder on the basis of reckless indifference, or of manslaughter through criminal negligence. If, as Wilson argued, intent is construed in its narrow (more natural) meaning as acting in order to bring about a consequence, Taber ought not to be convicted of murder, even if he did not care whether his victim lived or died. Such an outcome Wilson would find disagreeable, and so Wilson suggests that an additional category of cases meriting a murder label are those in which the defendant kills in the course of another serious crime (Wilson, 2006: 480).

We have already discussed cases in which murder is committed in the course of other serious crimes earlier in this chapter, and it is clear that Wilson's suggestion does not represent a radically new approach.[40] A key issue here is the minimum

[39] *R v Taber; R v Styman; R v Styman* (2002) 56 NSWLR 443.

[40] The concept of felony murders in jurisdictions such as the USA is undeniably characterised by less moral blameworthiness than the kind of murder-in-furtherance-of-serious-crime that commentators such as Wilson have in mind.

level of moral culpability that should be necessary in these cases. It seems that Wilson thinks that gross negligence rather than subjective recklessness as to causing death – which is favoured by Ashworth, for example (Ashworth, 2009: 248) – would be the appropriate fault element (Wilson, 2006: 480–81; Wilson, 2000: 52–3). The argument is that in the kinds of contexts in which the other serious crime is being committed – for example, a rapist briefly bereft of practical reasoning through lust or intoxication, or a robber high on adrenalin unaware of the dangers he is creating when firing warning shots at his pursuers – it would be unrealistic to expect the defendant to foresee the risk of death. The defendant's attitude is adequately expressed in his action. But that is not to imply a wholly objective test, for Wilson makes it clear that the fault element should be 'sensitive to the defendant's own capacities' (Wilson, 2006: 481).

Wilson is almost certainly right that many offenders (robbers or rapists etc) will not be thinking calmly and clearly, but it is arguable that requiring no more than gross negligence pitches the bar too low, given that the aim is to ensure that the law captures only those who display sufficient moral blame to merit conviction for the most serious forms of criminal homicide. The problem with Wilson's proposal is that it relies on aggregating the harm and culpability arising from the combination of the killing and the surrounding offence (the robbery or rape etc) for its justification. Arguably, cases in which the defendant kills a person through gross negligence in the course of some other serious crime would better be dealt with through prosecution for manslaughter and the other offence, and the totality of the harm and culpability reflected in the sentence. Conviction for murder – a truly uniquely heinous crime – should only occur where the defendant's *culpability for causing death* is high, and that clearly implies that awareness at least of the likelihood of death should be the minimum requirement.

V. CONCLUSIONS

Identifying the most serious forms of criminal homicide is almost certainly more difficult than might initially be expected. It is obvious that there are significant variations in the way in which different jurisdictions distinguish between the most serious and the less serious homicides. A review of current thinking suggests there is no single scenario or 'type' of murder that is undeniably and widely regarded as more serious than the others.

Any criminal or penal system must obviously make some fundamental decisions about how it wants to approach the issue of sentencing those who unlawfully kill their fellow human beings. All the systems that we are aware of take the view that recognising a single crime that encompasses all criminal homicides is inappropriate, because the circumstances and moral culpability vary so significantly that it would embrace too wide a spectrum of conduct. Thus, the issue is how we should distinguish between criminal homicides, and that is a potentially complex undertaking. First, we need to think about how far we want to distinguish on the basis of different forms of wrongdoing, as opposed to simply distinguishing on the basis of seriousness. In addition, we need to think about the breadth of individual offences – how far we want each definition to stretch. That in itself also means we must decide how much scope or discretion should be left by the definition for the courts to determine the precise limits of the offence.

It is difficult to criticise English criminal law insofar as it seeks to stress the importance of the killer's moral blameworthiness for causing the victim's death, but there are good reasons to argue that the current legal definition does not adequately encapsulate the most serious cases. It is to be hoped therefore that the government will address this in the near future.

2

Origins of the Mandatory Life Sentence for Murder

OVERVIEW

Having grappled with the problem of trying to define the most serious forms of criminal homicide, we turn in this and the next chapter to examine the sentencing of offenders convicted of murder. This chapter provides background context, explaining how the current sentencing law – namely, a mandatory sentence of life imprisonment – came about. The following chapter then looks at the way in which the sentence is operated in England and Wales and makes some limited comparisons with sentencing provisions for murder in other jurisdictions.

I. THE ABOLITION OF THE DEATH PENALTY

A. Before the Homicide Act 1957

The law that presently governs the sentencing of convicted murderers in England and Wales is a relatively recent one, originating in 1957. Before this date the sentence for murder was automatically the death penalty, death being brought about by hanging. Historically, the death penalty was a common feature of our sentencing law, and concerns about whether it really was necessary or desirable only became apparent during the eighteenth century. Even at that time, and in something of a contrast with the situation in continental Europe, there seemed to be a good deal of support for capital punishment across a range of crimes, some of which were not particularly serious by today's standards. Gradually though, in the early part of the nineteenth century the execution of offenders for relatively minor crimes was increasingly regarded as unjustified. More significantly for the criminal justice system, juries began to refuse to convict defendants for lesser offences so as to avoid the death sentence being imposed.

The principal rationale behind the death penalty was always its alleged deterrent effect, and its supporters claimed that its abolition would lead to an increase in crime. But in fact during the nineteenth century the crime rate generally fell. By the start of Queen Victoria's reign in 1837 the number of capital crimes was drastically reduced, from 220 to 15, and it was further reduced to four (viz murder, piracy with violence, treason, and arson in the royal dockyards) over the following 20 years or so. Indeed, by the second half of the nineteenth century the death penalty was, in practice, largely confined to murder. At this time there was a widespread appreciation that whilst all murders were serious, some were much more serious than others – compare carefully planned and deliberate killings with murders committed in the heat of passion or on sudden impulse. So, unsurprisingly, there was a growing school of thought that argued against an automatic death penalty, if only because some prospective murderers clearly would not be deterred by any sentence, whatever its severity.

Abolitionists and those who were not wholly wedded to retention of the death penalty began to see if distinctions could be made in the substantive homicide law; some considered the law in the United States of America and Canada where degrees of murder[1] were recognised. Various initiatives were launched during the last 30 or 40 years of the nineteenth century but they all found it impossible to draft a new law of murder without creating innumerable anomalies. Notwithstanding this problem, and although the death penalty remained the mandatory sentence, in practice many convicted murderers were not executed. Instead, the jury recommended that the Home Secretary be merciful so that the offender was sentenced to life imprisonment. However, the Home Secretary's decision was taken in private and no reasons had to be given for it. In this way, the penal system in England and Wales adopted what has sometimes been described as 'the least bad solution' (Hollis, 1964: 14), but one that no one – abolitionist, retentionist or those somewhere in between – supported.

An all-party House of Commons Select Committee was set up in 1929 to review the matter, but its report the following year showed divisions of opinion broadly along party lines, with the only significant support for abolition coming from Labour members. Subsequently, in 1938 the government introduced a Criminal Justice Bill that would address a wide range of criminal procedure issues, although abolitionists failed to get a clause in it. Then the Second World War broke out and all questions of criminal law reform were suspended till the war was over. In the 1947–48 parliamentary session the then Labour government introduced another Criminal Justice Bill. A motion to insert an abolition clause was narrowly carried in the Commons and the Home Secretary announced that henceforth all murderers would be reprieved. But there were difficulties for the government. Abolition was not part of its policy: it was assumed that public opinion apparently strongly favoured retention of the death penalty; and the government was more interested in getting other aspects of the Bill on to the statute books. After the Lords rejected the abolition clause the government drafted a compromise clause that would retain the death penalty for some murders but not others. But the Lords rejected this as well, and the government accepted defeat in order that the rest of the Criminal Justice Bill could be enacted.

[1] For example, murder in the first and second degree where the former usually refers to the most serious cases with multiple aggravating features.

i. The Gowers Commission

A further dimension of the compromise approach adopted by the government in accepting defeat on the abolition clause so as to get the remainder of the Criminal Justice Bill onto the statute books in 1948 was the setting up of a Royal Commission under the chairmanship of Sir Ernest Gowers. This was surely designed to go some way towards compensating the abolitionists, although the Commission was impliedly forbidden from tackling the question of abolition of the death penalty directly.[2] Instead, its task was

> to consider and report whether liability under the criminal law in Great Britain to suffer capital punishment for murder should be limited or modified, and if so, to what extent and by what means, for how long and under what conditions a person who would otherwise have been liable to suffer capital punishment should be detained, and what changes in the existing law and the prison system would be required; and to inquire into and take account of the position in those countries whose experience and practice may throw light on these questions.

In effect, the Commission was being asked to consider the same issue that had already been addressed on previous occasions, namely whether murder could be categorised by degrees, or something very similar, so as to narrow the scope of the death penalty.

Among a range of conclusions and recommendations made by the Commission, some are particularly noteworthy. First, they rejected the proposals to divide murder into two degrees, to redefine murder more narrowly than it then was, although they did propose the abolition of the doctrine of 'constructive malice' (whereby killing in furtherance of certain serious crimes automatically constituted murder), and to give the judge the discretion to decide whether the death sentence or some lesser punishment should be imposed on a convicted murderer (Royal Commission on Capital Punishment, 1953: para 610). On the other hand, the Commission felt that, given the wider decision to retain capital punishment, the only way to eliminate the defects in the law would be to give discretion to the jury to decide whether there were sufficient extenuating circumstances to justify a lesser sentence. If that should prove unacceptable (because it would add a wholly new function to the role of the jury), nothing more could be done to limit the impact of the death penalty and the question of abolition would have to be reconsidered (ibid: para 611).

[2] In its report the Commission expressly recognised this – 'The natural construction of [our terms of reference] precludes us from considering whether the abolition of capital punishment would be desirable; and the Prime Minister (Mr Attlee) stated in the House of Commons that they were intended to have this effect'. Nevertheless, it is interesting to note that the report immediately goes on to say that 'we have not thought it necessary on this account to exclude all evidence tending to establish or to refute the proposition that capital punishment should be abolished; evidence relevant to this issue may often also be relevant to the question whether the existing scope of capital punishment should be restricted, and we have not attempted to draw nice distinctions in this field'. (Royal Commission on Capital Punishment, 1953: para 13).

With regard to the proposal to divide murder into two degrees – in a broadly similar fashion to murder as defined in the USA – the Commission approved the summary found in a Home Office memorandum: 'there are not in fact two classes of murder but an infinite variety of offences which shade off by degrees from the most atrocious to the most excusable'. The determination of the suitability of the death sentence in any given case is too complex to be shoehorned into a legal formula (ibid: para 498). One illustration used by the Commission was the suggestion that first-degree murder should require premeditation (with or without deliberation). Again, however, the Commission adopted the observations of a Home Office memorandum:

> Among the worst murders are some which are not premeditated, such as murders committed in connection with rape, or murders committed by criminals who are interrupted in some felonious enterprise and use violence without premeditation, but with a reckless disregard of the consequences to human life. Some of the murders for which the death penalty is most obviously inappropriate are premeditated, for example, so-called 'mercy' murders, suicide pacts and murders of children by mothers in pitiful circumstances not covered by the Infanticide Act.[3] There are also many murders where the killing is clearly intentional, unlawful, and unaccompanied by any mitigating circumstances, but where there is no evidence to show whether there was or was not premeditation. (ibid: para 500)

Furthermore, the courts would naturally have to decide the precise meaning of premeditation – its exact scope and limits – and that would ultimately be regarded as an impossible task. The Commission cited the interpretations given by various jurisdictions that revealed significant variations in what might be assumed to be a simple concept – for example, in Belgium, premeditation required the lapse of two or three hours between initial consideration of the act and its execution; whereas in many parts of the USA it implied no more than a few seconds.

Although it was seemingly impossible to satisfactorily distinguish those murders that merited the death sentence from those that did not, the Commission felt strongly that the offence encompassed such a broad range of circumstances and contexts that the provision of a single punishment constituted an 'outstanding defect of the law of murder (ibid: para 790.1). The use of the royal prerogative of mercy provided a means of minimising this defect, but it was nevertheless unsatisfactory. The existence of the Court of Criminal Appeal to correct any possible injustices arising out of decisions made in lower courts, implied that the use of the prerogative should be exceptional. Yet at that time, approximately half of all convicted murderers were in fact spared the gallows and sentenced instead to life imprisonment. Thus, the exercise of the prerogative was far from rare, and the Secretary of State effectively became another appeal court, although he reached

[3] The *Infanticide Act 1938* makes it an offence for a woman to kill her natural child under the age of 12 months where the balance of her mind was disturbed because she had not fully recovered from the effects of giving birth or because of the effects of lactation, and she will be punished as if convicted of manslaughter.

the decision in private and gave no explanation for his decisions. Not surprisingly, the Commission reported that 'to entrust so wide a discretion to the Executive, who cannot be effectively questioned about the manner of its exercise, does not fit into the constitutional framework of this country' (ibid: para 47). In addition, even in cases where the defendant was reprieved the death sentence was still initially passed and that was highly undesirable (ibid: para 48).

As to the question of who should decide whether the particular facts of a case warranted a lesser sentence, the Commission concluded that the responsibility for so doing was too great for a single individual.

> The sentence of death differs absolutely, not in degree, from any other sentence: and it would be wholly inconsistent with our traditional approach to such issues to lay on the shoulders of the Judge a responsibility so grave and so invidious. It is more in accord with the instinct of our people to entrust to the men and women of the jury a joint responsibility for decisions which will affect the life of the accused. The responsibility of the Secretary of State is heavy enough, but it is not so heavy as would be that of a Judge; for in our view there is a real distinction between a positive decision to impose the death penalty and a negative decision not to interfere with the death penalty automatically imposed by the law. (ibid: para 549)

Account was also taken of the experience of other jurisdictions where such an unfettered discretion is given to juries. The Commission accepted that the system in those jurisdictions seemed to work satisfactorily – the discretion not to impose the death sentence was not used by juries excessively or with unjustifiable leniency. It further accepted that giving juries this discretion would represent a significant change from our traditional view of their role in the criminal justice system, that it would place a real onus on them and that it ran the risk of inconsistency. But since capital punishment was being retained, the Commission felt that the most satisfactory solution was to let the jury decide (ibid: paras 594–95).

Perhaps the other noteworthy conclusion of the Commission concerned the function of the death penalty. Whilst acknowledging the expectation of the public that the penal system should and would exact retribution from offenders, it was argued that the dominant aim of capital punishment was deterrence. Yet, having considered much research material, especially from the USA, Australia and New Zealand, and comparing jurisdictions where the death penalty had been abolished with those in which it had been retained, the Commission concluded there was 'no clear evidence' that abolition was followed by 'any lasting increase' in the number of homicides and other crimes of violence (ibid: para 790.3). This undoubted questioning of the deterrent effect of capital punishment, taken in conjunction with the various other recommendations for reforming the law, was treated by some as implying that the only really satisfactory reform would require abolition of the death penalty (eg Hollis, 1964: 25).

ii. The Impact of High-Profiles Cases: Bentley, Evans *and* Ellis

Although in the early- and mid-1950s the Conservative party was in government it seems that there were some potentially significant changes in the political landscape. There were a number of relatively young Tory MPs who approached the issue of capital punishment with a more open mind than many of their predecessors or older colleagues. Some expressed support for abolition, and even some of the Tory 'old guard' began to express serious doubts about retention. It has been suggested (Hollis, 1964: 41–8; Blom-Cooper and Morris, 2004: 63; Morris and Blom-Cooper, 2011: 198) that, against this background, three high-profile cases that occurred at this time and which all resulted in executions and attracted a good deal of public reaction, probably also played a part in the legislative change that was shortly to begin.

In the first of these cases two teenagers, Derek Bentley (aged 19) and Christopher Craig (aged 16) broke into a warehouse in November 1952, and the police were called. Bentley was physically apprehended by a constable, PC Miles, and was offering no resistance. He was then alleged to have called out to Craig 'Let him have it Chris', whereupon Craig fired a gun, and PC Miles was killed. The words 'Let him have it' were clearly ambiguous: did they mean 'shoot him', or as Bentley's defence subsequently argued, did they mean 'hand over the gun'?

Both defendants were convicted of murder, Bentley on the basis that he had encouraged Craig to shoot and was thus an accomplice. But because of his youth Craig could not be sentenced to death. Bentley, on the other hand, was that bit older – just old enough to be hanged – even though he was mentally retarded. The jury had recommended that mercy be shown to him, and it was believed that the judge felt the same. Moreover, even though it was assumed at the time that offenders would be spared from the gallows whenever there was an element of doubt about the case – and here the ambiguity of Bentley's words was all too apparent[4] – the then Home Secretary, Sir David Maxwell-Fyfe, declined to do so, and Bentley was duly hanged. The reason for declining a reprieve is not known, though it may have been that the Home Secretary wanted to show support and reassurance to the police.[5]

Then came the notorious Timothy Evans and John Christie case. It started towards the end of 1949 when Evans confessed to the police that he had killed his wife and disposed of her body down the drain at their house in Rillington Place in London. His wife's body and that of his small child were subsequently found, although in the wash-house rather than the drain. Evans subsequently tried to withdraw his confession, but since no-one else was suspected of having committed the murders, Evans was convicted and executed. The principal evidence

[4] It is worth noting that Bentley was physically under arrest when he uttered these words and was offering no resistance.

[5] For a full discussion of the case see Yallop (1990). Interestingly, Bentley's conviction for murder was quite recently quashed by the Court of Appeal after the case had been referred to it by the Criminal Cases Review Commission; *R v Bentley (deceased)* [2001] 2 Cr App R 307.

against Evans came from Christie who lived in the same house, and at that time he was regarded as a reliable witness. A few years after Evans's trial, however, Christie himself fell under suspicion for murder. Six bodies, including that of his wife, were found in the house, and Christie confessed not only to killing these victims but also to killing Mrs Evans. Not surprisingly, Christie was then seen in a completely different light, and the possibility that in the same house had lived two men who both sought pleasure from killing was dismissed as fanciful.[6]

The third case involved Ruth Ellis who, in 1955, had been having an affair with Daniel Blakely when she shot him dead outside a London pub. She admitted doing so and having intended to do so as an act of revenge. Ellis had recently become pregnant and about three days before killing him she said he had hit her in the stomach, causing her to miscarry. The defence argued that as a consequence of this assault she had become so hysterical that she was not wholly responsible for her actions.[7] But she was convicted of murder and subsequently hanged.[8]

Each of these three cases produced a very strong and intense public reaction. For the first time, ordinary members of the public began to stop and think more carefully and in more detail at how the criminal justice system dealt with murder and with those who committed it. Many seemed to feel that the system was far from satisfactory, especially by leaving it to one individual whether to grant a reprieve[9] and without asking for any reasons for the decision. People also appeared to realise some crucial home-truths about the unreliability of verdicts – that even if the verdict appeared to accurately reflect the law, there might still be an injustice perpetrated. Even more crucially, they realised the obvious point that whereas in all other areas of the criminal law a wrongly convicted man could be pardoned and compensated so that to some extent the system could make good the injustice it had inflicted, there was nothing to be done when an innocent defendant had been wrongly executed.

B. The Homicide Act 1957

The Gowers Commission concluded that '[t]he outstanding defect of the law of murder is that it provides a single punishment for a crime widely varying in culpability' (Royal Commission, 1953: para 790.1), and that although this was mitigated by the use of the royal prerogative of mercy the situation was unsatisfactory. The Commission also made various recommendations to amend the substantive law, some of which are identified later in this section. Nevertheless, in the

6 For further reading on the case see, for example, Kennedy (1961) and Simpson (1978).

7 It is impossible to say whether she might have been able to rely on diminished responsibility had that defence been introduced into English law sooner than it was.

8 For further reading, see, for example, Hancock (1963) and Mark and Van den Bergh (1990).

9 It is worth noting here that recent survey research by Barry Mitchell found some public support for having a panel of judges presiding over murder trials (rather than a single judge as under the current system). The obvious preference was for an odd number of judges, so that if one judge had an 'off day' the others could redress the balance (Law Commission, 2005: 263).

immediate aftermath of the *Bentley and Craig*, *Evans* and *Christie*, and *Ellis* cases and the public reaction thereto, the Tory government remained predominantly in favour of capital punishment, and in November 1955 the then Home Secretary rejected the recommendations of the Gowers Commission. At the same time, the government was in a difficult position since some of its most prominent members, including the Home Secretary, were professed abolitionists. Furthermore, a senior member of the government and former Attorney-General led a group of Tory lawyers to produce a pamphlet. This document pleaded with the government to retain the death penalty but to accept the Gowers Commission's proposals to abolish constructive malice, to introduce a partial plea of diminished responsibility and to extend the partial defence of provocation (Inns of Court Conservative and Unionist Society, 1956).

The government decided to support these proposals and introduced a motion in the House of Commons. This motion was debated in February 1956 and was carried with nearly four times as many Tory MPs supporting it than had voted for abolition in 1948. Indeed, the motion was carried by just 31, so the votes of the Tory MPs were significant. This effectively created further embarrassment for the government which reacted by permitting ample parliamentary time and a free vote to consider a full abolitionist bill.

MPs were effectively divided into three groups – abolitionists, retentionists, and those who favoured abolition for some murders but not others. The Homicide Bill passed through the Commons but was then rejected by the Lords. But as time went by MPs and members of the House of Lords increasingly came to the view that whatever their own personal views it would be wrong to vote against the (perceived) will of the public, and the Homicide Bill of 1956 was passed without any real difficulty. Royal assent was granted on 21 March 1957.

As signalled earlier the Act made some changes to the substantive criminal law in England and Wales. It abolished constructive malice – whereby killing in the furtherance of certain serious offences automatically constituted murder (*Homicide Act 1957*, section 1). It introduced the partial defence of diminished responsibility to murder, which effectively provided certain mentally abnormal killers with the possibility to reduce their liability to manslaughter (section 2).[10] It expanded the provocation plea – the other main partial defence to murder – by including provocative words as well as deeds (section 3). It also provided a third possible route to conviction for manslaughter rather than murder for survivors of a suicide pact (section 4).[11] Interestingly, though, as Hollis commented, in the period after the Homicide Act, a time when most types of crime were increasing, there was no obvious change in the murder rate (Hollis, 1964: 57).

[10] It is worth noting here that Scottish law already recognised a plea of diminished responsibility which, if successful, reduced the defendant's liability from murder to culpable homicide.

[11] A suicide pact is an agreement between two or more people that they should all die.

i. Emergence of Categories of Murder

But arguably the most significant provision in the Act for our present purposes was section 5, subsection (1) of which identified specific types of murder that should continue to attract the death penalty. These were:

(a) any murder done in the course or furtherance of theft;
(b) any murder by shooting or by causing an explosion;
(c) any murder done in the course of or for the purpose of resisting or avoiding or preventing a lawful arrest, or of effecting or assisting an escape or rescue from legal custody;
(d) any murder of a police officer acting in the execution of his duty or of a person assisting a police officer so acting;
(e) in the case of a person who was a prisoner at the time when he did or was a party to the murder, any murder of a prison officer acting in the execution of his duty or of a person assisting a prison officer so acting.

By section 6(1) of the Act those convicted of murder with a previous conviction for the same offence also continued to automatically receive the death sentence. But all other ('non-capital') convicted murderers would henceforth escape the gallows (*Homicide Act 1957*, section 7).

Given that the idea of distinguishing between categories (capital and non-capital) of murder had previously been rejected as unwise, it may seem odd that the government pressed ahead with section 5, which identifies forms of murder. But the government was in a difficult position. The vast majority of the public were thought to have traditionally been in favour of capital punishment for murder yet recent cases such as *Bentley*, *Evans* and *Ellis* prompted public disquiet with the way in which the system worked. Moreover, the dominant purpose of the 1957 Act was not so much to punish the most heinous murderers but to prevent the most deterrable murders (see also Hart, 1968: 60).

Sadly, but not surprisingly, the capital versus non-capital distinction under the Act proved far from satisfactory, both to lawyers and to the general public.[12] Not only were various murders that were widely regarded as particularly heinous, such as sexual or sadistic murders of children, placed in the 'less serious' category, but so too there was no apparent authority for the assumption in the Act that, for example, the poisoner was less easily deterred than the robber who shot his victim. Two commentators summed up the impact of the legislation thus: 'Quite apart from the uncertainties of interpretation that were never entirely absent from the minds of either judges or juries, the public increasingly perceived its workings as frequently capricious' (Blom-Cooper and Morris, 2004: 71).

Blom-Cooper and Morris rightly suggest that the case of *Vickers*[13] provides a useful illustration of the problems that the Act created. The defendant (aged 22) killed a 72-year old woman when she assaulted him as he was burgling her shop.

[12] Even though, in the years following its enactment, there was an apparent rise in the incidents of crime generally, the frequency of murder and manslaughter was relatively steady.

[13] *R v Vickers* [1957] 2 QB 664 (CA).

Her death was caused when he punched her and knocked her to the floor. He had wanted to steal money but left empty-handed. Vickers had one previous conviction, for theft, when aged 11. The forensic evidence suggested that no great force had been used in punching the deceased, clearly implying that Vickers had not intended to kill and even raising some doubt that he had really intended to cause serious harm. Nevertheless, he was convicted of murder in the furtherance of theft, and he became the first person after the 1957 Act came into force to be executed.

C. The *Murder (Abolition of Death Penalty) Act 1965*

There was undoubtedly more to be done in order to find a more satisfactory solution to the issue of the sentence for murder, and Sydney Silverman MP introduced a private member's bill that was supported by the government. The bill subsequently became the *Murder (Abolition of Death Penalty) Act 1965* and it marked the demise of capital punishment for murder. It is interesting to note that when the Bill was at the committee stage in the House of Lords the Lord Chief Justice, Lord Parker, succeeded in getting an amendment passed that would have given the judge the discretion to pass whatever sentence he thought appropriate to reflect the seriousness of the offence and the extent of public revulsion. This would obviously have brought the sentencing of murder into line with other serious offences (manslaughter, attempted murder, rape etc), but the government opposed it and in order to ensure that the bill was not lost – ie, to ensure that the death penalty was abolished – the amendment was abandoned.

By section 1(1) of the 1965 Act a mandatory sentence of life imprisonment replaced capital punishment for all offenders convicted of murder,[14] initially for a period of four or five years, but confirmed indefinitely by both Houses of Parliament in 1969. It is sometimes claimed by those who resist any change to the mandatory sentence that support for the abolition of the death penalty was only secured by a promise to put the mandatory life sentence in its place, and that any change to that would constitute an act of betrayal and be unacceptable.[15] Blom-Cooper and Morris (1996), however, note that no such compromise or understanding existed. They examined not only the parliamentary debates surrounding

[14] For the sake of completeness, those aged under 21 years at the date of conviction must be sentenced to 'custody for life': *Powers of Criminal Courts (Sentencing) Act 2000*, s 9. If section 61 of the *Criminal Justice and Courts Services Act 2000* is brought into force, the sentence of 'custody for life' would be abolished and replaced by life imprisonment. But offenders aged over 10 years but under 18 years when the offence was committed must be sentenced 'to be detained at Her Majesty's pleasure' under section 90 of the 2000 Act. Like life imprisonment, these are indeterminate sentences.

[15] As Blom-Cooper and Morris indicate, in December 1995 a Home Affairs Committee argued that abandonment of the mandatory life sentence 'would betray those who voted to abolish the death penalty in 1965 and 1969, as well as those who vote against its re-introduction on the understanding that that the life sentence for murder will continue to be mandatory' (Blom-Cooper and Morris, 2004: 94).

the 1965 Bill in both Houses but also the Cabinet papers during that period and found not a 'scintilla' of evidence to support the claim.

II. CONCLUSION

By 1965, therefore, the mandatory life sentence that exists today finally replaced the death penalty. The road to achieving this result had been long and arduous, and although the law had been changed, it has never been doubted that the debate over the most appropriate way to sentence convicted murderers would nevertheless continue. Divisions of opinion remained in the minds of both the public and politicians across the political spectrum.

In the next chapter we examine the way that the life sentence for murder has evolved in the intervening half-century or so and how it currently operates. Our primary concern will be with the way in which the sentence works in England and Wales, although some comparisons will be made with the system in other jurisdictions.

3

The Mandatory Life Sentence for Murder: the Status Quo

OVERVIEW

In the previous chapter we explained how the mandatory life sentence came to replace the death penalty for murder in England and Wales. In this chapter we describe the nature of the sentence, especially what is actually meant by a 'life sentence'. It is usual to think of it as divided into two principal stages. The first is a period of detention which reflects the seriousness of the particular case: at the expiry of this period the offender can then formally apply to be released into the community on licence – ie to move on to the second stage. This second stage lasts until the offender dies – the sentence never expires. In practice, most prisoners serving life for murder spend a lengthy period in prison and are then released under supervision. A small number, however, remain in prison for the rest of their natural lives, so for them there is effectively no second stage.

The chapter describes how the length of detention in prison is determined. Readers will be introduced to the relevant legal provisions and how they are interpreted. Life-sentence prisoners are normally then released into the community on licence – ie they are released under supervision – and the chapter will outline the sorts of conditions that are commonly stipulated for this purpose. If they breach the terms of the licence they are liable to be recalled to prison. Whilst the chapter is almost exclusively concerned with the operation of the sentence in England and Wales, limited comparisons will be made with other jurisdictions. Further details of the response of other jurisdictions to murder (or its equivalent) are provided in Appendix A.

I. THE EVOLUTION OF THE MANDATORY LIFE SENTENCE

In the second volume of his books *Responses to Crime* Lord Windlesham includes a chapter entitled 'Life Imprisonment: A Sentence Nobody Can Understand?' (Windlesham, 1993). The difficulty in understanding stems from the fact that even from the period before the Homicide Act 1957, when the Home Secretary reprieved some convicted murderers, a sentence of life imprisonment did not require the offender to be detained in custody for the remainder of his/her natural life. The latter part of the sentence was usually served outside any penal establishment and under supervision in the community. In that sense it has long been legally accurate to think of the mandatory sentence as consisting of two distinct stages, and the fact that the second stage would only terminate on the offender's death is reflected in the inclusion of the word 'life' in the sentence label. If the offender breaches the terms of the licence, it is liable to be revoked and the offender will be returned to prison. Further release on licence is possible, but equally it may be revoked again if the terms are not adhered to. The responsibility for deciding whether an offender should be released on licence and for recalling licensees to prison rests with the Home Secretary.[1]

The *Criminal Justice Act 1967* set up the Parole Board to which offenders had to formally apply for release. The Home Secretary could only order an offender to be released on licence if recommended to do so by the Parole Board,[2] but even if the Board did recommend release the Home Secretary was not obliged to implement the decision. If he did decide to do so, he first had to consult the Lord Chief Justice and (if available) the trial judge.[3]

Over the years, senior politicians have sought to shed light on the nature of the mandatory life sentence. Perhaps one of the relatively early and most useful indications is found in the statements made to the House of Commons in October 1983 by the then Home Secretary, Leon Brittan.[4] In setting out various new procedures relating to the management of life-sentence prisoners, he explained that the first stage of the sentence meant that the offender should be detained in custody for a period of time that was necessary to 'meet the requirements of retribution and deterrence'. This period was known as 'the tariff', though under the current law it is now called the 'minimum term'. The Home Secretary should, after consulting the judiciary, determine the earliest date at which the offender could first apply to have his case formally reviewed. This review should normally take place about three years before expiry of the tariff, so as to provide sufficient time for preparations for release on licence in the event that the Parole Board recommended release.[5] Mr Brittan added that for certain types of murder, such as the murders of police or prison officers, terrorist murders, sexual or sadistic murders of children, and murders by firearm in the course of robbery, the tariff would normally be at least 20 years or possibly longer.[6]

[1] By virtue of section 57 *Criminal Justice Act 1948*.

[2] Originally Part III *Criminal Justice Act 1967*, but repealed by the *Criminal Justice Act 1991*.

[3] Section 2 *Murder (Abolition of Death Penalty) Act 1965*.

[4] For written answers that provided the same information, see *Hansard*, HC, cols 505–508 (30 November 1983). The legality of this was confirmed by the House of Lords in *Re Findlay* [1985] AC 318.

[5] Offenders had to make a preliminary application to what was called the 'Local Review Committee' in their prison, and then to the Parole Board.

[6] The list of murders was not meant to be exhaustive. But it is interesting to note that regardless of the hitherto impossibility of satisfactorily distinguishing between capital and non-capital murders, senior politicians were still intent on formally categorising murders which merited a particularly severe punishment.

The second stage consists of release from custody into the community but under licence: in other words, the offender serves the remainder of the sentence outside prison but under supervision. Other than in truly exceptional cases, the offender must serve the tariff period in prison, at the expiry of which he can be released on licence. But the mere fact that the tariff period has expired does not automatically signal release: the offender's release on licence will only be sanctioned if there is no unacceptable risk to the public. Thus, whereas the first stage of the sentence is primarily concerned with punishment (and deterrence), the second stage is influenced by the need for public protection.

Other serious crimes such as manslaughter, rape and robbery may attract a discretionary sentence of life imprisonment – ie, life imprisonment is the maximum penalty that a court may impose. Since the courts had acknowledged the basic similarity in the two-stage structure of the mandatory and discretionary life sentences, one might expect that the right to a judicial determination of the length of the stages which had been granted to discretionary lifers[7] would also be available to their mandatory counterparts. But during a parliamentary debate on the Criminal Justice Bill in July 1991 the Minister of State, Angela Rumbold, drew a distinction between the two kinds of life sentence. She asserted that once a period of detention had passed so that the offender had been adequately punished, the decision to release a discretionary lifer was solely concerned with whether he continued to represent an unacceptable risk to the public. On the other hand, the issue of risk was not the main reason for imposing a mandatory sentence in murder. Rather, the offence was one of such seriousness that his liberty had been forfeited for the rest of his natural life. The obvious problem with this was that the Minister's statement clearly contradicted the way in which mandatory life sentences were being administered in practice.

Not surprisingly, in *Doody v Secretary of State for the Home Department and other appeals* where the House of Lords was dealing with the fairness of the tariff-fixing procedure at that time, Lord Mustill concluded that he should leave the Minister's statement 'entirely out of account'.[8] Although clearly critical of the Home Secretary's statement the House stopped short of declaring it unlawful. Nevertheless, it was still rather surprising that the then Home Secretary, Michael Howard, subsequently indicated that he intended to exercise his discretion on the basis of the distinction made by Angela Rumbold.

[7] See the European Court of Human Rights' decision in *Thynne, Wilson and Gunnell v UK* (1991) 13 EHRR 666.

[8] *Doody v Home Secretary* [1993] 3 All ER 92, 103.

II. THE LEGAL CONSTRUCTION OF THE MANDATORY LIFE SENTENCE

A. Fixing the Tariff/Minimum Term[9]

The Home Secretary of the day had long exercised a considerable influence over the ultimate fate of persons convicted of murder in England and Wales, but a significant change was brought about by the decision of the House of Lords in *R (Anderson and Taylor) v Secretary of State for the Home Department.*[10] Adopting the rationale of the Grand Chamber of the European Court of Human Rights in *Stafford v UK*[11] the House concluded that the Home Secretary's power to fix the tariff (now called the minimum term) in murder cases was incompatible with Article 6 of the Geneva Convention on Human Rights (the right to a fair trial).[12] Essentially, the argument was that the imposition of a sentence is part of the trial process and that fixing the tariff of a convicted murderer is indistinguishable from imposing a sentence. The tariff should thus be determined by an independent and impartial tribunal (in accordance with the wording of Article 6(1)), but the Home Secretary does not fulfil this requirement.

The minimum term is now fixed by the trial judge who states it in open court, in the defendant's presence and hearing. It is widely believed that at the time of the House of Lords' decision in *Anderson and Taylor* the Home Secretary of the day was deeply unhappy that the Executive had had this power taken away. It was therefore unsurprising that shortly afterwards the *Criminal Justice Act 2003* (CJA) made a major attempt to regain significant political influence over the punitive part of a mandatory life sentence. The relevant provisions came into force on 18 December 2003.[13]

There is no right of appeal against the setting by a judge of the minimum term, although the Attorney-General can refer a case to the Court of Appeal to have a minimum term reviewed. One potentially interesting issue is whether a minimum term is reducible in, say, cases where an offender makes exceptional progress whilst in prison. In the recent case of *Gill*[14] the Court of Appeal made it clear that

[9] 'Minimum term' is currently the correct term to use. It replaced 'tariff' which was historically the term used to denote the punitive part of a mandatory life sentence because there was a perceived need to make it clearer that release at the expiry of the punitive period is not automatic but depends on the Parole Board being satisfied that the risk to the public is sufficiently low.

[10] *R (Anderson and Taylor) v Home Secretary* [2003] 1 AC 837.

[11] *Stafford v UK* (2002) 35 EHRR 121.

[12] Article 6 states: '1. In the determination of his civil rights and obligations or of any criminal charge against him, everyone is entitled to a fair and public hearing within a reasonable time by an independent and impartial tribunal established by law. Judgment shall be pronounced publicly but the press and public may be excluded from all or part of the trial in the interest of morals, public order or national security in a democratic society, where the interests of juveniles or the protection of the private life of the parties so require, or to the extent strictly necessary in the opinion of the court in special circumstances where publicity would prejudice the interests of justice'.

[13] These *Criminal Justice Act 2003* provisions apply to all cases where the court imposes a mandatory sentence for murder (life imprisonment, custody for life, and detention at HM's pleasure).

[14] *R v Gill* [2011] EWCA Crim 2795.

offenders sentenced under the *Criminal Justice Act 2003* can only be released earlier than originally expected (ie before the minimum term has elapsed) under section 30 of the *Crime (Sentences) Act 1997*. This provision gives the Home Secretary the power to release a life-sentence prisoner on licence on compassionate grounds. Other life-sentence prisoners, though, seem to be treated differently in this respect. Those sentenced before the 2003 Act came into force could apply to a High Court judge to determine their minimum term and they had a right to appeal against the judge's decision. That appeal could take account of any exceptional progress they had made in prison

The imposition of a sentence of life imprisonment on an offender in the knowledge or expectation that he will subsequently be released into the community (albeit under conditions and supervision) is by no means peculiar to England and Wales. But the length of detention before the prisoner can formally apply for release does vary between jurisdictions. In Canada, for example, those convicted of murder in the first degree are statutorily ineligible for parole until they have served 25 years in prison, while those guilty of second-degree murder must serve between 10 and 25 years.[15] In Germany all those serving life sentences must be detained for at least 15 years.[16] The MLS has been abolished in New Zealand and replaced with a presumption in favour of life imprisonment, and if the presumption is not rebutted the offender must serve a minimum of 10 years in prison. In what are regarded as the most serious cases, release may not be granted until at least 17 years' detention have elapsed.[17] Further details of the punishments of those convicted in other jurisdictions of the most serious forms of criminal homicide are set out in Appendix A.

B. Schedule 21

According to section 269(5) of the CJA 2003 the court 'must have regard to' the principles set out in Schedule 21 to the Act. In *Sullivan and others*[18] the Court of Appeal subsequently explained that this means what it says but no more – the judge must bear the principles in mind but is not bound to follow them. If he chooses not to follow them, he should explain his reasons for so doing. The length of the minimum term should be determined by reference to the seriousness of the offence, and not the dangerousness of the defendant – the indeterminate nature of a life sentence in itself provides the necessary element of public protection.[19]

Schedule 21 originally identified three possible starting-points in the judge's calculation of the minimum term – a 'whole life' (which means that the offender

[15] See section 745(a) and (b) Canadian *Criminal Code*. The precise length of this period of parole ineligibility is determined by the trial judge who may, in so doing, take into account the views of the jury; (see section 745(2)).

[16] Clause 57a *Strafgesetzbuch (German Penal Code)*.

[17] Sections 103 and 104 *Sentencing Act 2002*.

[18] *R v Sullivan and others* [2004] EWCA Crim 1762.

[19] *R v Leigers (George)* [2005] 2 Cr App R (S) 104.

spends the rest of his/her natural life in prison), 30 years, or 15 years. Paragraphs 4 and 5 provide lists of offence characteristics to assist the judge in deciding the appropriate starting-point, but the wording is not prescriptive so that murders containing other characteristics may warrant similar starting-points.[20]

Under paragraph 4(2), cases of 'exceptionally high' seriousness call for a starting-point of a whole or natural life tariff.[21] Defendants in these cases should be aged at least 21 years. Indicators of this level of seriousness are:

(a) there were two or more people murdered and each of the murders involved either
    (i) a substantial degree of planning or premeditation, or
    (ii) the abduction of the victim, or
    (iii) sexual or sadistic conduct; or
(b) the victim was a child[22] who was abducted or the murder of the child was sexually or sadistically motivated; or
(c) the murder was motivated by the advancement of a political, religious, racial[23] or ideological cause; or
(d) the defendant had previously been convicted of murder.

The legality of whole life minimum terms was first challenged in the courts in England in *R v Secretary of State for the Home Department, ex parte Hindley*,[24] and they were upheld on the ground that the Home Secretary had a discretion to review and reduce the term if appropriate. But all minimum terms are now, of course, imposed by the judiciary and there is no right of Executive review. This therefore raised the question whether a whole life minimum term conflicts with Article 3 of the European Convention on Human Rights that seeks to guard against inhuman or degrading treatment. This was considered by the Grand Chamber in *Kafkaris v Cyprus*.[25] It was held that in Cyprus since a prisoner with a whole life minimum term retained some, albeit limited, prospect of release, there is no conflict with Article 3.

That decision was effectively followed by the English Court of Appeal in *Bieber*,[26] where the defendant was convicted on one count of murdering a police officer together with two counts of attempted murder and various firearms offences. The judge imposed a whole life minimum term after choosing a starting-point of 30 years. The Court of Appeal quashed the sentence on the ground that the aggravating factors did not justify the uplift to whole life, but the Court also confirmed that

[20] See *R v Duncan* [2007] 1 Cr App R (S) 126.

[21] According to a statement made by Lord De Mauley, as at 20 September 2011 there were 42 mandatory life prisoners held in prisons in England and Wales and a further five detained in hospital under the *Mental Health Act 1983* who had been given a whole life minimum term. See *Hansard*, 3 October 2011, col WA185.

[22] A 'child' means a person under the age of 18 years.

[23] 'Racial' was added by section 75(2)(c) *Counter Terrorism Act 2008*.

[24] *R v Home Secretary, ex parte Hindley* [2000] 1 QB 152.

[25] *Kafkaris v Cyprus* (Application No 21906/04, 12 February 2008, Grand Chamber).

[26] *R v Bieber* [2008] EWCA Crim 1601.

a whole life minimum term does not breach Article 3 because it is potentially reducible. The fact that the offender *may* be detained for the rest of his/her life is irrelevant.

Subsequent case law suggests that whole life sentences are unlikely to be *automatically* illegal. The European Court is clearly very critical of irreducible sentences, but in light of the recent decision in *Vinter and others v UK*[27] it seems that the ultimate criterion is whether a whole life sentence is 'grossly disproportionate'. The obvious implication behind this is that such a sentence does not necessarily constitute inhuman and degrading treatment.[28] A whole life minimum term should only be imposed where there is no doubt that the case is of exceptionally high seriousness. But, particularly if one or more of the factors listed in paragraph 4(2) are present, such a sentence might well be appropriate – though not necessarily automatic. For example, credit should be given for an early guilty plea,[29] and that might indicate a (high) finite term.

Alternatively, by virtue of paragraph 5(2), a 30-year starting-point is indicated if the defendant is aged at least 18 years and

(a) the victim was a police officer or prison officer acting in the course of his duty; or
(b) the murder involved the use of a firearm or explosive;[30] or
(c) the murder was carried out for gain (as in the furtherance of robbery or burglary, or in the expectation of gain); or
(d) the murder was meant to obstruct justice or interfere with the course of justice; or
(e) sexual or sadistic conduct was involved; or
(f) there were two or more people murdered; or
(g) the murder was racially, religiously aggravated or aggravated by sexual orientation; or
(h) the murder would have attracted a whole life starting-point but the defendant was under 21 years old.

Murders committed on or after 2 March 2010 are also subject to paragraph 5A, which was recently inserted into Schedule 21.[31] If neither paragraph 4(2) nor

[27] *Vinter and others v UK* (Application Nos 66069/09 and 130/10 and 3896/10); 17 January 2012, European Court of Human Rights.

[28] Nevertheless, the legality of whole life minimum terms is likely to be raised again in the near future in *Ahmad and others*, Application Nos 24027/07 and 11949/08 and 36742/08, albeit in the context of prisoners extradicted to very strict maximum security prisons.

[29] The extent of the reduction in sentence warranted by a guilty plea should be significantly influenced according to the stage at which it was made; see section 144(1) *Criminal Justice Act 2003*, and Sentencing Guidelines Council, *Reduction in Sentence for a Guilty Plea* (Revised 2007) para 4.3.

[30] The use of a firearm or explosive usually (but not necessarily) implies that the defendant had it so that s/he could kill or cause serious injury, and thus a 30-year starting-point is warranted. But the judge must always look at the facts of each case carefully and not assume that the defendant possessed the firearm or explosive for that reason.

[31] By the *Criminal Justice Act 2003 (Mandatory Life Sentence: Determination of Minimum Term) Order 2010* (SI 2010/197).

paragraph 5(2) is applicable and the defendant was aged at least 18 years at the time s/he committed the murder, the starting-point will be 25 years

> if the offender took a knife or other weapon to the scene intending to
>
> (a) commit any offence, or
> (b) have it available to use as a weapon,
>
> and used that knife or other weapon in committing the murder.

If the defendant was aged 18 years or over when s/he committed the murder and the case does not fall within paragraph 4, 5 or 5A, then by paragraph 6 the starting-point for determining the minimum term is 15 years. On the other hand, where the defendant was aged under 18 years, paragraph 7 indicates a starting-point of 12 years.

It is worth recalling here that prior to Schedule 21 judges were guided in their determinations of the minimum terms through various non-statutory sources. In February 1997 the then Lord Chief Justice, Lord Bingham, sent a letter to judges who had to make recommendations about the lengths of minimum terms. He indicated that his personal approach was that the 'average', 'normal' or 'unexceptional' murder would merit 14 years. He then offered two non-exhaustive lists of mitigating and aggravating factors that would take the minimum term below or above the average 14 years. That letter was followed in 2000 by a Practice Statement issued by Lord Woolf CJ,[32] which re-iterated that the average for an adult offender would be 14 years.

In March 2002 the Sentencing Advisory Panel (SAP) issued its advice on the matter. Since cases varied enormously, the SAP preferred to identify three starting-points. The middle starting-point was 12 years; the higher was 15/16 years, and the lower was eight/nine years. The middle figure was aimed at cases arising out of a quarrel or loss of temper between two people known to one another.[33] The lower figure was thought to apply to cases where the defendant's moral culpability was greatly reduced, where the case was close to the borderline between murder and manslaughter. Although the middle figure, 12 years, is prima facie slightly lower than the 14 years for an average or normal murder favoured by Lord Bingham, the Court of Appeal subsequently suggested that the murders in the SAP's middle group were slightly less serious than those which Lord Bingham had in mind, and that therefore there was no inconsistency between the two.[34]

The advice given by the SAP was then set down in a *Practice Statement*[35] by the former Lord Chief Justice, Lord Woolf. This Statement was to apply to judicial recommendations made after 31 May 2002. Lord Woolf indicated that a 'substantial

[32] *Practice Note* [2000] 4 All ER 831.

[33] Official homicide statistics published over the years have consistently indicated that quarrelling or loss of temper are the most common circumstances in which murders are committed.

[34] See the Lord Chief Justice's judgment in *Sullivan and others*, n 18 above.

[35] *Practice Statement (Crime: Life sentences)* [2002] 3 All ER 412, subsequently incorporated as part of a consolidated *Practice Direction* [2002] 3 All ER 904, 938.

upward adjustment' (ie up to 30 years) in the minimum term would be appropriate in the most serious cases, and in cases of 'exceptional gravity' a whole life would be proper. In *Sullivan and others* the Lord Chief Justice acknowledged that there are differences between the statutory and non-statutory figures, but thought they are at the upper end of the scale, when dealing with the more serious murders. But the Court of Appeal stressed that

> it would be wrong to assume that Parliament had intended to raise minimum terms over those recommended by the expert Sentencing Advisory Panel by merely applying the 15-year starting-point to all murders other than those whose seriousness is exceptionally or particularly high.[36]

Nevertheless, some commentators have argued that a consequence of Schedule 21 has been an increase in the length of the minimum term, and that the Executive has used the statute to interfere with judicial decisions on the matter.[37]

Paragraphs 10 and 11 of Schedule 21 offer illustrative lists of aggravating and mitigating factors[38] respectively which the judge should then take into account. Potentially aggravating factors are:

- significant planning or premeditation;
- victims who are vulnerable through age or disability;
- the infliction of mental or physical suffering before death;
- abuse of trust; the use of duress or threats to facilitate the murder;
- the fact that the victim was providing a public service or performing a public duty; and
- concealment, destruction or dismemberment of the body.

Mitigating factors include:

- an intent to cause serious harm rather than kill;
- lack of premeditation;
- the fact that the defendant was suffering from a mental disorder or disability (not amounting to diminished responsibility) which reduced his culpability;
- the fact that the defendant was provoked (for example, by prolonged stress) but not sufficiently for a plea of (formerly provocation but now) loss of control;
- the fact that the defendant acted to any extent in self-defence;
- a belief by the defendant that the murder was an act of mercy; and
- the offender's age.

[36] ibid, para 35.

[37] Arguments that Schedule 21 has led to an increase in the length of sentences in homicide cases can be found in, for example, Creighton and Arnott (2009: 470); and Jeremy (2010).

[38] Thus, in *R v Richardson* [2006] 1 Cr App R (S) 240 the Court of Appeal held that the trial judge had rightly treated the defendant's possession of a knife at the time of the murder as an aggravating feature, even though it is not mentioned in paragraph 10. This case was, of course, heard before paragraph 5A, which added another starting-point where the killer was in possession of a knife or other weapon, was inserted in Schedule 21; (see n 31 above).

As the Court of Appeal has remarked, the gap between the starting-points indicated in Schedule 21 is considerable;[39] the Act provides only a very broad framework. When determining the minimum term – especially when looking at paragraphs 4, 5, 5A and 6, and then taking account of any aggravating and/or mitigating elements – the judge must be careful not to 'double count' any of the relevant factors.

According to section 269(2) of the CJA 2003 the court must normally make an order that the early release provisions in section 28(5) to (8) of the Crime (Sentences) Act 1997 apply to the defendant. This reflects the fact that most murders are expected to be of a degree of seriousness that results in the offender's release on licence. If no such order is made the minimum term will be a whole life. The court should also indicate whether any, and if so what, allowance is being given for time spent on remand.[40] The minimum terms are subject to the normal process of appeal against sentence[41] – ie the defendant can initiate an appeal or the Attorney-General can refer a case to the Court of Appeal.

Comparison of the former Lord Chief Justice's Practice Direction of 2002 with Schedule 21 (a summary of which is provided in Appendix B) may help to explain why some commentators fear that the 2003 Act has lengthened minimum terms for convicted murderers. The following points of contrast are worth noting:

- Whereas paragraph 4 of Schedule 21 identifies factors that would indicate a starting-point of a whole life, the Practice Direction does not expressly recommend a whole life but says 'rather than setting a whole life minimum term [the judge] can state that there is no minimum period which could properly be set in that particular case' (para 49.19).
- Paragraph 5 of Schedule 21 lists individual factors (for example, the murder of two or more victims) that would warrant a 30-year starting-point; the Practice Direction states that such cases should involve 'a *substantial* number of murders' or '*several* factors indicating a higher starting-point' (emphasis added) (para 49.19).
- Some of the characteristics in paragraph 5 are listed in the Practice Direction as indicative of a 15- or 16-year starting-point (para 49.13).
- For what might be described as a 'normal' murder by an adult, Schedule 21 identified the starting-point as 15 years (para 6); but the Practice Direction's recommendation is 12 years (para 49.10).
- The shortest starting-point indicated in Schedule 21 is 12 years (para 7); the Practice Direction suggests that where the offender's culpability is significantly reduced, the starting-point should be eight or nine years (paras 49.11 and 49.12). (Both then state that the actual minimum term may be above or below the starting-point when all the other aggravating and mitigating factors have been taken into consideration.)

[39] See *R v Jones* [2006] 2 Cr App R (S) 121.
[40] Section 269(3) *Criminal Justice Act 2003.*
[41] See sections 270 and 271 *Criminal Justice Act 2003.*

Since the factors listed in paragraph 4 of Schedule 21 all indicate the same starting-point (whole life), the obvious implication is that they all have a similar impact on the seriousness of the murder. But that does not seem to necessarily follow when we examine those factors. Some of the wording is ambiguous and in our view paragraph 4 appears to permit varying degrees of seriousness to justify a whole life starting-point. We will subsequently argue (in Chapter eight) that murders of multiple victims are invariably very serious because of the significant increase in both the harm and culpability. Yet under paragraph 4 such cases would only warrant a whole life starting-point if there were even further aggravating factors in the form of substantial planning or premeditation, abduction of the victim, or sexual or sadistic conduct. On the other hand, the murder of a child accompanied by similar additional aggravation is put into the same category. Thus, in essence the murder of a child is equated with the murder of multiple victims, and whilst child murder is rightly condemned for its heinousness, it is difficult to see how it can justifiably be placed into the same sentencing bracket as a multiple-victim murder.

Murders motivated by the advancement of political, religious, racial or ideological causes (paragraph 4(2)(c)) could encompass a broad spectrum of cases. At one extreme it is not hard to envisage an instance in which not only the motivation is regarded as highly offensive and undesirable but there is also an implied threat to the lives of others. In contrast, cases in this group might be characterised by an intent to cause no more than serious injury and carry no apparent risk to the well-being of anyone other than the deceased.

Moreover, the factors listed in paragraph 5 which indicate a 30-year starting-point should presumably imply a lower level of seriousness than those in paragraph 4. But examination of the contents of the two paragraphs does not necessarily bear this out. Thus, for example, compare a case in which the offender deliberately killed three adults, with a second case in which a 21-year old offender abducted a child and killed him having intended to cause serious injury. The former results in a 30-year starting-point, whereas the latter leads to a whole life.

C. Judicial Interpretation of Schedule 21

Paragraph 11 of Schedule 21 indicates that an intent to cause serious harm (rather than to cause death) is a potentially mitigating factor, but the case law stresses that we should be careful not to draw any immediate conclusions from the nature of the defendant's intent. In *Peters; Palmer; Campbell*[42] Judge LJ remarked that there is no starting-point for intent-to-cause-serious-harm cases, and that such an intent will not necessarily mitigate the sentence.[43] The courts must look at all the facts. Mercy killing, for example, is characterised by an intent to kill; yet it 'repre-

[42] *R v Peters; R v Palmer; R v Campbell* [2005] EWCA Crim 605.

[43] ibid, para 14.

sents an act of mercy, motivated by love and devotion'. This is identified in paragraph 11(f) as a mitigating factor, and it led Judge LJ to comment:

> It is unlikely that the mitigation in such a case will be less than the mitigation allowed to an offender who involves himself in an unlawful violent incident and, intending to do really serious harm, causes death. Similarly, there are cases in which death, even if unintended, is a possible or likely consequence of the offender's premeditated conduct. For example, those who abduct a child intending to blackmail the parents into providing a large ransom may deliberately make the parents aware that the child is being tortured, to encourage a positive response from the parents. In the course of torture the child may die. Just because the very objective of the criminal is a ransom, death may not be intended. If it is a consequence of the abduction or torture, we doubt whether much, if any, allowance would normally be made in mitigation for the fact that the death of the child was an unintended consequence of the deliberate infliction of bodily harm.

Note that the mere fact that death was not intended is inconclusive partly because it may nonetheless have been quite likely or foreseeable.[44] Indeed, the nature of the defendant's intent may be given less weight than other offence characteristics. Thus, in *Connor*[45] the Court of Appeal held that since the appellant had set fire to a house with petrol, killing two people and badly injuring a third, it made little difference whether the intent was to kill or seriously injure.

Schedule 21 clearly identifies different starting-points by reference to the defendant's age, but again the courts have stressed that what is more important is the individual's maturity as a person rather than whether they have reached a physical age. In *Peters; Palmer; Campbell* Judge LJ referred to the need to approach Schedule 21 'with an acute sense of how inevitably imprecise the statutory criteria may sometimes be to issues of culpability, and ultimately to seriousness'.[46] More recently, the Court of Appeal underlined this by asserting 'there should be no sudden postponement or acceleration of a sentence due to age. In practice, there will be something of a continuum'.[47] Relying on *Peters et al*, the Court in *Taylor and Thomas*[48] stated that where two co-defendants of equal culpability murder in the course of robbery, and one was just over 18 years old whereas the other was just under 18, it would be quite wrong to identify significantly divergent starting-points.

Paragraph 5(2)(c) of Schedule 21 indicates a 30-year starting-point where the murder was committed for gain. In *Bouhaddou*[49] the defendant entered the deceased's home in the early hours. He was in the kitchen rifling through a handbag

[44] See also *Attorney-General's Reference (Nos 98 and 99 of 2006) (R v McGarry and Wells)* [2006] EWCA Crim 3177.

[45] *R v Connor* [2007] EWCA Crim 2591. This point was reinforced in *R v Blue* [2008] EWCA Crim 769 where, although the defendant intended only serious harm, the court was more influenced by the fact that he inflicted four stab wounds, and the degree of force used to inflict the fatal wound to the deceased's chest.

[46] See n 42 above, at para 11.

[47] See *R v Martin* [2009] EWCA Crim 1182 (Cranston J), at para 9. See also *R v Jonathan Clarke* [2009] EWCA Crim 2484 where the defendant, under 21 years of age, was convicted of a particularly sadistic murder and given a minimum term of 27 years.

[48] *R v Taylor and another* [2007] EWCA Crim 803.

[49] *R v Bouhaddou* [2006] EWCA Crim 3190.

when he was disturbed by the deceased. The defendant grabbed a knife from the drawer and in the course of a scuffle stabbed the deceased in the chest and fled. Lord Phillips rejected the argument that murder 'for gain' only arises where it is in order to facilitate the gain. This was regarded as mere 'sophistry': committing murder in order to escape from a burglary, the object of which is gain, constitutes murder for gain, because the escape is an integral part of the enterprise.

Under paragraph 5(2)(e) of Schedule 21, a 30-year starting-point is indicated where the murder involves sadistic conduct, and the meaning of this was considered by the Court of Appeal in *Bonellie, Miller and Hughes.*[50] Two defendants were in their mid-teens and the third was under 21 at the time of the offence. Their victim, aged 23, had spent the previous nine years in psychiatric hospitals and suffered from a learning disability and other psychiatric conditions. They repeatedly punched him, jumped on him, stamped on him and head-butted him. They tormented and ridiculed him. He was never aggressive towards them, and regarded his assailants as friends. In sentencing Hughes the trial judge identified the starting-point as 30 years, but the Court of Appeal thought this was unjustified. Goldring J explained that whilst many assailants get pleasure from what they do, that is not sufficient to bring the case within paragraph 5(2)(e). 'Sadistic conduct' 'contemplates a significantly greater degree of awareness of pleasure in the infliction of pain, suffering or humiliation'.[51]

III. THE MEANING OF LIFE: THE MANDATORY LIFE SENTENCE IN PRACTICE

Fortunately, the number of people convicted of murder has long been relatively small. According to the latest available government statistics, during the period 2000–01 to 2009–10 the figures varied from 195 in 2009–10 to 318 in 2004–05 (Smith et al, 2012; Table 1.02). As at 30 June 2010 there were 4,798 convicted murderers in prison in England and Wales, 211 of whom were females (Ministry of Justice, 2010; Table A1.6). The vast majority of them spend a period of time in prison and are then released into the community on licence. The length of the minimum term has been steadily increasing for several decades, and since the current provisions in the *Criminal Justice Act 2003* took effect on 18 December 2003 the average minimum term for convicted murderers has gone from 14.6 years (in 2004–05) to 19.0 years (in 2010–11).[52] Table 3.1 shows how the length of the minimum term has increased.

Convicted murderers, along with other life sentence prisoners ('lifers'), are housed with determinate sentence prisoners, although they should be accommodated on a landing with other long- or medium-term prisoners. (There is also one institution – Kingston prison in Portsmouth – which accommodates only lifers,

[50] *R v Bonellie; R v Miller; R v Hughes* [2008] EWCA Crim 1417.

[51] ibid at para 16.

[52] We are grateful to the Ministry of Justice for supplying these statistics to us.

Table 3.1 Average Minimum Terms for Murder

Year	Average minimum term (years)
2000	14.32
2001	14.00
2002	13.19
2003	13.68
2004	14.52
2005	16.14
2006	17.54
2007	15.91
2008	17.96
2009	17.54
Average over the decade	*15.50*

Source: NOMS, Ministry of Justice; data to 5 February 2010

where some convicted murderers may spend part of their detention.) Following conviction, offenders are likely to be returned initially to the local prison where they were detained awaiting trial on remand and which serves the court where they were sentenced – though some may have been held in a high-security establishment. They may well spend the first few months in the local prison, but within 16 weeks of sentence a sentence planning and review meeting (SPRM) should be held which should produce a plan for the management of the offender's imprisonment.

The principal aim of this plan should be to identify the needs of the individual and assist them in reducing the risk of causing serious harm to the public. Risk assessment and reduction is not a perfect science, but the factors that are likely to be taken into account include the nature and circumstances of the offence, the level of aggression shown, and special or unusual (for example, pathological) behaviour during or after the offence, the offender's criminal history, the motivation for the offence, information relating to the victim, the offender's lifestyle, his/her behaviour and attitude, any substance or alcohol abuse, and the offender's mental health.

The progress of lifers through their time in prison is regularly reviewed by a variety of staff – SPRMs must be held at least once a year. Those who contribute to this ongoing process of review include appropriate police officers and probation officers as well as prison staff. Not long before the expiry of the minimum term each lifer will be referred to the Parole Board who ultimately, in light of the reviews and assessments, will decide whether they think it is safe for them to be released on licence. There are, of course, different dimensions to the reduction of the risk that any lifer might pose to the public.

One of the objectives entailed in reducing risk is the promotion of re-integration into society, and as part of the effort to achieve this many lifers are encouraged to enhance their prospects of employment, during their detention, by gaining appropriate educational and/or vocational qualifications and experience. In addition, and especially where they have spent a long time in prison, they may need assistance to re-adjust to life in the community and to re-establish family links. Again, provided it is felt safe to do so, in the later stages of detention they may well be allowed or perhaps encouraged to spend limited amounts of time outside prison escorted by prison staff – attending courses, re-familiarising themselves with community life, or engaging in community projects etc.

IV. RELEASE OF MANDATORY LIFERS ON LICENCE

At the appropriate stage in the sentence, lifers can formally apply to the Parole Board to be released from prison on licence. If the Parole Board is satisfied that the lifer's continued detention is no longer necessary for the protection of the public and the application is successful, the Secretary of State is then under a duty to release him.[53] Not surprisingly, public protection is the principal consideration in deciding whether to sanction the release of a life sentence prisoner in various jurisdictions. Lifers will obviously still be in prison when they are informed of the outcome of their parole application, and it is important to stress that (if successful) any date they are given for their release on licence will always be provisional. If there are any concerns about the risk that the lifer would pose to the public, the release date is likely to be withdrawn. Nonetheless, if there are no such concerns and the lifer is released into the community the licence will remain in force for the remainder of the lifer's natural life, though it may be revoked and the lifer (licensee) returned to prison if s/he ceases to be regarded as a small enough risk to the public.

Table 3.2 sets out the numbers of mandatory life sentence prisoners first released on licence in England and Wales and the average time they have spent in prison (Ministry of Justice, 2010; Table A3.5).

Table 3.2 Numbers of Mandatory Life Sentence Prisoners First Released and Average Time Served in Prison

Year of first release	2000	2001	2002	2003	2004	2005	2006	2007	2008	2009	2010
Number	101	111	117	185	152	156	100	90	98	73	115
Average number of years served	13	13	14	15	14	14	14	16	16	17	18

[53] See section 28(5) of the *Crime (Sentences) Act 1997*.

A. Licence Conditions

There are seven standard conditions subject to which a lifer may be released (Ministry of Justice, 2006; para 13.3 and Annex 1). These are:

- S/he is supervised by whichever supervising officer is nominated for the purpose;
- On release s/he reports to the nominated supervising officer and keeps in touch with that officer in accordance with the officer's instructions;
- If so required by the supervising officer, the lifer will receive visits from that officer where s/he is living;
- S/he will reside only where approved by the supervising officer;
- S/he will undertake work, including voluntary work, only where approved by the supervising officer and must inform the supervising officer of any change in or loss of employment;
- S/he will not travel outside the United Kingdom without the prior permission of the supervising officer; and
- S/he must be well behaved and not do anything that would undermine the purposes of the supervision, ie the protection of the public and ensuring that their safety would not be put at risk, and to secure the lifer's successful re-integration into society.

If recommended by the Parole Board, the licence may also include additional conditions, the purpose of which should be to ensure continued public safety by providing a means of assisting the assessment and management of the risk that the lifer represents, or to help the lifer's re-integration into the community as a law-abiding citizen.[54] Examples of such additional conditions include:

- Requiring the lifer to undertake work related to the offence;
- Prohibiting contact with members of the victim's family;[55]
- Requiring the lifer to remain in regular contact with a named doctor or psychiatrist;
- Preventing contact with young people under a certain age; or
- Excluding the lifer from specific geographical areas or zones, so that they cannot come into contact with the victim's family.

Whilst there is no absolute prohibition on routinely electronically monitoring lifers on licence, it is expected that this will not be used, if only because the risk of harm to the public must have been judged to be sufficiently low in order for the lifer's release to be sanctioned in the first place.

Any condition which excludes a lifer from entering a geographical area or zone must be reasonable, necessary and proportionate, so as to achieve a balance

[54] The Board will usually do this if the appropriate member of staff has so recommended in his or her report. Reasons for any additional conditions must be provided.

[55] Where possible, anyone with whom there should be no contact should be named in the condition.

between the rights of the lifer under Article 8 (the right to privacy and family life) and those of the victim's family. This may require ascertaining precise details of where the family members live, work and socialise etc, and balancing those against corresponding details of the lifer's family and lifestyle. The licence should identify the exact limits of the exclusion zone very clearly, so that all parties have an accurate understanding of the restriction.

B. Supervision and Monitoring in the Community

Upon release the National Identification Service (the NIS) at New Scotland Yard is notified of the lifer's address and the supervising probation area. Indeed, the local police should liaise with the supervising probation area before release takes place. According to information supplied to the authors by the Ministry of Justice in December 2011 there are 1,345 convicted murderers being supervised on life licence in the community in England and Wales. Within a month of release, a report must be sent to the Lifer Review and Recall Section (LRRS) of the National Offender Management Service at the Ministry of Justice. Subsequent reports are required at quarterly intervals for the first two years. If it is thought that good progress has been made, reports may then only be required every six or 12 months.[56]

During the course of the supervision in the community licence conditions may be varied, cancelled or even re-imposed. As one might expect, whenever this happens, reasons must be given. It is particularly noteworthy that the supervision part of the licence may be cancelled 'after a minimum of four years of trouble-free existence in the community'. This may occur in cases where there is evidence of:

- a stable lifestyle, good integration, a balanced outlook and an open relationship with the supervising officer;
- gradual reduction in the requirement for contact with the Probation Area;
- crises, if any, having been faced and dealt with sensibly, with proper involvement of the supervising officer; and
- where appropriate, an indication that the licensee would turn to the Probation Area for assistance on a voluntary basis in necessary. (Ministry of Justice, 2006: para 13.9.2).

Then again, a supervising officer may feel that whilst the standard supervisory conditions of the licence can be cancelled, the additional conditions should remain in place.

In the interests of ensuring there is no unacceptable threat to public safety and of maximising the prospects of the lifer's re-integration into the community, it is important that the element of risk is regularly monitored, and that the possibility

[56] These reports should address: risk factors and risk management; compliance with licence conditions and reporting requirements; general response to supervision; current employment, training or education; current domestic circumstances, etc.

of old factors re-emerging or of new factors becoming apparent is regularly addressed. That said, it is possible that a lifer may be allowed to travel abroad temporarily, provided it is felt that he can be trusted to return. Approval for this is obviously not readily given and there must be good reason to feel confident that the lifer will repay the trust placed in him or her. Similarly, it is possible for a lifer to be allowed to reside permanently abroad, but only following a very thorough risk assessment.

C. Licence Revocation and Recall to Prison

Section 32(1) of the Crime (Sentences) Act 1997 gives a power to the Secretary of State to revoke the licence if recommended to do so by the Parole Board and the lifer is recalled to prison. In what might be described as emergencies a further power is provided under section 32(2) which enables the lifer to be recalled without the need to obtain the Parole Board's prior recommendation if it would be in the public interest so to do. It should be made clear though, that the LRRS should then refer such a case to the Parole Board so that the Board can then decide whether the lifer should remain in prison.[57]

Predictably, a licence should only be revoked where there is perceived to be too high a risk to the public in allowing the lifer to remain in the community. In 2010 some 63 convicted murderers who had been released were recalled, according to information supplied to the authors by the Ministry of Justice. The normal power under section 32(1) – where the Secretary of State acts on the Parole Board's recommendation – should be used where the circumstances allow the matter to be referred to the Board. For example, the lifer is in breach of the terms of his licence, perhaps through failing to keep in touch with his supervising officer, but it seems there is no imminent threat to the public. The emergency power under section 32(2), by-passing the Parole Board, should be reserved for cases where the circumstances make time of the essence, although (again) this need not be because the lifer is suspected of re-offending. As for the 63 mandatory lifers in England and Wales who were recalled in 2010, the vast majority (54) had their licence revoked because of 'poor behaviour'.[58]

If the licence is revoked, the LRRS should inform the NIS. Whichever power is used to make the recall, the lifer should be given the opportunity to make representations against it. If the decision is that he should not be re-released, the LRRS should fix a date for a subsequent review which should take place not later than two years.

[57] See section 32(4) of the *Crime (Sentences) Act 1997*.

[58] We are grateful to the Ministry of Justice for this information.

V. CONCLUSIONS

On reflection, it seems fair to observe that the sentence partly lives up to its name but partly does not. It is mandatory in that it is automatically imposed on all convicted murderers, and it is a sentence that endures for the remainder of the offender's natural life. But in the majority of cases the offender does not spend the rest of his or her life in prison. It is also quite clear that the duration of the first stage of the sentence is gradually increasing; both the length of the minimum terms imposed by the judges and the actual periods being served in prison are getting longer. Finally, having been released, most mandatory life-sentence prisoners appear to re-integrate into society successfully, at least in so far as their licence is not revoked.

4

Making the Case For and Against the Mandatory Life Sentence

OVERVIEW

In Chapter three we described the way in which the MLS for murder has evolved in England and Wales since it came into being in the middle of the last century. As we have seen, the Westminster Parliament is not alone in legislating for such a sentence; almost all western nations have created a mandatory life sentence for murder. The purpose of this chapter is to examine the arguments in favour of and against the MLS.

I. THE UNIQUENESS OF MURDER

It is often said that murder is a unique offence and that this justifies the imposition of a special kind of punishment, namely the MLS. But we need to be clear about just what this uniqueness is that necessitates a special sentence, one which, as we shall later argue, violates important sentencing principles.

It is, of course, quite justifiable to argue that taking the life of another human being is a special kind of harm. In contrast to the harm in other crimes, death can never be undone or made good. As Paul Rock explained, there is no shortage of evidence indicating that the family and friends of the deceased suffer in a way that is quite different from that of other crime victims (Rock, 1998: 30). Further, as George Fletcher remarked:

> causing death is a harm of a different order. Killing another human being is not only a worldly deprivation; in the Western conception of homicide, killing is an assault on the sacred, natural order. In the Biblical view, the person who slays another was thought to acquire control over the blood – the life force – of the victim. The only way that this life force could be returned to God, the origin of all life, was to execute the slayer himself (Fletcher, 2000: 235, 236).

This special, fundamental 'difference' between homicide and other offences continues to be reflected in the law. For example, consent is not recognised as a defence to criminal homicide, whereas the opposite is true of some non-fatal offences against the person and many property offences. One reason for this,

Fletcher suggests, is that the 'religious conception of human life still prevails against the modern view that life is an interest that the bearer can dispose of at will'. (Fletcher, 2000: 236) Even if we ignore the religious conception of life, it is difficult to argue against the proposition that human life has the highest secular value, for it is undeniably 'necessary for the enjoyment of all other goods' (Kadish, 1976).

These arguments are not unique to murder, however. Indeed, the points made in the previous paragraphs apply to a variety of situations in which human life is lost, both lawfully and unlawfully. What distinguishes murder – or, perhaps more accurately, what *ought* to distinguish murder from any other circumstances in which a human life is taken – is the combination of causing death and a high degree of moral blame for doing so. It is this combination of the 'ultimate harm' and high moral culpability which is said to constitute a unique form of heinousness that can only be adequately reflected by a mandatory life sentence. In the minds of many leading criminal law practitioners and commentators, this is in fact the principal justification for the MLS.

Yet it is all too easy to find scathing attacks on the MLS for murder, especially from senior members of the judiciary with considerable experience of dealing with such cases. In delivering the annual Frank Newsam memorial lecture in March 1998, Lord Bingham, the former Lord Chief Justice, began his critique by pointing out that arguments based on this ground simply do not stand up to close scrutiny. As illustrated in Part 1 of Chapter one, similar comments have been publically made by other senior members of the judiciary. It is abundantly clear from the discussion of the law in Chapter one, especially Part 4, that murders vary considerably not only in their circumstances but also in the killer's level of moral blameworthiness, so that it would be wholly wrong to 'lump all murderers together and treat them all as uniquely heinous'.

II. THE CONSEQUENCES OF THE LAW'S FAILURE TO ENSURE THAT MURDER IS UNIQUELY HEINOUS

Several adverse consequences ensue from the law's failure to ensure that the offences committed by convicted murderers are uniquely heinous.

A. Mislabelling Offences and Offenders

Cases such as *Cocker*[1] and the more recent decision in *Inglis*,[2] which were described in earlier chapters, indicate that concerns that mercy-killers – whose homicides are widely regarded as amongst the less serious cases (Mitchell, 1998) – might be unable to avoid a conviction for murder are well-founded. This exposes a funda-

1 *R v Cocker* [1989] Crim LR 740.
2 *R v Inglis* [2010] EWCA Crim 2637.

mental but inescapable problem with the MLS – it makes it imperative that offenders are only convicted of murder if the homicide they committed truly was one of the worst examples of unlawful killing. This in fact means (1) that the *only people convicted of murder* are those who have committed one of the most serious forms for criminal homicide, and (2) that *all those who commit one of the worst forms of criminal homicide* are convicted of murder. We have argued in Chapter one that the current legal definition of murder is so imperfect that it fails on both counts.

A consequence of some people being undeservedly convicted of murder and others undeservedly not being convicted of murder is that some cases are inaccurately labelled. The imposition of a life sentence regardless of the individual circumstances of the case labels all offenders convicted of murder in the same way when in fact their levels of culpability may vary widely. An MLS places a serial murderer such as Peter Sutcliffe[3] in the same legal category as Frances Inglis, who took the life of her own severely disabled son: both Sutcliffe and Inglis were convicted of murder and sentenced to imprisonment for life. Few would argue that these two crimes were equally serious, or that these two offenders were equally culpable, yet the law appears to treat them as such. Supporters of the MLS might seek to defend the status quo by pointing to the judge's ability to reflect the individual circumstances of a case in the minimum term, but the offender must always remain at risk of recall to prison for the rest of his natural life, and that may be for several decades. Maintaining the sentence to the end of the offender's life is also justified on the basis that they may represent a risk of re-offending. Considering cases such as Sutcliffe and Inglis highlights the weakness of this argument; the former may continue to represent a threat, but no-one would argue this for the latter offender.

B. Undermining Public Confidence in Sentencing

A further potential risk of the law's failure to consistently ensure that a MLS is fully merited by the facts and circumstances of the case is that it will undermine rather than promote public confidence in sentencing – which, ironically, is another central concern of the supporters of the status quo. Politicians may claim that an MLS maintains public confidence in sentencing for murder, but surely not in light of the way that it is currently administered. Consider the case of a 30-year-old offender who is convicted of murder and sentenced to life imprisonment with a minimum term of eight years. This offender will probably spend eight years in prison and then be released into the community under the licence of the court for the remainder of his natural life – which may last for another 50 years. Few members of the public would accept this arrangement as a sentence of 'imprisonment

[3] Sutcliffe (labelled the 'Yorkshire Ripper' by the media for the brutality of his crimes) was convicted of several murders of women in Yorkshire in the 1980s.

for life'. The public may well regard such an arrangement as lacking truth in sentencing – a criticism which is less likely to arise for a definite term of custody where the offender and the public have a precise idea of when release from prison will occur.

III. THE NEED TO MAINTAIN PUBLIC CONFIDENCE IN THE CRIMINAL JUSTICE SYSTEM

A second major reason for replacing the death penalty for murder with the MLS was the assumption that nothing less than mandatory life would maintain public confidence in the criminal justice system. Half a century ago when the legislation was passed that enacted the MLS public sensitivity to murder was possibly even greater than it is today. It may be that the impact of the media over the years has meant that instances of murder and other criminal homicides are more familiar to us than they used to be, but we are understandably still horrified by these crimes even though they are less of a rarity to us than they were 50 years ago.

Sentencing offenders is a particularly visible and controversial stage in the criminal process, and it has long attracted the attention of the public, politicians, policy-makers and advocacy groups. These constituencies have inter-related interests: the public expects legislators to create appropriate sentencing laws, and politicians and policy-makers craft policies with an eye on the likely public reaction. Indeed, the evolution of sentencing policy has reflected a complex interplay between politics, populism and penology. Public interest has tended to focus in particular on the sentencing of the more serious offences, and no crime generates as much public concern or as many sentencing-related headlines as murder.

In the circumstances, therefore, it is not at all surprising that both when the MLS was introduced into English law and throughout the period since then there has been a keen political desire to ensure that the relationship between legal and popular opinion on the sentence for murder should be sufficiently close. It is worth noting, however, that political sensitivity to the subject seems to have reached new heights. For example, when the Law Commission was asked to review the law relating to murder, manslaughter and infanticide in 2005, the terms of reference expressly excluded consideration of the MLS (Law Commission of England and Wales, 2005: para 1.1) – one suspects on the ground that there would be a strongly adverse reaction from the public if the government were even seen to be thinking about the subject. More recently, at a relatively late stage in the passage of what was then the Coroners and Justice Bill through the House of Lords, an amendment was considered that would effectively have replaced the MLS with a discretionary life sentence. But the suggestion was summarily dismissed in light of the anticipated reaction it would receive in certain quarters of the media.

One of the reasons why it was so disappointing to find this continued reluctance to question or even review the MLS is that there has, for some time, been an ample body of research evidence that the public are sensitive to variations in the seriousness of offences, including murders (see, for example, Mitchell, 1998: 2000). This has been repeatedly demonstrated in the empirical research on public sentence preferences. When asked to sentence offenders, most people follow the principle of proportionality, imposing harsher sentences for the more serious crimes (see Roberts and Hough, 2005; Roberts, 1992). Thus, it is hard to see why we should be sure there would be a loss of public confidence in the criminal justice system if the mandatory sentence became discretionary.

The mandatory life sentence for murder was introduced in 1965; yet before we conducted our survey in August 2010 there had been no scientific attempt in this country to undertake an objective analysis of public opinion on the sentence for murder. The only apparent explanations are that politicians were either so sure of their assumption about the state of public opinion that no such survey was deemed necessary, or were deterred by the prospect of adverse media reaction if seen to be even re-examining the status quo.

A. Further Undermining of Public Confidence

As indicated in the previous section (on the alleged uniqueness of the heinousness in murder), one could argue that the need to maintain public confidence in the criminal justice system points more to the abolition of the MLS than to its retention. There are yet additional reasons for this, one of which arises out of the dubious representation of the sentence. At the start of Chapter three reference was made to Lord Windlesham's description of the MLS as 'A Sentence Nobody Can Understand'. In his 1998 lecture Lord Bingham made the uncontroversial assertion that the sentence for murder (as for any crime) should be 'intelligible, transparent and certain'. Yet none of these adjectives accurately describe the MLS. True, the sentence is mandatory – where the conviction is for murder the record must show that the sentence was 'life imprisonment' (or equivalent). And the sentence only comes to an end, at least formally,[4] when the defendant dies. But in reality the indeterminacy of the sentence is usually much more difficult to identify. The vast majority of murderers are released from prison before they die, so that what substance remains in the sentence thereafter – even where the supervisory conditions of the licence are not relaxed – is not readily apparent. Thus, Lord Bingham's description of the MLS as 'no more than a formula which gave no real clue to the offender, to the victim's family, the media or to the public at large what in practical terms of years to be served in prison the sentence meant' is surely very apposite.

As a final note on the issue of public confidence, it is interesting that Lord Bingham suggested that ordinary people are generally unaware that an intention

[4] If the offender is successfully released into the community on licence, then certainly after four years the supervisory conditions of the licence will probably be abandoned, so that the only remaining impact of the sentence is the threat of recall to prison.

to merely cause serious but not necessarily fatal or life-threatening harm will suffice for a murder conviction. Indeed, in talking to members of the public we have found that they were both surprised to discover this and unable to understand the justification for it. Like the Lane Committee (Committee on the Penalty for Homicide, 1993: at 19) Lord Bingham thought that most convicted murderers did not intend to kill, which clearly implied that the homicides committed by most of those found guilty of murder contained a significant element of mitigation. As noted in Chapter one, we simply do not know how many or what proportion of murder convictions are recorded on the basis that the defendant intended no more than serious injury. But it is difficult to avoid the suspicion that there is a divergence of opinion between the law and popular sentiment about where we should draw the bottom line in murder. In short, we suspect that members of the public think the law makes it too easy for a killer to be convicted of murder, and that is obviously unlikely to boost public confidence in the criminal justice system.

IV. PUBLIC PROTECTION AND DANGEROUSNESS

One of the principal aims of the penal system is to protect the public from further offending in the future – by the offender appearing for sentencing or other potential offenders. This is true for all forms of offending, including murder. Indeed, these aims are given statutory authority by section 142 of the *Criminal Justice Act 2003*. This provision states that the courts 'must have regard to' the protection of the public when sentencing offenders (aged 18 or over). Protection of the public can, of course, be achieved in various ways – for example, by incapacitating those who are considered to represent a danger to others, by deterring potential offenders, and by the rehabilitation of offenders.[5] There is nothing in the law which stipulates that an MLS should be imposed in murder cases because the offender is regarded as a danger to society. Being given a whole-life minimum term does not mean the offender is viewed as an indefinite danger to the community.

As far as the MLS is concerned, dangerousness becomes relevant at the later stage, when the offender formally applies for release on licence after serving the minimum term. Release will only be permitted if the offender is no longer regarded as dangerous. It is worth emphasising that the fact that a murderer is given a finite minimum term does not necessarily mean that he will be released at some future date. If, having been released on licence, there are concerns that the offender might constitute a risk to members of the public, the licence will be revoked and he will be recalled to prison. Assessing the risk that any prisoner – not just a convicted murderer – would pose if released into the community is not a perfect science. It is interesting to note that government statistics show that dur-

[5] Section 142(1) of the *Criminal Justice Act 2003* lists the punishment of offenders, deterrence, rehabilitation and the making of reparation along with protection of the public as legitimate purposes of sentencing.

ing the period 2000–01 to 2010–11 there were 6,053 convictions for murder or manslaughter, and only 30 cases (<0.5 per cent) of persons who had previously been convicted of such an offence (Smith et al, 2012: Table 1.13). Ultimately, of course, the only way to guarantee the public's safety from the individual would be through indefinite incarceration, but that is clearly not a feature of the MLS.

Crime may be prevented and the public protected through deterrence. The sentence may either deter the individual defendant who is being punished or it may send out a general message seeking thereby to deter others through the penalty imposed on the defendant. Frustratingly, we simply do not know how many potential murderers are deterred. Some might like to think that because the police devote an unusually high level of human and financial resources to murder detections and investigations, the detection rate is high – in other words, the vast majority of murders that are committed are subsequently discovered. But the inescapable fact is that we do not know that this is true. Moreover, nor do we know how many of those cases categorised as 'missing persons' in fact relate to undetected murders and manslaughters.

Official government statistics indicate that the number of recorded murders (and manslaughters) does not fluctuate very markedly over the years. Retentionists might claim this means that the MLS is having some deterrent effect by keeping the incidence of murder at a fairly stable level, but there is no evidence of cause and effect here. It is interesting to note that in other common law jurisdictions (such as Victoria and New South Wales) where the MLS has been abandoned there has been no apparent increase in the murder rate (Law Reform Commission of Victoria, 1988: para 94; Yeo, 1987). Although the number of recorded murders initially increased slightly at the start of the twenty-first century, reaching a high of 318 in 2004–05 – a figure that appears to have been heavily influenced by the London bombings – it then dropped to 195 in 2009–10 (Smith et al, 2012: Table 1.02).

In addition, there are specific reasons to think that the MLS has little or no deterrent effect. First, it has long been the case that significant numbers of homicides are spontaneous, spur-of-the-moment offences, resulting from quarrels, arguments or loss of temper: truly planned or premeditated homicides are not especially commonplace (Smith et al, 2012: Table 1.07).[6] In his 1998 lecture Lord Bingham expressed the belief that many murders occur because of a specific set of circumstances that are very unlikely to be repeated. Secondly, as the House of Lords Select Committee recognised, the popular perception that a life sentence is really a misnomer means that the deterrent value of the MLS is undermined (House of Lords Select Committee, 1989: para 114B). The clear implication of all this is that the MLS is unlikely to have a markedly deterrent effect on the murder rate.

Furthermore, there are reasons for believing that a discretionary life sentence would provide adequate public protection. As Lord Bingham remarked, judges

[6] For statistics relating to earlier years, see, for example, Mitchell (1990).

have considerable experience and expertise in deciding when a life sentence is appropriate when punishing offenders convicted of other serious crimes such as manslaughter.[7]

V. THE NEED TO DISTINGUISH BETWEEN MURDER AND MANSLAUGHTER

A further reason given in support of the MLS is that the significance attached to the distinction between murder and manslaughter would otherwise be seriously undermined. It is argued that if the courts were given the same sentencing powers when dealing with either crime the perception of murder as encompassing the more serious, more heinous homicides would be severely compromised. Against this, it may be said that when determining the appropriate sentence the courts will invariably be intent on evaluating the seriousness of the particular facts and circumstances of the case. This evaluation will be seen in the punishment imposed by the court so that variations in gravity between cases will be reflected in the sentences. As a general proposition, therefore, assuming offence definitions are sufficiently well drafted, convictions for murder would attract tougher sentences than those for manslaughter, and the comparative seriousness of the crimes would be maintained.

VI. PROBLEMS IN ASSESSING THE CORRECT LENGTH OF DETERMINATE SENTENCES

It used to be argued that if the MLS were replaced with a discretionary life sentence so that some murderers could be given a determinate prison sentence, judges would find it difficult to assess the appropriate length of the imprisonment and that in turn would lead to inconsistency (see, for example, House of Lords Select Committee, 1989: para 113A; and the Criminal Law Revision Committee, 1980: para 47). However, a body of case law which contains guidance from the Court of Appeal has been established. As this continues to grow it will provide further and more detailed guidance for trial judges that should both ease their task and minimise the risk of inconsistencies. In addition, there is general guidance from the Sentencing Council on the impact of aggravating and mitigating

[7] In respect of those offences not listed in Schedule 15 of the *Criminal Justice Act 2003* the criteria in *R v Hodgson* (1967) 52 Cr App R 113 still govern the imposition of a discretionary life sentence – the offence must have been sufficiently grave, the offender must have been suffering from some form of mental instability, and s/he must be thought to pose an unacceptable risk to the public for the foreseeable future. The *Criminal Justice Act 2003* contains provisions relating to the sentencing of what are regarded as 'dangerous offenders' and it enables the courts to impose life sentences in such cases. Schedule 15 identifies a list of offences for this purpose, and section 225(1)(b) states that if the court thinks there is a significant risk of serious harm to the public through the commission of further crimes by the offender, a life sentence *must* be imposed – ie the sentence effectively becomes mandatory.

factors (Sentencing Guidelines Council, *Overarching Principles: Seriousness*, 2004) Moreover, any concerns that individual sentences for murder might be unduly lenient can be addressed through the right of the Attorney-General under section 36 of the *Criminal Justice Act 1988* to refer such cases to the Court of Appeal where the judges are free to substitute what they regard as the appropriate punishment.

VII. FURTHER REASONS FOR ABANDONING THE MANDATORY LIFE SENTENCE

A. The MLS Violates the Sentencing Principles of Proportionality and Restraint

Any mandatory sentence subjects all offenders to the same penalty regardless of the seriousness of the specific offence or the offender's level of culpability. Mandatory sentences thus risk violating the principle of proportionality in sentencing – the fundamental principle of sentencing in all common law jurisdictions (Roberts and Baker, 2007). How does this occur? Proportionality requires a calibration of the seriousness of the crime which is then matched with an appropriately severe sentence. Yet seriousness and culpability cannot be determined in the abstract by Parliament. The exercise is individualised – to reflect the characteristics of each crime, each offender. It can only be accomplished by a sentencing court after hearing a detailed account of the crime and the offender. Imposing the same sentence on all offenders means that important differences in terms of harm and culpability are ignored, or at least not given adequate reflection – hence the loss of proportionality. Granted, a degree of discretion is permitted by the MLS to the extent that the judge should reflect the individual aggravating and mitigating factors in the minimum term, but in all cases the sentence only terminates on the death of the offender, who may remain liable to recall to prison (without necessarily committing any further offence) for many decades.

The MLS also violates the principle of restraint or parsimony in sentencing. This principle requires courts to impose the least intrusive or onerous penalty that will be sufficient to achieve the objectives of sentencing, and is found in section 153(2) of the *Criminal Justice Act 2003*. This provision states that if a custodial sentence is passed, it should be for 'the shortest term . . . that in the opinion of the court is commensurate with the seriousness of the offence'. The operative phrase here is surely 'in the opinion of the court'; this suggests that sentence length should be established by the judicial determination of seriousness, rather than by Parliament in the abstract. Thus, if a five-year term of custody is sufficient to denounce the crime, deter the offender from further offending and achieve other potential objectives such as rehabilitation, a court should not impose an eight-year sentence. Mandatory sentences violate this principle of sentencing because they involve a legislature deciding, a priori, that *all* cases of, say murder, must attract an MLS. In reality there will always be some offenders for whom the MLS is not warranted and who accordingly merit some lesser penalty. The most obvious candidates to fall within this category are 'mercy killers', and there is clear evidence that the public does not regard the MLS as an appropriate way for the criminal justice system to deal with them (Mitchell, 1998).

B. Undermining Rehabilitation

Rehabilitation of the offender is one of the most fundamental purposes of sentencing. This objective is found in all western sentencing systems and was placed on a statutory footing in England and Wales by section 142 of the *Criminal Justice Act 2003.*[8] Some offenders may actively resist rehabilitation, others may be incapable of reform, but the vast majority of offenders have the potential for reformation. Their efforts in this direction should be actively encouraged, and offenders convicted of murder are no exception to this sound principle of corrections. The imposition of a sentence which never expires, however, can only impede the individual offender's efforts. How can he rejoin the community as a law-abiding citizen when he carries the sentence to the grave? Regardless of the lengths they may go to, offenders convicted of murder will always remain offenders.

C. Blind Retribution

There is one final point about the imposition of a life sentence which highlights the paradox of current arrangements. The alleged unique nature of murder – its inherent seriousness – justifies the imposition of a sentence which never expires. Yet some offenders convicted of murder receive minimum terms of less than 10 years in prison and are released into the community within a decade. Some cases with a significant degree of mitigation attract minimum terms of less than five years. This creates an obvious paradox: the gravity of the crime requires on the one hand a life sentence, yet at the same time the offender may be released after only a few years. Penologists have described this as 'bite and bark' sentencing: the sentencing process barks loudly by announcing a life-long sentence, yet in reality the 'bite' on the offender is much less severe. As the gap between the time actually served in prison and the label of life increases, the sentence will become increasingly implausible to the community.

D. Inappropriate Convictions for Manslaughter

The organisation Victim Support argued in its evidence to the House of Lords Select Committee that the existence of the MLS meant that sometimes the courts

[8] It is significant that the sentencing objectives enumerated in section 142 are not rank-ordered, suggesting that no single objective is primary, and therefore that rehabilitation is potentially as important as deterrence or any other statutory sentencing objective.

return inappropriate verdicts of manslaughter (House of Lords Select Committee, 1989: para 117). This accords with unpublished research data obtained by Barry Mitchell that in a small number of cases the evidence available to the court indicates there is a reasonable prospect of conviction for murder, yet the defendant is convicted of manslaughter. Although our basic sense of justice and the principle of fair labelling imply that the offence of which the defendant is convicted is very important, it may be that in practice more attention is focused on the sentence. Those involved in criminal trials for homicide, be they legal practitioners or laypersons, are keen that the punishment should reflect their perception of the seriousness of the case in hand. An MLS may seem a rather crude and inappropriate response, and so a murder conviction has to be avoided in order to provide the necessary sentencing discretion.[9]

VIII. CONCLUSIONS

In our view, the arguments in its favour are ultimately unpersuasive. The claim that murder is a uniquely heinous crime – the principal argument on which retentionists rely – could obviously be boosted by redefining the offence so as to remove from its ambit those cases that simply do not reflect particularly serious instances of homicide. But whether even then a MLS would be justifiable is by no means clear; for the very nature of a mandatory sentence places such enormous stress on the ability of the statutory draftsman to devise a set of provisions which will invariably distinguish the worst from the not-quite-so-bad homicides without producing any anomalies – ie injustices – along the way. That may well be asking too much.

The irony will hopefully not be lost on readers that there are more reasons to fear that the MLS undermines public confidence in the criminal justice system than to believe it is necessary to uphold such confidence. Making adjustments to the MLS simply would not be adequate to remedy this. There is abundant evidence that the public wants 'the punishment to fit the crime' and that can only be assured through a system which permits greater flexibility and discretion than the MLS. Moreover, public protection cannot rescue the case for the MLS, since there is no apparent reason to believe that public safety would necessarily be jeopardised if the sentencing law were to be reformed. Thus, focusing our attention on the arguments in favour of the status quo to the exclusion of the counter-arguments does not provide a convincing case for retention of the MLS. It is too crude and blunt an instrument, and its deficiencies cannot be adequately addressed by tinkering with other parts of the criminal justice system.

[9] This tendency has long existed in the administration of justice. For centuries jurors have avoided convicting in accordance with the facts established in court if a conviction would result in imposition of a sentence, eg the death penalty, which seems disproportionately harsh. In extreme cases juries acquit the defendant if they believe that a conviction would result in excessive punishment – a phenomenon referred to as 'jury nullification'.

5

Public Knowledge of Trends in Crime and Punishment

OVERVIEW

In this chapter we review public knowledge of a number of statistics relating to sentencing for murder, including crime trends and sentencing patterns. Before discussing the empirical findings, however, we note some reasons why public opinion is relevant to the debate about the future of sentencing arrangements for murder. This is followed by a brief discussion of measurement issues in the context of public opinion. We set out some of the limitations on public opinion polls as an adequate measure of community values and then describe the methodological approach we adopted, by summarising the specific research components of the project.

I. WHY ARE PUBLIC VIEWS RELEVANT?

Before describing and discussing the findings from our empirical research into public attitudes to sentencing for murder, it is important to provide some justification for this research. Why are public views relevant to the question of how to punish offenders convicted of murder – or any other offence for that matter? What role, if any, should public opinion play in determining sentencing policy and practice?[1] One short answer is that public opinion has long been cited as a justification for retaining the mandatory life sentence, both in this country and other jurisdictions. It has been argued that removing the mandatory element – for example, making a life sentence discretionary – would undermine public confidence in the administration of justice and in particular sentencing. Whether this is in fact true is an empirical question, and the one we have addressed in our research.

But there is a more principled reason for wanting to know how the public reacts to sentencing for murder. Systems of legal punishment do not exist in a vacuum; it is a truism to say that state responses to offending are culturally determined.

[1] For further discussion of this issue, see Ryberg (2011); Roberts (2011; 2008).

Sentencing practices reflect the larger society within which they are embedded. This suggests the need for some relationship between the sentencing practices of the courts and the communities on whose behalf legal punishment is imposed. Some link between community values and sentencing practice is surely necessary. More specifically, from a utilitarian perspective it is important to maintain an adequate level of public confidence in the sentencing process without which it would be harder for the justice system to function (see discussion in Robinson (2007; 2008)).

Retributive sentencing takes a different approach, one which is less concerned with preventing crime and which places heavy emphasis on proportionality. From a retributive perspective it makes little sense to overlook community values if they contain principles which may be relevant to proportional sentencing. Locating a place for the public requires finding some middle ground, where the community's views are considered, but with significant qualification.

We believe, however, that community views should only be considered when they are the views of an *informed* sample of the public – generally defined as those people who have been given some time and information to arrive at a decision.[2] It would be no more reasonable to use a public opinion poll to determine a penal policy than to use a public opinion survey to replace a criminal jury: in both cases we require a decision taken by a representative sample of the public[3] with adequate time to consider relevant evidence.

Three principal justifications exist for considering public views at sentencing: (i) to enhance perceptions of legitimacy and to encourage compliance with the law; (ii) to amplify the censure conveyed by a legal sanction; (iii) to reflect the social element of criminal wrongs.

A. Perceived Legitimacy

If sentencing policy and practice completely ignores public opinion, the legitimacy of the sentencing system will be threatened. More than this, the legitimacy of a state which punishes individuals without considering the community will be called into question, with adverse consequences for the criminal justice system. This consequentialist argument is most closely associated with the writings of Paul Robinson. In addition, compliance with the law is dependent upon the extent to which the community perceives the system to be legitimate. It is clear that compliance with the law cannot be achieved by threats alone. Research by Tyler and others has demonstrated the important role of perceived legitimacy in eliciting compliance with the law (see Tyler, 2006).

[2] See Golash and Lynch (1995) for a discussion of the use of surveys in shaping sentencing policy, and Roberts, Hough and Feilzer (2011); and Green (2006) for a discussion of research methodologies.

[3] Of course juries are not statistically representative of the general public; many people are either not eligible for jury duty or excused from serving on a jury. Nevertheless, the intention is for them to be as representative as possible.

These twin, related arguments are essentially consequentialist in nature: ignoring the views of the community will undermine perceptions of legitimacy as well as levels of compliance with the law. Both arguments assert a benefit (legitimacy, and consequently compliance) which is contingent upon a degree of concordance between opinion and practice. Thus if the practice of the courts drifts too far from the views of the community, this will create a gulf which may ultimately undermine the functioning of the system. Paul Robinson (Robinson, 2007; 2008; 2009) distinguishes 'deontological' from 'empirical' desert. By the term 'empirical desert' he refers to the responses of the community as measured by empirical research rather than positions derived from moral philosophy (deontological desert). Robinson advocates restructuring sentencing policies and practices to reflect to a far greater degree the intuitions about punishment held by members of the public. Robinson argues that the credibility of the criminal law is essential to effective crime control, and is enhanced if the sentencing process assigns punishment in a way that is consistent with 'shared intuitions of justice'.

B. Effective Censure

A related justification for public input at sentencing invokes the censuring function of the criminal sanction. Regardless of their specific nature and severity, all punishment systems reflect and interact with the social context in which they are set. The nature and perceived severity of specific sanctions, the factors that are considered to aggravate or mitigate, and indeed the overall objectives and principles reflect, in large measure, the culture of the society in which sentencing takes place. Moral blameworthiness – whether as a function of crime seriousness or culpability – also has a social component. Conceptions of what is blameworthy must to some degree be empirically derived from the community, or no blame will be communicated to the offender.

Retributivism involves the collective censure for criminal wrongs (see von Hirsch, 1976; 1993). The phrase 'collective censure' implies some social consensus about the kinds of conduct worthy of legal censure. Advocates of this perspective would argue that a sentencing framework derives its *coherence* from adhering to a theoretically sound model, but its *legitimacy* from its relationship to the community on whose behalf legal punishments are imposed. The degree of censure that we experience when censured is affected by the legitimacy of the censuring power. Penalties imposed by forces or governments considered illegitimate may be harsh, and may be experienced as harsh punishments, but the individuals on whom they are imposed are unlikely to feel censured – just punished. For example, the penalties imposed by an occupying foreign power will be perceived as punishments, yet lack all legitimacy – they are totally decoupled from the community to which the punished individual belongs.

If all consideration of public opinion were jettisoned, the censuring function of a court-imposed sentence would be divorced from the community on whose behalf censure is expressed. A purely theoretical account of sentencing would ultimately drift away from community views and the result will be a failure in the censuring power of the sentencing process. Ewing (1929) observed almost a century ago that when the sentencing system fails to impose adequate punishment 'the moral judgements of those who represent the State . . . will cease to be taken seriously' (p 95). The expression of legal censure is different from the blame we assign in daily life for non-criminal transgressions, but there must be some relation between the two systems.[4]

C. Recognising the Social Dimension of Moral Wrongfulness

The final justification for introducing public views into the determination of sentencing policy and practice invokes the social component of state punishment. The gravity of crimes, the legitimacy of legal defences, and many other components of the criminal law are influenced by community values. With respect to the determination of punishment, this means that cultural factors cannot be overlooked in favour of some abstract or purely theoretical model. This justification for the introduction of community input is therefore internal to a retributive rationale. Seriousness ratings and sentencing factors (for example) should reflect public opinion not for instrumental reasons – because the public will have more confidence in or respect for sentencing – but because community views constitute an inherent element of crime seriousness. To a degree, the moral wrongfulness of criminal acts is determined by the extent to which these acts depart from consensual norms, and these are derived from the culture. For all these reasons, therefore, it is important to understand what the public thinks about sentencing for murder.

II. WHY HAS THE SUBJECT BEEN OVERLOOKED?

Having noted the arguments supporting some community consultation or input into sentencing policy for murder, it is worth asking why, if public opinion is relevant, there has to date been no systematic exploration of public attitudes? Politicians and government departments have conducted a vast amount of research into public attitudes to sentencing and related issues such as parole, yet no one has ever commissioned a study of this most visible sentencing question. People seem to have simply accepted that the public endorses the use of a mandatory life sentence.

[4] The censure-amplification argument is susceptible to some critiques. Collective censure can easily become unprincipled – for example if the majority expresses its greater disapproval of crime committed by minorities. For this reason, the public's position on any punishment-related issue should be subject to careful scrutiny rather than imported blindly into the practice of sentencing, and should be subject to strict limits.

Three explanations may be offered for this failure to determine the true position of the public. First, few – if any – politicians appear interested in proposing to relax the mandatory requirement for the imposition of a life sentence in cases of murder. To do so may be to court electoral disaster for appearing soft on crime (and in particular the most serious crime). Secondly, there has been a slavish adherence to public opinion surveys as a tool of measuring public opinion, and a couple of these have been conducted on the issue of sentencing murder. Thirdly, governments and law reform agencies around the world have evinced little interest in addressing the sentencing of offenders convicted of murder.[5] As noted, the government's terms of reference for the Law Commission's homicide review of 2005 expressly directed the Commission to 'take account of the continued existence of the mandatory life sentence for murder' (Law Commission of England and Wales, 2006: 1).

What is needed is a careful analysis of the nature of public attitudes to sentencing for murder using an appropriate research methodology. At this point we discuss some of the methodological challenges and options confronting researchers in the field.

III. DEFICIENCIES OF OPINION POLLS AS A MEASURE OF PUBLIC OPINION

A. Question Format

Most empirical studies of public attitudes to crime and criminal justice have used a public opinion survey (see Roberts and Hough (2005a) for a review and Roberts, Feilzer and Hough (2011); Viki and Bohner (2009); and Stalans (2002) for discussion of methodological issues). Sample sizes, sampling strategies and modes of contact (face to face; telephone; internet-based) all vary, but the essential element is constant: respondents are asked to respond rapidly to a question which, given the time constraints of the survey, must be clear and simple. Unfortunately, the simplicity of the question undermines polling as a methodology for exploring public attitudes to criminal justice. Although most issues in the area of crime and justice are complex and controversial, they often seem straightforward. Everyone has an opinion about subjects like mandatory sentencing for knife-crime, parole or the role of the victim at sentencing; a simple question such as 'are you in favour of or opposed to mandatory sentencing' immediately taps into an intuitive reservoir of opinion about sentencing. These intuitions then guide the individual's response.

[5] The response of the Ministry of Justice to media coverage of the research reported in this book offers a good example of the indifference to criminal law reform in this area. A Ministry spokesman noted: 'We have no plans to abolish the mandatory life sentence for murder. The most serious crimes deserve the most serious sentences'. (Cited in *The Guardian*, 6 December 2011).

The use of focus groups and related qualitative research methods addresses this deficiency, at least to some degree. By holding a deliberative discussion around the issue it is possible for researchers to uncover the complexities and nuances of public reaction. However, the focus group methodology carries its own deficiencies and limitations. Focus group discussions are seldom recorded, and if they are, the reader of a research report or scholarly article is unlikely to have access to a recording of the group discussions. The conclusions of the report are therefore taken on trust; we rely on the ability of the researcher to render an accurate account of what the focus group participants said. The discussion is filtered through the moderator, who may or may not have done a good job in directing and summarising the discussions. Often the focus group is conducted by a general qualitative researcher, one who may not be a substantive expert in the issue being discussed. Focus groups therefore represent a useful adjunct to the use of opinion polls, but they do not resolve all the problems.

B. Context of Questions

A second deficiency of criminal justice polling concerns the context – independent of how the specific questions are constructed or how much time respondents have to answer. Almost all pollsters adopt a very narrow, client-directed approach to research, one which rewards brevity and ignores the context in which the questions are posed. The respondent's level of knowledge about the issue being explored is a most important contextual element in many areas of public policy, yet this dimension of public opinion is routinely overlooked by pollsters. Consider the question of sentencing severity. The most frequently posed sentencing-related question is probably '*Are sentences too tough, too lenient or about right?*' The response pattern to this question varies little across jurisdictions or over time within the same jurisdiction.

For example, the British Crime Survey (BCS) has repeatedly shown that between three-quarters and four-fifths of the public express the view that sentencing is too lenient. Moreover, the public perception of leniency has persisted for some time. Thus, in 1990 the British Attitudes Survey found that four out of five respondents agreed with the statement that 'too many convicted criminals are let off lightly by the courts' (Dowds, 1995). Over two-thirds of the British public held this view in 1981. Thirty years later, the most recent polling in Britain found that approximately three-quarters of the polled public held the view that sentencing was too lenient (Dawes et al, 2011).

Similar trends emerge in other countries. Thus 85 per cent of respondents in South Africa and 74 per cent in Scotland expressed the view that sentences were too lenient (Schonteich, 1999; Justice 1 Committee, 2007). Comparable findings emerge from other countries, including Belgium (Parmentier et al, 2004), Germany (Kury et al, 2002) and Barbados (Nuttall et al, 2003). US polls also reveal little variation over time in the percentage perceiving sentences to be too lenient. This percentage did not vary outside a narrow range from 79 per cent in 1975 to 67 per cent in 2002 (Sourcebook of Criminal Justice Statistics, 2011). The same pattern emerges from Australian and Canadian polls over the same period (see Roberts and Indermaur, 2009; Roberts et al, 2007). Taking this finding – that most people see courts as too lenient – without considering the context – would lead to the conclusion that the public are much harsher than the courts, but when public knowledge of sentencing patterns is explored, we gain insight into the responses to the severity question (see below).

Repeated administrations of the BCS and other surveys around the world have shown that most people underestimate the lengths of custodial sentences handed down by the courts, and underestimate the amount of time that offenders actually serve in prison prior to being released on licence. Public estimates of the imprisonment rate for specific offences are significantly lower than the actual rates (eg, Doob and Roberts, 1983; Hough and Roberts, 1999; Mattinson and Mirrlees-Black, 2000; Walker, Hough and Lewis, 1988). The public in many countries also underestimates the average length of sentences of imprisonment (Hough and Roberts, 1998; Home Office, 2001; Paulin et al, 2003). The consequences of these trends for attitudes trends is clear: when people say sentencing is too lenient, their attitude is based upon an inaccurate perception of actual trends. This is also true for murder, as we shall shortly demonstrate.

IV. MURDER AS A SPECIAL CASE

In our view, conventional opinion poll questions are particularly inappropriate for exploring public attitudes to sentencing for murder. First, respondents are never given specific cases to consider; this can only exacerbate the punitiveness of responses. Research has demonstrated that when asked about sentencing, people tend to think of the worst cases – those which are most likely to attract media stories.[6] Thinking about the worst cases of murder will lead to the most punitive responses. Most members of the public are unaware of the range of culpable conduct that can give rise to a conviction for murder and subsequent imposition of a life sentence. The British public is likely to associate murder with high-profile cases such as Ian Huntley, Myra Hindley or Frederick West which have many aggravating features; cases of a less serious nature are unlikely to come to mind when people think about murder.

Most people would be surprised at the diversity of criminal conduct which can give rise to a conviction for murder; even relatively common cases such as those in which a person intends serious bodily harm but who does not intend to kill would strike the public as atypical. And the concept of joint enterprise murder, in which an individual can be convicted of murder on the basis of a quite limited

[6] For example, Doob and Roberts (1988) and Indermaur (1987) found that when people responding to a general question about sentencing severity were asked to identify the offender that they had in mind, most respondents said they had been thinking of violent, repeat offenders.

degree of actual involvement in the killing (see Chapter six), will likely strike many people as constituting a crime other than murder – as our data will demonstrate later in this book. Secondly, in most polls about sentencing for murder in Britain, respondents were, unrealistically, allowed to select a sanction long abolished (capital punishment). This restricted and selective set of response options then distorts the image of public attitudes emerging from the survey.

In the course of this volume we shall demonstrate significant public support for definite terms of imprisonment rather than mandatory life imprisonment for offenders convicted of murder. This finding emerges when people are asked to impose sentence having been given specific cases to consider (eg, Schonteich, 1999).[7] This methodology comes much closer to capturing the nature of public opinion, and of course more closely matches the task facing a sentencing court. Although prior research has explored public reactions to sentencing in specific cases (see Roberts and Hough, 2005a), it has never been used with respect to murder.

V. SURVEYS OF ATTITUDES TO THE DEATH PENALTY

We cannot ignore polls posing general questions completely, however, since they influence politicians. Most polls containing questions on sentencing for murder have explored the issue in the context of the death penalty. The focus has been on that specific sanction rather than the broader issues surrounding murder and terms of imprisonment. Opinion polls asking whether respondents favour or oppose the death penalty for murder constitute a very imperfect measure of public attitudes. They may be compared to an inaccurate set of scales – offering useful guidance as to *changes* in a person's weight over time, but no reliable estimate of the objective weight of the individual.

Polls permit the tracking of public support for capital punishment over time by recording the percentage in favour of executing murderers, but provide little insight into the true nature of public attitudes to sentencing. Such surveys preclude inferences about the *absolute* level of support for capital punishment in the general population, or the level of support for the death penalty relative to sentencing alternatives such as life imprisonment (with or without parole) or fixed-term lengthy terms of custody. People need to be given alternatives to the death penalty to consider, and they should evaluate the options while contemplating actual cases of murder, not a categorical description such as 'murder'.

While this observation applies to all sentencing-related questions, it is particularly applicable for murder. Most people subscribe to a relatively simple conception of murder: Ask a member of the public to describe the offence and they will

[7] Schonteich (1999), for example, found that when asked a general question, three-quarters of his sample of South African respondents favoured the death penalty. However, when given specific cases of murder to sentence, the percentage supporting execution of the offender dropped to less than half, even for a case with aggravating circumstances.

probably include the elements of intentionality as well as the loss of human life. Premeditation is often cited by members of the public as an element of the offence of murder (see, eg Mitchell, 1998). Moving beyond an intuitive offence description to ask people to describe the typical murder they will likely generate an image of an offender with prior convictions, who planned the death of his victim, probably for profit, revenge or other bad motives. In other words, the worst forms of murder will come to the public mind when they are asked questions about sentencing offenders convicted of this offence.[8]

An accurate calibration of public support for the death penalty or the mandatory life sentence requires certain conditions, all of which are absent in conventional opinion polls which pose general policy questions. The deficiencies of simple polls introduce systematic error into the measurement of public attitudes. By allowing respondents to create their own image of the crime, and by restricting their freedom to choose from among a range of sanctions, polls over-estimate the level of public support for both the death penalty and the more punitive alternatives such as mandatory life imprisonment or life imprisonment without release on parole. Researchers in the field of capital punishment have demonstrated this by the simple expedient of asking people both a simple question about whether they support the death penalty and then whether they support capital punishment in specific cases. When this is accomplished the results reveal (a) high levels of support for the death penalty in the abstract; and (b) much lower levels of support when people are asked to make decisions in actual cases (see Roberts and Hough, 2005a).

To summarise, opinion polls which use questions with little concrete information give a partial and misleading representation of public views of sentencing, particularly for murder. For this reason a more sophisticated methodology is required. Opinion polls are useful for establishing public levels of knowledge of a particular issue. An important component of our research therefore involved putting questions with known factual answers to members of the public, with a view seeing what proportions would be correct. Focus groups cannot establish population levels of knowledge.

VI. OUR RESEARCH

There were two related stages to this research project, reflecting the importance we attached to both quantitative and qualitative research perspectives.

[8] Some of the less serious forms of homicide also get included in the public's generic definition of murder; frequently people will unthinkingly refer to someone convicted of dangerous driving causing death as a murderer. This is a consequence of the public emphasis on harm – the loss of human life. In all probability, however, premeditated killings more often come to the public mind when asked to describe the typical case of murder.

A. Quantitative Survey

The first research element was quantitative in nature. The survey fieldwork took place between 12 and 24 May 2010, and 1,027 face-to-face interviews were conducted by a well-known research firm (GfK/NOP). Interviewing took place in 102 sampling points across England and Wales. Each sampling point was a Census Output Area, and these were selected from a list of all Output Areas, stratified by Government Office Region, local authority, urban/rural character and Index of Multiple Deprivation score. The target was for 10 interviews to be conducted in each sampling point, with quota controls set for age and gender interlocked with working status. Interviewing took place in respondents' homes by means of Computer Aided Personal Interviewing (CAPI), and the interviews took about 30 minutes each to complete.

The questionnaire – a copy of which can be found in Appendix C of this volume – involved a number of split sample variations in wording; each respondent was randomly allocated to one of the variants by the CAPI script. This method provides a relatively accurate guide to the attitudes of the population, although the level of accuracy is related to the sample size. Thus, for example, if the whole sample was used and 50 per cent expressed a given response, we can be 95 per cent sure that the proportion of the population in England and Wales giving the same response would be between 47 per cent and 53 per cent, although it is more likely to fall near the sample statistic than more extreme values. For the purposes of exploring social attitudes such as sentencing this level of accuracy is more than sufficient.[9]

B. Qualitative Focus Groups

The second stage of the research involved a qualitative research approach. The survey organisation Plus Four was engaged to convene six focus groups to facilitate further exploration of public opinion and murder. Two sessions were held in Leeds, two in Hinckley, and two in Bath. Five groups consisted of nine members of the public and the sixth comprised 10 people. Participants were screened so as to exclude market researchers, members of the police or armed forces, the legal profession and the media; also excluded were those who reported having a family relative or close friend involved in a murder case. To the limited extent possible with small numbers of participants, the composition of the groups reflected the national population in age, marital status and domestic circumstances, occupation, and socio-economic grouping.

Each group was asked to consider the following scenario which had been used in the quantitative survey:

[9] If we were hoping to predict the outcome of a general election, a much larger sample would be necessary.

Jim decided to rob a bank. He bought a shotgun and was prepared to kill anyone who tried to prevent him. He entered the bank, pointed the gun at the cashier and demanded money. When the cashier pushed the alarm bell, Jim shot him dead and then fled.

Having discussed the sentencing options in that case the participants then considered other relatively serious types of murder (such as the murder of a police officer, the murder of a baby, and the murder of multiple victims).

The second purpose of the focus groups was to obtain a more detailed picture of the public's knowledge and understanding of the current sentencing arrangements for murder, and in particular to gauge their views about the value and appropriateness of the release of most prisoners serving life for murder on life licence at the expiry of the minimum term. The discussions were audio-recorded and each lasted for between 75 and 90 minutes. Each stage of the methodology was reviewed in advance by the ethics committee at Coventry University.

At this point we turn to review levels of public knowledge.

VII. PUBLIC KNOWLEDGE OF MURDER TRENDS AND THE MANDATORY LIFE SENTENCE

Attitudes must be considered with some awareness of levels of public knowledge. This is particularly the case when the goal of research is to evaluate public reaction to sentencing policies – such as the mandatory life sentence. For this reason, prior to exploring people's attitudes we measured respondents' awareness of the crime and punishment of murder in this country. We posed several questions to explore respondents' knowledge of current statistical trends. First, however, we set the findings within the context of previous research on public knowledge of sentencing. Research on public knowledge of sentencing represents a small percentage of all public opinion research in this area; most researchers have seemed content to measure opinions without exploring the knowledge on which those attitudes are based. However, there is a limited literature from several countries from which we can learn.

A. Knowledge of Overall Crime Trends

Surveys have asked respondents in many countries to estimate recent crime trends. These studies go back many years, and the results are strikingly consistent. Crime rates in most western nations have been declining steadily since the mid-1990s – although that is not the way the public see things. For example, between 1992 and 2008 the property crime rate declined in the United States from 325 to 134 incidents per 1,000 households, a decline of 59 per cent (US Bureau of Justice Statistics, 2011). Violent crime declined from 51 incidents per 1,000 population to only 19 over the same period, a drop of almost two-thirds (US Bureau of Justice

Statistics, 2011). Yet when asked about the crime trends most Americans continued to believe that there was more crime than during the previous year. By 1997, approximately two-thirds of respondents to a nationwide poll held this view, and the percentage was almost the same a decade later. Similar trends are repeatedly observed in other countries including Canada, New Zealand and Australia (eg, Roberts and Indermaur, 2009).

B. Knowledge of Murder Trends

If people over-estimate general trends in crime, it seems likely that they will also over-estimate murder trends. Unfortunately, the BCS has not asked any questions to explore public perceptions of murder trends or rates. However, in other jurisdictions the public clearly over-estimated the volume of murder (eg, Weatherburn and Indermaur, 2004). Indermaur (1987) found that four-fifths of the public believed that the murder rate in Australia had increased when in fact there had been no change. Vandiver and Giacopassi (1997) found that US residents over-estimated the true number of homicides; some by a very considerable margin: 15 per cent of their respondents estimated that one million or more murders occurred annually across the United States There is no reason to believe that the public in Britain would be any more accurate in their estimates of murder trends, and as we shall see, people are no more accurate in this country.

C. Knowledge of Statutory Maxima and Sentencing Trends

The first surveys to systematically explore public knowledge of sentencing trends were conducted in North America. Almost 40 years ago a survey in California explored public knowledge of maximum penalties. The results demonstrated that most people underestimated the severity of statutory maxima – possibly reflecting public estimates of penalties imposed (see California Assembly Committee on Criminal Procedure, 1975; Williams, Gibbs and Erickson, 1980). Surveys have shown that Canadians and Australians also under-estimate the magnitude of statutory maxima by a considerable margin and this was true even for well-publicised offences such as drink driving, rape or robbery (see Roberts, 1988; Indermaur, 1987). Other research has explored public estimates of current sentencing practices.

Polls conducted in Canada, Britain, and Australia all converge on the same result: most people systematically under-estimate the severity of sentencing trends, and this has long been the case. For example, Doob and Roberts (1982) found that fully three-quarters of a sample of Canadians provided a 'large under-estimate' of the percentage of convictions for robbery, rape and assault. British data (from the British Crime Survey (BCS)) collected in 1996 and 2000 sustain the same conclusion: large majorities of respondents provided estimates of imprisonment rates which were much too low for all categories of crime (Hough and Roberts, 1998; see also Australian data reported by Roberts and Indermaur, 2009; Indermaur, 1987). Questions about imprisonment rates were repeated a decade later using the BCS and with the same result: most people underestimated the incarceration rate for common crimes (Hough and Roberts, 2012). These statistics are all the more surprising since over the period 1996–2008 sentencing became more severe in England and Wales, although this obviously escaped the attention of the public. The common element, over time and across jurisdictions is of course news media coverage. News media reports of sentencing are highly selective and over-represent sentences which appear lenient.

In our study we were interested in two related domains: public knowledge of murder trends in Britain, and public awareness of punishment of persons convicted of murder.

VIII. MURDER TRENDS IN ENGLAND AND WALES: PERCEPTIONS AND REALITY

Previous research has revealed that societal beliefs about crime trends affect public perceptions of the sentencing process (see Roberts and Hough, 2005a). People often perceive a relationship between crime rates and sentence severity; many people have an intuitive belief in the power of severe sentences to deter offenders. If the public perceives crime rates to be high and/ or rising, they also infer that sentences are too lenient. We therefore included two questions on the survey to explore public knowledge of recent murder trends in England and Wales. One question asked about trends in murder over the past few years, while the second probed perceptions of the murder rate in this country compared to other jurisdictions.

A. Reality of Murder Trends

Surprisingly, perhaps, determining the number or rate of murders is not straightforward; a portrait of murder trends in Britain must be composed from two sources: offences reported to the police and classified as homicide, and convictions for murder. The homicide statistics reveal a decline over recent years. The 608 offences officially recorded as homicide in 2009–10 represented the lowest number since 1997–98 (Smith et al, 2012). Statistics published by the Home Office[10] show that having reached a peak of 942 in 2002–03,[11] the number of

[10] These statistics distinguish three different sets of figures, namely (1) offences initially recorded as homicide, (2) offences currently recorded as homicide, and (3) convictions for murder and manslaughter. For a variety of reasons a proportion of the first two groups are ultimately not regarded as murders or manslaughters.

[11] As Smith et al (2012) note, statistics from 2002–03 are misleading because they include 172 homicides attributed to Harold Shipman. The total of 172 was derived from homicides committed over a range of years. If we ignore the year 2002–03, the highest number recorded was 793, in 2001–02.

offences officially recorded as homicide (ie, murder and manslaughter combined) has since declined.

The average for the latest three years for which complete figures are available (2007–10) was 661, a decline of nearly 17 per cent since 2001–02 (Smith et al, 2012: Table 1.01). The average number of homicides recorded as murder over the latest three years for which reliable data are available (2007–10) is 241 – a decline of more than 18 per cent over the previous three years (2004–07 (Smith et al, 2012: Table 1.02). Convictions for murder reached a high of 318 cases in 2004–05 and have also since declined to a record low in 2009–10, when 195 were recorded. The number of recorded murder convictions in 2009–10 was nearly 19 per cent lower than a decade earlier.

B. Public Perceptions of Murder Trends

How accurate are the public when asked to estimate murder trends? The exact question we posed respondents was the following: '*Has the number of murders in this country over the past decade increased greatly, increased somewhat, stayed about the same, declined somewhat, declined greatly?*' On the basis of the homicide and murder statistics just summarised we would conclude that the correct answer to this question is 'declined somewhat'.

Public responses to the murder trends question are summarised in Table 5.1,[12] from which it can be seen that only five per cent of the sample chose the correct answer (ie, 'declined somewhat'). In total, almost two-thirds (64 per cent) of the sample expressed the view that murder rates had actually increased over the decade. This sub-group of respondents was equally divided: 32 per cent thought that murder had increased *greatly* and the same percentage expressed the view that it had increased 'somewhat' (see Table 5.1). Approximately one-fifth held the

Table 5.1 Public Perceptions of Murder Trends in England and Wales

Over the past decade, the number of murders in this country has . . .	
Increased greatly	32%
Increased somewhat	32%
Stayed about the same	21%
Declined somewhat (correct answer)	*5%*
Declined greatly	1%
Don't know	10%
Total	*100%*

Question: 'Over the past decade has the number of murders in this country...?'

12 For most questions in this survey the percentage of 'don't know' responses was 2% or fewer. For this reason all tables exclude these responses, presenting them only when they account for 3% or more of the sample.

view that the murder rate had stayed the same while 10 per cent responded 'don't know' (see Table 5.1).

C. Comparisons with Other Jurisdictions

The second question testing levels of knowledge asked respondents to compare the murder rate in England and Wales to other western European nations. Smith et al (2012) provide homicide rate comparisons for a limited number of European jurisdictions which show that the homicide rate for England and Wales is generally in line with those for other Western European nations. The rate in England and Wales was 1.35 per 100,000 population which is lower than Finland (2.34); Scotland (2.14); Ireland (2.00); Belgium (1.97); Luxembourg (1.61); Northern Ireland (1.52); Portugal (1.46); and France (1.37); but higher than Denmark (1.22); Italy (1.13); Sweden (1.06); Greece (1.04); Netherlands (1.02); Spain (1.02); Germany (0.84); and Austria (0.61) (see Smith et al, 2012: p 18). The specific question we posed to respondents was: '*Do you think the murder rate in this country is higher, lower or about the same as in other western European nations?*' The correct answer – based on official statistics – is therefore that the murder rate is 'about the same' in this country as in other western European countries.

Table 5.2 shows that public knowledge is out of step with trends regarding this question as well. By a margin of approximately two to one, respondents were more likely to believe that the murder rate is higher here than in other western nations. Thus almost a third of respondents believed that the rate was higher in England and Wales, compared to 18% who thought that it was lower. Public knowledge levels were higher for this question than some others: however, significantly less than half (38 per cent) of the sample chose the correct answer, namely that the murder rate was about the same here as in other western jurisdictions.

Table 5.2 Public Perceptions of the Murder Rate in England and Wales Compared to Other Nations

The murder rate is…	
Much higher in this country than in other western European nations	9%
Somewhat higher in this country	22%
About the same in this country (correct answer)	*38%*
Somewhat lower in this country	16%
Much lower in this country	2%
Don't know	13%
Total	*100%*

Question: 'Is the murder rate in this country much higher, somewhat higher, about the same, somewhat lower or much lower than in other western European nations?'

These public misperceptions about murder trends are troubling. It would be unreasonable to expect the public to have accurate opinions about crime trends in general or trends for specific offences. After all, the annual crime statistics released by the Home Office are often reduced to a few brief newspaper headlines. In many cases the headline bears little relation to the contents of the statistical report. In light of its importance to public confidence, murder statistics should be the focus of more attention from statistical agencies. Public knowledge of murder trends would appear to be affected by two important trends. First, the statistics are not easily compiled, even by professional researchers; secondly, the news media coverage of murder is very unrepresentative of statistical trends. Is it any wonder that most people subscribe to misperceptions?

IX. PERCEPTIONS OF TIME SERVED IN PRISON BY OFFENDERS CONVICTED OF MURDER

If members of the general public are misinformed about murder trends, they also have inaccurate views about the punishment of offenders convicted of murder. As noted, research has demonstrated that members of the public in this country and elsewhere tend to under-estimate the length of time that offenders serve in prison. There are at least two explanations of this tendency. First, people generally under-estimate the average length of sentences imposed at sentencing. One explanation for this is the rather cynical view that most people have about criminal justice in general – the system is seen as being lenient on offenders in several ways.

Secondly, many people *over*-estimate the extent to which early release provisions such as parole reduce the proportion of a custodial sentence served in prison. This tendency reveals itself in survey findings which show that people under-estimate the proportion of a prison sentence that is served in prison. Data collected in the United States found that 93 per cent of a representative sample of the public believed that inmates serve significantly less time in prison than they actually do (Florida Department of Corrections, 1997). This study also confirmed the tendency of the public to see the system as becoming more lenient: while the public believed that the percentage of time served in prison had decreased, in reality it had doubled in the five years preceding the survey (Florida Department of Corrections, 1997). Curiously, no research of which we are aware has explored public knowledge of time served statistics in Britain.[13]

[13] Anecdotal evidence derived from many conversations with members of the public suggests that they assume that some portion of a sentence of imprisonment is served in the community. This is of course accurate. However, with respect to murder, the public appear to assume that the life prisoner is released automatically, and once in the community is as free as any other citizen. People appear unaware of the conditions of the life licence, as well as the impact of those conditions on the offender.

A. Reality of Time Served in Prison by Offenders Convicted of Murder

How long do offenders convicted of murder and sentenced to life imprisonment in Britain actually spend in prison? This question may be answered by examining minimum terms imposed by courts, or by the number of years that mandatory life prisoners have served prior to their release on licence. The latter statistics will obviously be somewhat longer because some prisoners – for a variety of reasons – will be released later than at the end of their minimum term.

Table 5.3 summarises statistics from the National Offender Management Service (NOMS) at the Ministry of Justice previously presented at Table 3.1. This table provides the average minimum number of years imposed on mandatory life prisoners convicted of murder and released in each calendar year.[14] As can be seen, between the years of 2000 and 2009, on average, offenders sentenced to a mandatory life sentence could expect to spend at least 15½ years in prison before being released on licence.[15] These statistics also reveal that the minimum number of years lifers are required to spend in prison has been increasing: the average for the last 10 years (15½ years) is higher than the 13 years recorded over the previous decade 1990–99 (see Home Office, 2001).

Table 5.3 Average Minimum Terms Imposed on Offenders Sentenced to Mandatory Life Sentence

Year	Average minimum term (years)
2000	14.32
2001	14.00
2002	13.19
2003	13.68
2004	14.52
2005	16.14
2006	17.54
2007	15.91
2008	17.96
2009	17.54
Average over the decade	*15.50*

Source: NOMS, Ministry of Justice; data to 5 February 2010

[14] These minimum terms under-estimate to some degree the amount of time that life prisoners actually serve in prison, as some prisoners are detained beyond the minimum term. Another source of data is therefore the average number of years actually served; these data reveal the same general pattern as the minimum term statistics summarised here: they demonstrate an increase in the amount of time prisoners serving life for murder have spent in prison prior to release.

[15] The statistics were taken from the Public Protection Unit database in the NOMS. We would like to thank Tony Macgregor from NOMS and Ransford Fiti, Prison and Probation Statistics for their assistance in providing the statistics.

We posed two questions about time served in prison by offenders convicted of murder. Half the sample was asked to estimate the amount of time that offenders convicted of murder spend in prison in this country before being released on licence, while the other half was asked whether the average time served in prison by convicted murderers was higher or lower in Britain compared to other western nations.

It is more challenging to provide an authoritative answer to the question of comparative amounts of time served. Homicide definitions vary considerably across jurisdictions and this alone has inhibited comparative analyses. One limited comparative study conducted a decade ago would suggest that offenders convicted of murder in England and Wales spend somewhat longer in prison than offenders convicted of murder in other jurisdictions (Public Safety Canada, 2000). The average number of years served by persons convicted of murder in England and Wales in that study was 14 years, significantly higher than many other jurisdictions. For example, the study reported that the average number of years served by life prisoners convicted of murder was 12 years in Sweden and Norway, 13 years in Belgium and Denmark, and 11 years in Ireland (Public Safety Canada, 2000). Moreover, looking at the ficures previously given in Table 3.2 the average number of years served in prison in England and Wales prior to release on licence has increased over the past decade from 13 to 18 years. The correct answer to the second question we posed is most likely that offenders convicted of murder and sentenced to life imprisonment spend more time in prison in England and Wales.

B. Public Perceptions of Time Served in Prison

Table 5.4 summarises public responses to the first question. As can be seen, there is a clear tendency for the public to under-estimate the amount of time that life prisoners served in custody: more than four respondents in 10 believed that offenders convicted of murder spent 10 years or less in prison.[16] Thus most respondents underestimated the severity of the life sentence in terms of the number of years served in prison prior to release on licence: 48 per cent gave a response which we have classified as roughly accurate, namely one between 11 and 20 years.

In response to the question about comparative time served in prison statistics, more than six respondents in 10 (61 per cent) believed that persons convicted of murder in this country spend less time in prison than prisoners elsewhere in the western world. Sixteen percent believed the amount of time spent was about the same and six per cent thought that convicted murderers in this country spent more time in prison.[17] Thirteen per cent of the sample failed to respond or

[16] The British public is not the only one to misperceive trends in time served in prison. A survey conducted in the United States found that although the overall time served in prison had increased, 60% of the polled public believed the exact opposite (Justice Centre, 2007).

[17] This tendency to assume sentencing is more lenient in the respondent's own jurisdiction is also found in other countries. The custody rate in Canada has typically been higher than most other western

responded 'don't know'. If we consider only those respondents who expressed an opinion on the question, approximately three-quarters of the sample believed (incorrectly) that sentencing for murder is more lenient here than in other western nations.

Table 5.4 Public Estimates of Number of Years Served in Prison by Offenders Convicted of Murder

Number of years offenders convicted of murder actually spend in prison	*% of Respondents*	*Cumulative Percentage*
1 to 5 years	3%	3%
6 to 10 years	39%	42%
11 to 20 years (Correct answer)	48%	90%
21 to 30 years	8%	98%
More than 30 years	2%	100%
Total	*100%*	

Question: 'How many years do offenders convicted of murder and sentenced to life imprisonment actually spend in prison?'

X. PUBLIC ESTIMATES OF LIFE LICENCE RE-OFFENDING STATISTICS

The final knowledge question posed on our survey explored public estimates of the percentage of life licence prisoners in the community who are recalled to prison. We were interested in this issue because members of the public often make spontaneous comments about the danger to the community of allowing prisoners sentenced to life for murder out on licence. In light of these comments we thought it unlikely that people would have any accurate idea of the actual criminal recidivism rate of this small group of prisoners on licence in the community. Respondents were asked to estimate the percentage of life prisoners who were recalled to prison following an allegation of fresh offending.[18]

A. Reality

For the most recent year for which data are available (2009–10), 63 lifers or 4.7 per cent of the total population of 1,345 were recalled to prison for any rea-

nations (except the United States and England and Wales); however, when a sample of the public was asked about the use of custody in that country, the most common response was that the custody rate was lower (see Roberts, Nuffield and Hann, 2000).

[18] We recognise that prisoners may be recalled for breaches of conditions unrelated to allegations of fresh offending. Indeed, technical breaches account for the majority of recalls. However, the public generally believe that fresh offending is the cause, which is why we asked about this issue.

son.[19] (Of these recalls, almost all were for allegations of a breach of their licence conditions rather than for allegations of fresh offending). The recall rate has remained stable over the past decade. We therefore estimate the correct answer to this question to be 'approximately 2 per cent'.

B. Public Perceptions

As shown in Table 5.5, the public holds a relatively pessimistic view of re-offending by lifers, with the most likely response (held by four of ten respondent) being that 20 per cent of life prisoners released on parole are recalled for having re-offended. If we conservatively classify respondents who chose one per cent or five per cent as being more or less 'correct', this means that approximately three-quarters of the sample were incorrect, while a further nine per cent responded 'no idea'.

Table 5.5 Public Estimates of Percentage of Life Licence Recalls for Further Offending

Response	*% of respondents*	*Cumulative %*
1% (Correct answer)	*2%*	*2%*
5%	15%	17%
10%	17%	34%
15%	17%	51%
20%	40%	91%
No idea	9%	
Total	*100%*	*100%*

Question: 'What percentage of offenders convicted of murder and who have been released on licence to live in the community are recalled to prison for committing another offence? Would you say it is closest to . . .?'

This is the first time that a survey has measured public perceptions of life licence recalls. However, the over-estimation of recidivism rates is consistent with research which has explored public perceptions of recidivism rates for other categories of offender (eg, Redondo, Luque and Funes, 1996; Roberts and White, 1986). Public over-estimates of recall statistics are relevant because they are presumably related to public support for a life sentence; if people believe that re-offending is likely when a prisoner is released on licence they may well be opposed to release provisions.

[19] These figures were kindly provided by the National Offender Management Service.

XI. KNOWLEDGE LEVELS OF THE MANDATORY LIFE SENTENCE IN FOCUS GROUPS

Our focus groups provided an added opportunity to probe public knowledge of sentencing for murder, and in particular the way that the mandatory sentence functions, a topic which is hard to explore within the limits of a quantitative survey. It was clear from the focus group discussions that participants had only a very imprecise idea of what the mandatory life sentence for murder actually means. Predictably, when asked about the life sentence, they generally responded that 'life doesn't mean life', and most suggested that murderers are sent to prison for fixed periods before being automatically released – the periods they suggested varied from as little as 10 years. What was especially notable was the comments made; participants clearly implied that the phrase 'life sentence' (or perhaps 'life imprisonment') is misleading and that some more accurate label should be substituted. These reactions highlight the self-defeating nature of a mandatory life sentence with release after a minimum period. Created to ensure maximum denunciation and confidence in sentencing, in reality it may well have the opposite effect, namely of fuelling public cynicism about sentencing.

Focus group participants were also unsure about who is responsible for determining the minimum term. One person thought that there is a separate hearing specifically for this purpose. Many participants were aware that the Parole Board of England and Wales has an important role in deciding whether a murderer should be released on life licence, but appeared to have little or no knowledge of the nature of this role, or of the process by which the decision is made. Some participants were aware that licensees are supervised or monitored, although very few had any clear idea of what this actually means – an issue to which we shall return in a subsequent chapter. Several participants knew that licensees are released under certain conditions but very few participants were able to suggest what these conditions entail.

XII. CONCLUSIONS

Taken together, these findings demonstrate the prevalence of several misperceptions about trends regarding murder and the life sentence. It would be unreasonable to expect people to have an accurate sense of many criminal justice statistics, particularly those that relate to sentencing. The sentencing process is one of the most complex stages of the criminal justice system, and one which has been reviewed and amended many times in recent years in this country. Nevertheless, it is regrettable that the public is so misinformed about the crime which, understandably, causes most public concern. To a degree, this widespread public misinformation can be attributed to the news media; yet it is significant that neither the justice system nor central government has made any effort to dispel some of these public misperceptions. We shall return to the important issue of public education in our concluding chapter.

In the next chapter (six) we turn to public attitudes to the sentencing of murder, and in the chapter after that (seven) we bring together the two domains of knowledge and opinion. It is important to recall however, that the attitude data that we now describe reflect, for many people, a number of misperceptions about the mandatory sentence for life and the prisoners serving this sentence.

6

Public Attitudes to Sentencing in Cases of Murder

OVERVIEW

The previous chapter demonstrated (a) that many people under-estimate the severity of sentencing in cases of murder; and (b) that they have an overly pessimistic view of trends in the murder rate and recidivism statistics of offenders convicted of murder. Now we turn from documenting knowledge levels to an exploration of public opinion. Before describing our findings we summarise the limited research into public attitudes to sentencing murder in this and other common law jurisdictions, bearing in mind the weaknesses of polls as an instrument to measure attitudes. Since many politicians have cited polls addressing the issue of murder, we begin by reviewing findings from this literature. We shall return at the conclusion of this chapter to consider these trends in light of our empirical findings.

I. POLL TRENDS IN ATTITUDES TO SENTENCING FOR MURDER

The few polls that have explored public attitudes to sentencing for murder generally find strong support for capital punishment or life imprisonment without parole.[1] For example, in 2007, Ipsos-MORI asked a representative sample of the public in this country the following question: '*Which punishment do you prefer for people convicted of murder?*'. Respondents were given a short list of sentencing options from which to choose. In response, 34 per cent favoured the death penalty, 44 per cent life imprisonment without parole (LWOP), while only 19 per cent chose 'a long prison sentence with the chance of parole' (Ipsos-MORI, 2007). A few years earlier the same company asked respondents to choose between the death penalty, imprisonment for natural life or 'a long prison sentence' as possible sentences for the murder of 'an adult stranger'. In total, over four-fifths of the

[1] Some polls fail to identify specific custodial options such as fixed terms of imprisonment or life imprisonment, thereby making it hard to know where the public stands on the mandatory life sentence. Recent polling research in Australia asked people to choose between the death penalty and 'imprisonment', and found that approximately two-thirds of the sample favoured the latter (Roy Morgan Research, 2010).

sample favoured the death penalty or natural life (Ipsos-MORI, 2000). These polls asked questions about 'murder', leaving the respondent to decide what this offence entails, and to construct for him or herself an image of the crime and the offender. As we have noted, this is less appropriate as a methodology than asking people about specific cases. In our view these polls fail to provide an adequate test of levels of public support for the mandatory life sentence.

Our literature review uncovered only a single poll which provided respondents with specific cases of murder to sentence. That survey – now over 35 years old – found considerable variation in support for the death penalty, depending on the nature of the specific form of murder. Respondents who had agreed with the general proposition that the death penalty was 'sometimes justified' were then asked whether it was 'suitable' for a list of specific categories or exemplars of the offence. For example, when asked about the murder of a police officer or 'terrorist murders', three-quarters of the sample responded that the death penalty was suitable; however, the percentage finding capital punishment appropriate as the penalty declined to 57 per cent for the planned killing of a spouse (Ipsos-MORI, 1978).

This poll has not, to our knowledge, been repeated; it represents the first empirical evidence in the literature of public sensitivity to variation in the forms of murder, and suggests a kind of proportionality implicit in their judgements, with support for the death penalty being strongest for the most serious cases of murder where aggravating circumstances are usually present. We shall return to this point when we discuss public sentencing preferences in our own survey. These previous poll findings suggest little public support for fixed-term alternatives to a mandatory life sentence, or even for the status quo, namely a mandatory sentence of life imprisonment with variable minimum periods of imprisonment. In light of these poll trends, it is easy to understand why politicians have declined to reform the murder sentencing provisions.

The research on community-based alternatives to custody also carries lessons for public opinion research. Research upon public attitudes to imprisonment has demonstrated high levels of public support – except and until people are asked to consider a range of sanctions. In one US study Doble (1987) asked members of the public to sentence offenders, without giving them a list of different sentences to employ. Under these conditions Doble found high levels of support for imprisoning offenders convicted of a range of offences. However, when he asked members of the public to sentence offenders using a list of disposals including prison and a range of community sentences, large percentages of the public chose the alternatives rather than custody. The lesson of the research was simply that the first sanction that comes to the public's mind – usually custody – is not necessarily the one that they favour when all the options are on the table. Similarly for sentencing in cases of murder, the public may support the mandatory life sentence or the death penalty in part because they have not considered possible alternatives such as fixed-term sentences. This research demonstrates the importance of providing respondents with a range of sentencing alternatives, and not simply a choice between the death penalty and life imprisonment.

II. PREVIOUS RESEARCH ON PUBLIC ATTITUDES TO SENTENCING IN CASES OF MURDER

A great deal of polling has been conducted in the United States upon the death penalty. This research tells us more about attitudes to capital punishment than the crime for which it is imposed. Surprisingly, few polls have explored attitudes to sentencing murder, and then only in ways that we feel are inadequate (see Chapter five). More to the point, prior to this research, no survey of national opinion had tested the assumption underlying the current law in England and Wales, namely that the overwhelming majority of the public believes that a sentence of life imprisonment should automatically follow from a murder conviction.

The only previous academic research of relevance to this issue consisted of two small-scale qualitative studies (each involving about 60 participants) by Mitchell which suggested that only about half the public favours some form of mandatory sentencing for murder (Law Commission, 2004; 2005). But those previous studies did not explore the issue in any detail; they did not, for example, test views on whether any alternative determinate sentences might be preferable. Finally, since these studies employed small numbers of subjects, their findings cannot be generalised to the larger UK population from which participants were drawn. Nevertheless, they do provide the first evidence that public support for a sentence of life imprisonment in all cases of murder may not be overwhelming.

Although no research has explored public reactions to sentencing in cases of murder, findings from studies exploring other forms of mandatory sentencing suggest that the conventional wisdom about public support for the mandatory life sentence may be erroneous. First, research in this and other western jurisdictions has demonstrated that public support for mandatory sentences in general is far from strong (Roberts, 2003; ICM Research, 2005[2]). Secondly, research in this and other jurisdictions (eg, Roberts et al, 2009) has revealed strong public support for judicial discretion, even if people feel that sentencing 'in general' is too lenient. This suggests that there may be public support for more flexible sentencing arrangements for murder. Finally, the received wisdom about public attitudes to sentencing murder is founded upon rather simplistic surveys in which respondents are asked a single general question.

[2] When given a choice between mandatory sentences and judicial discretion, the public is divided, with significant proportions of respondents favouring judicial discretion. For example, ICM research (2005) asked a sample of the British public the following question: 'Do you approve or disapprove of new directions to judges that a person should not be automatically sent to prison for mugging?' Approximately 40% of the public expressed their approval.

III. PURPOSES OF SENTENCING

Our exploration of public attitudes to sentencing in cases of murder begins with some questions dealing with sentencing purposes. We asked respondents to identify the most important purpose of sentencing offenders. They were given a list of potential purposes from which to select a single objective. In case some of these purposes were unfamiliar to respondents, the survey instrument provided a brief definition of each sentencing purpose (see survey instrument in Appendix C). For example, rehabilitation was described as: '*Change behaviour and/ or attitudes of an offender to prevent them re-offending (rehabilitation)*'.[3] After providing a response for sentencing in general, participants were asked to specifically consider offenders convicted of murder. The results are set out in Table 6.1.

Table 6.1 Most Important Purpose of Sentencing: All Offences and Murder

Most Important Purpose of Sentencing		
	All Offences	*Murder*
Punishment	35%	40%
Rehabilitation	25%	10%
Incapacitation	16%	25%
General Deterrence	11%	11%
Individual Deterrence	7%	4%
To make amends to the crime victim	4%	4%
To express society's disapproval of the crime	2%	4%
Total	*100%*	*100%*

Notes: Excludes 'don't know' responses; Questions: 'Looking at this card, what do you think is the most important purpose of sentencing offenders?' 'And what do you think is the most important purpose of sentencing offenders convicted of murder?'

For sentencing offenders in general, punishment emerged as the most popular single purpose – supported by 35 per cent of the sample, and followed by rehabilitation which was identified as the single most important purpose by 25 per cent of respondents. Deterrence (general and individual) and incapacitation attracted significantly smaller proportions of respondents – 18 per cent and 16 per cent respectively. It is rather surprising that such a small percentage of the sample chose 'making amends to the victim' as the principal goal of sentencing 'all offenders'. This may reflect the structure of the question; many people may see

[3] Some previous surveys have adopted a slightly different approach, in which respondents are asked to rate the importance of all principal sentencing options, but comparison of findings across different questions suggests that it makes little difference to the outcomes (see Roberts and Hough, 2005a).

victim compensation as an important goal of sentencing, without necessarily regarding it as the *single* most important purpose.

Unsurprisingly, when respondents were asked to consider sentencing in cases of murder, their sentencing priorities changed.[4] Public support for punishment and incapacitation rose, while support for rehabilitation declined (from one quarter of the sample to one tenth). This shifting of support from rehabilitation to the more punitive purposes of punishment and incapacitation has been found in other surveys in which respondents have been asked to sentence offenders convicted of minor and serious crimes (see Roberts, 1988; Paulin et al, 2003).

It is interesting to note that even for the most serious crime of murder, fully one tenth of the sample identified rehabilitation as the single most important purpose of sentencing. If respondents had been asked to identify more than a single sentencing purpose, there presumably would have been considerably more support for rehabilitation. This finding, which underlines the support for rehabilitation among the public and is consistent with other jurisdictions, is also the first evidence in our survey that the public is not exclusively punitive in its approach to sentencing, even in cases of the most serious crime.

IV. PERCEPTIONS OF SENTENCING LENIENCY

As noted in the previous chapter (Chapter five), the most well-documented finding in the field of public opinion and sentencing is that people perceive sentencing to be excessively lenient. This trend emerges across jurisdictions, using different methodologies, as well as over time (see Roberts and Hough, 2005a for a review). The British Crime Survey has repeatedly demonstrated this public dissatisfaction with the sentencing process. Thus in 1996, 79 per cent of the public expressed the view that sentencing was too lenient, and a decade later the figure was almost the same (75 per cent; Hough and Roberts, 1998; Hough, 2010). The latest British survey using a representative sample of the public (conducted in 2011; see Dawes et al, 2011) found that 81 per cent of the polled public held the view that sentencing is too lenient. As with many other issues, however, researchers have not to date explored the issue as it applies to murder.

In order to see whether perceptions of leniency are comparable for murder, we divided the sample at random into two sub-samples and asked half the respon-

[4] Respondents were warned at the outset of the survey that they would be asked questions about murder. This necessary warning was provided to ensure that anyone who had been directly or indirectly affected by a homicide would be aware of the survey content and could decline participation from the outset. However, by sensitising people to murder just prior to asking about the purpose of sentencing, it is possible that respondents had murder in mind when they answered the general question, even though it asked about sentencing 'all offenders'. This 'priming' may well explain why there was not greater differentiation between the patterns of responses when people were asked about sentencing in general and sentencing for murder. Previous research has demonstrated that when the public is asked general questions about sentencing they often have in mind the most serious crimes, usually murder (Indermaur, 1987; Doob and Roberts, 1983).

dents about sentencing in general, and the other half specifically about sentencing patterns in cases of murder. Table 6.2 shows the typical pattern emerging for perceptions of sentencing in general: approximately four-fifths of the sample believed that sentencing was too lenient, only 16 per cent believed it was' 'about right'. Fully 40 per cent of the sample held the view that sentencing was much too lenient. An even higher proportion of the sample was critical of sentencing for murder: 45 per cent of the sample held the view that sentencing was much too lenient for this offence.[5] Fewer than one respondent in five held the view that sentencing cases of murder was 'about right'.

This finding is consistent with the limited number of previous polls: in 2006 79 per cent of the public believed that prison sentences for 'serious crimes such as murder' were too short (ICM Research, 2006). The widespread perception of leniency needs to be considered in light of the trends in knowledge reviewed in the previous chapter; those data showed that many people under-estimated the number of years that offenders convicted of murder serve in prison. Presumably, if the public had more realistic views of sentencing patterns at least some people would change their perception that the courts are too lenient. We shall explore the link between knowledge and opinion in the next chapter.

Table 6.2 Perceptions of Leniency in Sentencing, All Offences and Murder

Sentencing is…		
	All Offences	*Murder*
Much too lenient	40%	45%
Too lenient	39%	35%
About Right	16%	18%
Too harsh/ much too harsh	3%	2%
Total	*100%*	*100%*

Notes: split sample, n = 525 for each column; Excludes 'don't know' responses; Question: 'Is sentencing (sentencing in cases of murder) in this country…?'

V. PUBLIC REACTION TO SENTENCING IN SPECIFIC CASES OF MURDER

Earlier in this book we noted the methodological deficiencies associated with posing general questions to the public and the advantages of asking people to consider specific cases rather than general categories of offending. In order to explore public reactions to the mandatory sentence of life imprisonment we therefore gave each respondent three specific murder cases to consider, with the selection and order of the case being randomly determined.

[5] Several members of the focus groups volunteered similar criticisms.

It is a feature of homicide law that although there are different requirements for murder and manslaughter convictions it is frequently impossible to know in advance whether a case will result in a conviction for murder or manslaughter. One of the theoretical distinctions between the offences is that if the defendant *felt sure* that his actions would result in a person being killed or seriously injured he may be convicted of murder, whereas if he merely thought that death or serious injury was *probable or possible* – ie, he was not sure – then he should be convicted of the lesser offence manslaughter. The difference in the defendant's foresight of the consequences of his action should influence whether he is convicted of murder or manslaughter. But of course it is impossible to look inside the defendant's mind and know the extent to which he foresaw the consequences: instead, a court or a jury has to consider all the evidence – especially the evidence of what the defendant did, the circumstances in which he acted and what subsequently happened – and make what it thinks is the most accurate inference about the defendant's foresight. This is clearly not a scientific process in which the jury can be sure that they have drawn the empirically correct inference, and different juries may draw different inferences from the same facts.

For the most serious cases at the 'upper end' of the seriousness spectrum – ie, the most serious cases of murder – it is very likely that juries would reach the same verdicts. The same can be said for some of the least serious cases. But in the cases which we might describe to be of intermediate seriousness it is quite possible that different juries would draw different inferences about the consequences foreseen by the defendant. Whether a killer is convicted of murder or manslaughter may be determined by this or by other factors such as whether the jury is persuaded that he was *provoked* to kill or whether he was *sufficiently mentally abnormal*. Moreover, research suggests that whilst the evidence available to the court pointed to, say, murder, the defendant was in fact convicted of manslaughter – perhaps because the jury felt some sympathy towards the defendant (see Mitchell, 2007).

A. Murder Scenarios

The scenarios were all based on actual cases which had resulted in a conviction for murder in England (with the subsequent imposition of a mandatory life sentence) and were chosen to represent a range of offence seriousness, from the actions of a distraught parent who kills his severely disabled, suffering son, to a killing which occurred during an argument.

The nine murder scenarios provided to respondents are contained in Box 6.1:

Box 6.1
Murder Scenarios Used in the Research

1. *Frank, aged 18, burgled the home of Alex who was a 64-year-old widower. Alex disturbed Frank during the burglary, and Frank hit him several times over the head with a hammer, killing him. Frank said he just reacted without thinking.*
2. *Jess had recently ended her relationship with Mark, but he went to her house to try to persuade her to take him back. When she told him she did not love him anymore, he became upset and stabbed her to death with a kitchen knife.*
3. *Nick and Oliver ran rival minicab businesses. Nick thought that Oliver had sabotaged his radio system preventing him from contacting his drivers. Knowing he had a knife in his pocket, Nick went to Oliver's offices and confronted him about this. They argued and that led to a scuffle, in the course of which Nick fatally stabbed Oliver in the chest.*
4. *One evening Terry accused his partner Peter of having an affair with another man. They argued and Peter, who denied the allegation, called Terry a 'bastard'. Terry then picked up an ashtray and hit Peter over the head with it, killing him.*
5. *Jim decided to rob a bank. He bought a shotgun and was prepared to kill anyone who tried to prevent him. He entered the bank, pointed the gun at the cashier and demanded money. When the cashier pushed the alarm bell Jim shot him dead and fled.*
6. *Pete and Bert had an argument and Pete punched Bert in the face. Pete then left to walk home. Meanwhile Bert got into his car and set off after Pete. He approached Pete from behind and drove the car straight at Pete, tossing him high into the air. Bert then drove off leaving Pete lying dead on the pavement.*
7. *Gary and Jane had an argument at a party at their house. When Max intervened to try to calm things down, Gary picked up a knife and stabbed him with it.*
8. *Graham was six years old and suffered from a series of untreatable extremely serious mental and physical disabilities. His mother Jane testified that she could not bear to see him suffer any more. One day she walked into a side ward in the hospital and disconnected the life-support machinery from Graham.*
9. *Brian was 18 years old and he broke into the house of Fred who was 68. Brian was just about to pick up the TV set when Fred confronted him. Fred kept shouting out 'Help! Help!' and Brian picked up a cushion and suffocated him with it.*

Previous research by one of us (Mitchell, 1998) suggests that the public would regard scenarios 1, 5 and 9, which involve murders in the course of other serious offences (burglary and robbery), as being the most serious. In contrast, scenario 8 might be regarded as being much less serious: it is likely to be seen as a form of 'mitigated murder' and in practice such cases are often prosecuted as manslaughter, in order to avoid the imposition of a mandatory life sentence (usually by stretching the partial defence of diminished responsibility).[6] The other scenarios are of a broadly intermediate gravity, and the verdicts in these cases are likely to depend on whether the court felt that the killer was sufficiently aware of what s/he was doing that they intended to kill or cause serious injury.

For each case, respondents were asked to select a sentence from among a range of fixed-term sentences from 'up to four years' through to at least 30 years 'with release at some stage'. They were also given the alternative of imposing imprisonment for natural life, without release at any point. Respondents' preferences for sentencing the murderers in the nine scenarios are set out in Table 6.3. Several important conclusions may be drawn from this table.

Table 6.3 Public Sentencing Preferences in Murder Scenarios: Percentage Choosing Options

	Up to 9 years in prison	10 to 19 years	20 to 29 years	30 years or more, with release at some stage	Imprisonment for offender's natural life	Total
Scenario						
1	8	22	20	17	33	100%
2	3	24	25	20	30	100%
3	5	31	24	16	24	100%
4	20	39	18	8	14	100%
5	1	10	20	18	52	100%
6	3	28	25	13	33	100%
7	11	36	20	14	19	100%
8	79	9	7	2	4	100%
9	5	22	26	15	32	100%
Average across all scenarios	*15%*	*25%*	*21%*	*14%*	*26%*	*100%*

Question: 'Imagine you are a judge sentencing people convicted of murder. Please tell me which of the sentences on this card is most appropriate for this case?' Row totals are rounded.

[6] But as cases such as *R v Cocker* [1989] Crim LR 740 demonstrate, even though a homicide may be viewed as a compassionate or mercy killing, the defendant is sometimes convicted of murder and the current law permits no alternative to a life sentence. Cocker had taken the life of his partner, after she had demanded his help in terminating her life.

First, for all but one scenario at least two-thirds of respondents thought there should be some sort of finality to the murderer's sentence, in other words, only approximately one-third of respondents believed that a natural life sentence was the appropriate sentence to impose. This finding provides a very clear contrast with the polls which used general questions about sentencing murder; they had suggested a strong public demand for life without parole or the death penalty. Secondly, even in what was probably the most serious case (scenario 5[7]), only slightly over half the sample favoured the imposition of a natural life or indeterminate sentence. It was unsurprising, but nonetheless valuable, to find that the highest level of support for an indeterminate sentence was in what under current sentencing practice would be regarded as the most serious case of murder. This substantiates the public adherence to the principle of proportionality in sentencing. It also suggests public support for a natural life sentence for the most serious cases.

Thirdly, the public responses to the scenarios show wide variation, demonstrating the extent to which they are sensitive to characteristics of the case. Thus the percentage of responses falling into the least punitive range (up to nine years imprisonment) ranged from only one per cent for case 5 (the killing of a bank employee during the course of a robbery) to 79 per cent for scenario 8 (the case of a parent killing a critically ill child). Similarly, at the opposite end of the severity spectrum, the proportion of respondents endorsing imprisonment for the offender's natural life varied from only four per cent in the parent-child killing (scenario 8) to 52 per cent in the robbery homicide (5).

B. Public Attitudes to Murder under Conditions of Significant Mitigation

It is worth examining respondents' sentences for one case in a little more detail. Scenario 8 was an amalgam of two cases briefly described at the beginning of this volume. *Inglis*, the English case, involved a woman who took the life of her own son who had been incapacitated following a tragic accident. Robert Latimer took the life of his own severely disabled daughter. He freely disclosed to police how he had taken her life, but pleaded not guilty to a charge of murder. Upon conviction, he was sentenced, like Mrs Inglis, to life imprisonment.[8]

[7] The law regards this as a particularly serious murder because although he did not set out with the intent to kill, Jim had considered killing someone and was prepared to do so. He used a dangerous and lethal weapon to kill his victim who was simply doing his job; and the murder was committed in the furtherance of robbery, a serious crime which in itself carries a maximum punishment of life imprisonment.

[8] The trial judge attempted to circumvent the mandatory sentence for murder by declaring the case a constitutional exception. He then imposed a sentence of 3 years' custody. The Crown appealed this sentence and it was overturned by the Saskatchewan Court of Appeal which substituted the mandatory life sentence without parole for 10 years. This decision was then appealed by the offender to the Supreme Court which ultimately upheld the mandatory life sentence; see *R* v *Latimer*.

Graham was six years old and suffered from a series of untreatable extremely serious mental and physical disabilities. His mother Jane testified that she could not bear to see him suffer any more. One day she walked into a side ward in the hospital and disconnected the life-support machinery from Graham.

Table 6.4 provides a breakdown of the responses. In *Inglis*, the trial judge was constrained by the law and was required to impose the mandatory sentence of life imprisonment. Members of the public appeared to have the view that a relatively brief sentence (in terms of the usual sentences for murder) was appropriate.[9] Over two-thirds of the sample would have imposed a sentence of four years or less, and four-fifths selected a sentence of under 10 years' imprisonment.

Table 6.4 Sentencing Preferences for Scenario 8

	% of Respondents Choosing Option	Cumulative Percentage
Up to 4 years in prison	68%	
Between 5 and 9 years	11%	79%
Between 10 and 14 years	4%	83%
Between 15 and 19 years	4%	87%
Between 20 and 24 years	4%	91%
Between 25 and 29 years	3%	94%
At least 30 years but with release from prison at some point	2%	96%
Imprisonment for the rest of the offender's natural life; he will never be released.	4%	100%
	100%	*100%*

Scenario: *Graham was six years old and suffered from a series of untreatable extremely serious mental and physical disabilities. His mother Jane testified that she could not bear to see him suffer any more. One day she walked into a side ward in the hospital and disconnected the life-support machinery from Graham.*

One final element of the cases giving rise to scenario 8 is worth making. As noted in Chapter two, second-degree murder carries a mandatory life sentence. The sentencing court has the discretion to impose a period of parole ineligibility (the equivalent of the minimum term in England and Wales) of between 10 and 25 years. In Canada, juries who convict an offender of second-degree murder are allowed, if they so desire, to make a recommendation to the trial judge with respect to the number of years (between 10 and 25) that the offender should be

[9] The trial judge in *R v Inglis* imposed a minimum term of 9 years' imprisonment as part of the mandatory life sentence. On appeal the Court of Appeal reduced this to 5 years. Both sentences were therefore more severe than those favoured by most members of the public.

required to serve before becoming eligible for parole. After hearing the evidence in the Latimer trial, and having found the defendant guilty of second-degree murder, the jury recommended the court impose a term of two years. The actual jury reacted in a similar fashion to respondents to our survey, further underlying the importance of providing actual cases for participants to consider.

C. Focus Group Discussions

The quantitative survey showed that just over half of respondents thought that Jim (scenario 5) should receive a life sentence without the possibility of parole. All participants in the focus groups favoured some form of life sentence – the only difference of opinion was whether or not he should ever be considered for release on life licence. Similar responses about the sentence were given for the deliberate killing of a police officer, murder of a child, and the murder of multiple victims. It is worth noting that the majority of participants opposed the idea that killing a police officer who was acting in the course of his duty was in any way 'worse' – and therefore merited a longer period in prison – than the murder of any other individual.[10] This is in contrast to a poll finding from 1978 which found that people were more punitive when the murder victim was described as a police officer (see Chapter five).

In addition, it was interesting (although not unsurprising) to find that several participants expressed the view that the murder of multiple victims – either through a single act or by means of a series of separate acts – is significantly more serious than the other 'serious' cases they had considered. Nonetheless, they did not feel it was appropriate to moderate their views on the sentences that should be imposed in cases such as Jim's, or the murder of a police officer or a baby.

Participants in the focus groups expressed a clear preference for some sort of life sentence in the worst cases of murder. When discussing the most serious murder scenarios participants were keen that the penal system should ensure that offenders in these cases should not escape their 'just deserts' (ie, a life sentence). Almost invariably, they supported the idea that judges should be required to impose a life sentence – although, as stated above, there was divided opinion about the possibility of release on licence. But those who did recommend the possibility of release were equally anxious that the sentencing judges should have sufficient discretion to enable them to reflect the seriousness of the particular facts of the case in the length of the minimum term.

No clear conclusions were reached about how this should be achieved, but all participants – including those who supported a sentence of 'natural life' imprisonment – thought that all murders should be grouped or graded in some way

[10] A very few participants were aware that killing a police officer would be regarded as more serious because the police were protecting the public and thereby putting themselves in positions of danger. It is worth noting here that according to Schedule 21 of the *Criminal Justice Act 2003*, para 5, murder of a police officer in the course of his duty should indicate a starting point of a 30-year minimum term.

according to their relative seriousness. Those who did support the possibility of release on licence suggested that either there should be minimum and maximum tariffs which would be determined by reference to the presence of offence characteristics, or judges should have to adhere to legal guidelines as to the weight to be given to specific characteristics.[11] As well as wanting to ensure that offenders were not under-punished, participants also expressed a desire that judicial discretion in determining the tariff should be exercised in a consistent manner.

Very few participants volunteered support for the present system which required the imposition of an indeterminate sentence for serious murders but then gave judges some leeway in determining the length of the minimum term. In addition, there was general approval of the approach taken in the *Criminal Justice Act 2003*, which identifies starting-points based on offence and/or offender characteristics. Although they were not asked to comment expressly on the matter, one implication of the general desire to restrict judicial discretion is that the public favours some form of legal limitation on the potential impact of the remaining aggravating and mitigating factors (after the starting-point sentence has been determined).

Previous studies (see Law Commission, 2005) had revealed some support for substituting a single judge to preside over murder trials with some form of panel of judges, in order to maximise the likelihood that the appropriate sentence would be imposed (and to avoid the risk that a single judge would 'have an off day'). Participants in all focus groups were evenly divided in their views about this, but there was undoubtedly some degree of support for it as a 'safer' method of achieving a balance between compelling judges to impose sufficiently tough sentences and simultaneously giving them the ability to craft the punishment to reflect particular circumstances of the case. One person thought that a single judge should have the option of consulting other judges before formally passing sentence. A small number of participants expressed opposition to the idea of panels of judges, either on the general ground that all committees or panels struggle to genuinely reach agreement, or simply that it would lead to 'chaos'.

VI. PUBLIC REACTION TO 'JOINT ENTERPRISE' MURDER

The last issue we explore in this chapter is public reaction to homicides where there are two people who share an intent to commit a crime and one makes no attempt to stop the other from committing the lethal act, and may in some way appear to encourage or assist in it. These kinds of cases – which are sometimes referred to as 'joint enterprise' murders – have attracted considerable news media attention in recent years. A typical instance of joint enterprise would involve con-

[11] In addition, those who advocated life imprisonment without parole for defendants convicted of the most serious murders similarly felt that in the lesser cases of murder, offenders should be released after serving a term of imprisonment, and that judges should be given fairly tight guidelines (maxima and minima) within which to determine the length of the custodial term.

flicts between gangs which erupt into lethal violence. Under the current law, a person can be guilty of murder or manslaughter as an accomplice even though s/he did not physically contribute to the victim's death. Merely being present at the scene may be sufficient to support a conviction for murder – provided there is some sort of encouragement or assistance, and an intention to do so. It may be clear that the accomplice D expects the principal offender P to be violent, but not at all clear whether D expects P to use the precise nature and extent of violence that he does use.

Unfortunately, English homicide law is unclear partly because there are conflicting lines of legal authority. According to one line of authority[12] the court simply has to decide whether D foresaw the possibility of P's act. If the jury concludes that D did not foresee it, D is not guilty of murder or manslaughter. But if the jury believes that the defendant did foresee this possibility, the question is then whether they are sure that D foresaw that P might commit the act with the necessary intent for murder (ie intent to kill or cause serious injury). If they are unsure of this, D is guilty only of manslaughter.

According to an alternative legal view,[13] if D did not foresee the possibility of P's lethal act, D is not guilty of murder or manslaughter, provided that the lethal act was 'fundamentally different' from what D had envisaged. But if it was not fundamentally different, the fact that it was not foreseen by D is no defence to a murder charge. Once again we divided the sample to explore public reaction to two joint enterprise murder scenarios. Both scenarios were based upon actual cases which had given rise to convictions for murder and are contained in Box 6.2.

In case A, although on the face of it Pete offers only general encouragement to Jim by shouting 'Go on mate' and that obviously does not *necessarily* imply that Pete was aware that Jim had a knife, Pete made no attempt to prevent (or minimise) the harm that Jim would cause. It is quite possible that a jury would conclude that Pete anticipated that Jim would or might intentionally kill Steve – or that at the very least Jim would intend serious injury.[14] Thus, Pete too could be convicted of murder – although different juries might draw different conclusions about what he foresaw and thus the extent of his liability for murder or manslaughter.

In case B, Bob's liability as an accomplice to murder arises as a result of his knowledge that Mike has gone into the bank with a loaded gun and a court may well conclude that he knew that Mike might deliberately kill or seriously injure someone during the robbery. How did the public react to this? As Table 6.5 shows, the results are crystal clear: the vast majority of both samples rejected a conviction for murder, even having been told that the lesser and included offence of manslaughter carries a less severe sentence. Only approximately one-fifth of both samples favoured a murder conviction. The percentage supporting a manslaughter

[12] ie, the approach adopted in *Van Hoogstraten*, 2 December 2003 (CCC), unreported.

[13] ie, the approach adopted in *R v Powell and Daniels; R v English* [1999] 1 AC 1.

[14] This is the kind of anticipation or foresight that the law currently requires for guilt as an aider or abettor of murder.

Box 6.2
'Joint Enterprise' Murder Scenarios and Questions

Case A

Jim and Pete, two 16 year-old schoolboys, were walking home when they met Steve, also 16. Jim didn't like Steve and they argued. A fight began during which Jim pulled out a knife and stabbed Steve to death. Pete shouted to Jim 'Go on mate', but otherwise simply stood and watched, making no attempt to intervene. Jim was subsequently convicted of the murder of Steve.

I would like to ask you about Pete who simply stood and watched, making no attempt to intervene.

Question: Do you think Pete is:

- *Guilty of murder – just like Jim because he let Jim kill Steve;*
- *Guilty of manslaughter – a less serious offence than murder which carries a lighter sentence;*
- *Not guilty of murder or manslaughter.*

Case B

Bob and Mike decided to rob a bank. Bob drove them to the bank and waited outside in the car. Mike went in to the bank, waved a gun and demanded that the cashier hand over money. The cashier pressed the alarm bell. Mike shot her dead and ran out of the bank. He jumped into the car and was driven away by Bob. Bob knew that Mike had a loaded gun with him. Mike was subsequently convicted of the murder of the cashier and robbing the bank.

I would like to ask you about Bob who drove the car but who did not enter the bank.

Question: Do you think Bob is:

- *Guilty of murder – just like Mike he participated in the robbery even though he didn't shoot the cashier;*
- *Guilty of manslaughter – a less serious offence than murder which carries a lighter sentence;*
- *Guilty of robbery but not murder or manslaughter.*

conviction was higher in the case of the juvenile with a knife (case A, Pete) than the robbery driver (case B, Bob). This may be explained both by the closer proximity of the offender to the person responsible for the murder, and also by virtue of the fact that there was an alternate verdict of robbery possible in the case of Bob.

Table 6.5 Public Verdicts in Aiding and Abetting (Joint Enterprise) Murder Scenarios

	Case A: Pete	*Case B: Bob*
Verdict		
Guilty of Murder	21%	22%
Guilty of Manslaughter	57%	40%
Not guilty of murder or manslaughter	20%	37%
Don't know	2%	1%
Total	*100%*	*100%*

Notes: n = 517 per condition; Questions: 'I would like to ask you about Pete/ Bob . . . Is he guilty of murder, guilty of manslaughter or not guilty of murder or manslaughter?' (See text for offence descriptions).

VII. COMPARISONS WITH OTHER JURISDICTIONS

In 2011, these two scenarios[15] were used in a survey of residents of Trinidad (see Hood and Seemungal, 2011, for further information). The results reveal some parallels and some differences. For the stabbing incident (Case A), 40 per cent of the sample in Trinidad but only 21 per cent of our sample selected murder as the appropriate offence. However, in both jurisdictions the public were more likely to regard the offender as guilty of manslaughter than of murder. Support for manslaughter was marginally higher than support for murder in Trinidad (a seven per cent difference) and much higher in England and Wales (a 36 per cent difference; see Table 6.6).

The discrepancy between the pubic in the two jurisdictions was even higher for the bank robbery joint enterprise killing: for this offence 47 per cent of the Trinidad sample chose murder, compared to only 22 per cent of respondents in England and Wales (Table 6.6). In fact, respondents in Trinidad were significantly more likely to see this offender as being guilty of murder (by a margin of 16 per cent). This suggests cultural variation in perceptions of the appropriate sentence for murder.[16]

It is noteworthy, however, that even in the jurisdiction with more support for the murder conviction, the majority of respondents (60 per cent for case A and 53

[15] One scenario – the stabbing homicide – was described slightly differently in the Trinidad survey; the two defendants were adults, aged 23 rather than juveniles. This and the fact that the respondents were informed of the verdict of murder may have inflated public support for murder over manslaughter or the not guilty alternative (see discussion in text).

[16] Trinidad retains the mandatory death penalty for murder, although as the research by Hood and Seemungal (2011) demonstrates, approximately three-quarters of the polled public in that jurisdiction prefer a discretionary sentence or are opposed to capital punishment. Hood and Seemungal conclude that only a quarter of Trinidadians support the current law.

per cent for case B) saw the offence as something other than murder. In addition, the fact that respondents in Trinidad were informed that a court of law had convicted both defendants of murder may well have inflated the level of support for murder as the appropriate conviction. Respondents may have felt inhibited from selecting a conviction other than the ones determined by a court.

These trends are also consistent with a large body of public opinion research into felony-murder convictions in the United States and Canada. This research has demonstrated that the public sees an important distinction between accessories and principals which echoes the distinction between the offenders involved to varying degrees in joint enterprise murders in England and Wales (see, for example, Finkel and Duff, 1991; Focus Canada, 1987, and for a review Roberts and Stalans, 2000). We would conclude on the basis of this research that while there is clearly cross-cultural variation in public preferences for various sentences for murder, the public in a number of countries attempts to distinguish between degrees of involvement in offending.

Table 6.6 Comparison between Attitudes in England and Wales and Trinidad

	Case A	*Case A*	*Case B*	*Case B*
	Trinidad (Hood and Seemungal, 2011)	*England and Wales*	*Trinidad (Hood and Seemungal, 2011)*	*England and Wales*
Verdict				
Guilty of Murder	40%	21%	47%	22%
Guilty of Manslaughter	47%	57%	31%	40%
Not guilty of murder or manslaughter	12%	20%	23%	37%
Don't know	<1%	2%	<1%	1%
Total	*100%*	*100%*	*100%*	*100%*

Although there are few joint enterprise murder convictions each year, these findings suggest that for this relatively rare form of murder there is a clear departure between the views of the British public and the law of murder. The discrepancy between the law and public opinion is usually in the other direction – with members of the public favouring harsher treatment than sentencing law permits. With respect to joint enterprise, the criminal law is more severe than the views of a considerable majority of the community.

VIII. CONCLUSIONS

This chapter has addressed the most important question posed by our research: Is the public in this country strongly committed to the mandatory life sentence for all forms of murder? The results seem clear: the public support for fixed-term alternatives in several cases suggests that many members of the public find determinate sentences to represent an acceptable alternative. In light of the poll findings identified at the beginning of the chapter, this result may seem surprising. After all, the surveys using general questions found strong support for the death penalty and life without parole release. We explain the difference between the two outcomes by reference to the methodology employed. Given a choice, we believe that asking about specific cases would appear to be the most appropriate way of measuring public attitudes, and comparing public sentencing preferences to judicial practice. The public responses to the scenarios suggest that the discrepancy between community views and the law of murder is greatest with respect to the mitigated forms of murder, including the joint enterprise cases. The public and the courts appear closer together if we consider the more serious forms of murder.

The third message which emerges clearly from these findings is the public support for proportionality in sentencing cases of murder. The more serious cases attracted the harsher sentences from the public. This represents another way in which the current murder sentencing arrangements are at odds with community views; while courts may vary the minimum terms imposed to reflect variation in seriousness, the imposition of the same mandatory life sentence undermines proportionality. Schedule 21 creates only a very crude statutory form of proportionality. Yet proportionality can only be accurately established if courts are free to vary the length of the sentence imposed, and not just the likely period of detention. We shall return to this issue in the final chapter of this volume when we outline a revised sentencing regime for murder.

7

Exploring the Relationship Between Information and Attitudes to Sentencing

OVERVIEW

The previous chapter described the state of British attitudes to sentencing for murder, drawing upon the survey and the focus group discussions. We demonstrated that most people regard sentencing as being too lenient, particularly when asked about sentencing offenders convicted of murder. Yet when asked to impose sentence in specific cases, people respond more liberally and with a sense of proportionality in mind – favouring sentence lengths which reflect the relative gravity of particular cases, and opposing the use of a 'one sentence fits all' mandatory life sentence approach. In this chapter we explore in more detail the relationship between public knowledge and public opinions. This is accomplished in several ways.

Research upon the effects of knowledge on public attitudes serves two purposes. First, it sheds light on the nature and foundation of opinions: some attitudes – towards the courts or criminal justice professionals – may well be empirically derived. People are critical of the courts because they read media reports of sentencing decisions that appear excessively lenient. On the other hand, some attitudes may be based not on knowledge but more fundamental philosophical positions; support for the death penalty may be an example of this latter kind of opinion. The second purpose of research of this kind is applied: researchers test the hypothesis that short communications – of a length or duration that may be employed with a mass audience – can change attitudes to sentencing or improve levels of public confidence in the sentencing process. Usually researchers have only a few minutes with study participants and can therefore provide only a limited amount of information. This makes these studies particularly useful for the second purpose.

We explored the relationship between knowledge levels and opinions in three ways. One method involves an experiment conducted within the quantitative survey: we divided the sample randomly into smaller groups and then gave one group some information about the issue while the other groups were not given any additional information. Both groups then answer the same question to see whether respondents' level of knowledge affects their opinions.

A second approach involved comparing the views of respondents who are more informed about the issue with opinions of less well-informed participants. These analyses are both bivariate and multivariate in their nature, with the latter enabling us to isolate the effect of knowledge upon attitudes, having controlled the influence of other variables. These analyses draw upon the total sample of respondents.

The third source of insight into the relationship between knowledge and opinion is of course the focus groups; we describe the ways that discussions in the focus group evolved as people became more aware of the issues. Taken together, these findings address the question: do the more well-informed members of the public hold different opinions? To anticipate our findings, all analytical approaches point towards the same general conclusion: information changes opinions – and we shall return to the implications of these findings in the last chapter of our volume.

I. EFFECTS OF INFORMATION ON ATTITUDES: SOME PRIOR RESEARCH FINDINGS

Public opinion studies conducted in this country and elsewhere have explored the impact of information upon attitudes to sentencing other forms of offending (eg, Hough and Park, 2002; Roberts and Hough, 2005a). The typical finding from this international body of literature is clear: when people have more information about the sentencing process – or about the specific case – they are less inclined to respond punitively towards offenders. In addition, providing information about the justice system often increases public confidence in the system or criminal justice professionals. Although the pattern of findings is consistent – people become more positive towards the sentencing process or rate criminal justice professionals such as prosecutors more positively when provided with information – the differences between the responses of 'informed' respondents and those with less information are generally quite modest (eg, Roberts, 2001). The transitory nature of the experience presumably accounts for this fact; most researchers have provided subjects with information-based communications which take only seconds to read.

In a typical study a sample of respondents is divided in two. Both groups of people are asked to consider the same case or question, but one group is first given some information about the issue or case being sentenced. For example, Roberts and Hough and Roberts (2005b) asked equivalent samples of respondents to sentence a young offender with different levels of information about the case. Results demonstrated that participants who had the most information about the case were also the least punitive in their sentence recommendations. Sanders and Roberts (2000) manipulated the amount of information subjects were given about community penalties. This information was designed to dispel some misperceptions about community penalties (such as the view that they never carry onerous requirements for offenders). Subjects who were more informed of the nature and consequences of the community penalty were also more supportive of imposing the community-based penalty rather than custody. Other research which has demonstrated the effects of information on attitudes in Britain and elsewhere includes: Singer and Cooper (2008); De Keijser, van Koppen and Ellfers (2007); Salisbury (2004); Gainey and Payne (2003); Chapman, Mirrlees-Black and Brawn (2002); and St Amand and Zamble (2001). These studies demonstrate that it is possible to change attitudes through the provision of information.

We conducted a modest test of the information-attitude change hypothesis with respect to sentencing in cases of murder. Whether attitudes are likely to change in the context of murder was unclear; the highly emotive nature of the crime may mean opinions are impervious to the influence of information; this seems to be the case for death penalty attitudes. Opinions about capital punishment tend to remain stable even in the face of compelling evidence which calls the attitude into question. This intransigence regarding death penalty attitudes has been demonstrated in both laboratory and field research. Thus, in a now classic study Lord, Ross and Lepper (1979) found that when proponents of the death penalty were confronted with disconfirming research (demonstrating the failure of capital punishment to deter potential murderers), they became more, not less convinced of the rectitude of their views, and the same phenomenon was observed for opponents of capital punishment.

Hough and Park (2002) report findings from a so-called 'Deliberative poll' of the British public. A deliberative poll is a methodology which involves measuring attitudes before and after people receive information and have had the opportunity to deliberate upon some issue such as sentencing. The idea is that such a method uncovers reasoned rather than reflexive public reactions. In the poll studied by Hough and Park, respondents' attitudes towards a variety of sentencing-related issues were measured before and after participants had spent a weekend attending seminars and learning about criminal justice from academics and professionals. At the end of the weekend (and also months later) participants' attitudes were re-measured. Hough and Park found significant shifting for a number of attitudes (in a more liberal direction), but not with respect to the death penalty, suggesting support for capital punishment reflects more immutable moral views.

There are obvious policy implications of this prior research: if attitudes become less punitive when people have more information, efforts should be made to inform the populace about crime and punishment. However, the reason for providing information is not simply to compare informed and uninformed samples of the public; it is also to match the views of the public more closely to the decision-making of the courts – which are aware of issues such as the nature of a life licence, and the consequences for offenders on licence in the community. If we want to know how close or far apart the courts and the public are, it is necessary to ensure that the public has the same amount of information about the case or issue.

A. Impact of Information about the Life Licence

One of the popular misconceptions about prisoners serving life sentences for murder concerns the licence period after release from prison. People may well interpret a mandatory life sentence with a 10-year minimum term to be a sentence which leaves the offender free once he has served the decade in prison. In reality, life sentence prisoners are allowed to live in the community under licence only if they adhere to their licence conditions. They can be, and sometimes are recalled to prison for violations of conditions or to face allegations of fresh offending. Our focus group discussions confirmed these misperceptions; most people believed that the sentence effectively ended when the prisoner left the institution. In reality, offenders on life licence are subject to conditions and possible recall to prison in the event of non-compliance with conditions.

Our hypothesis was that if people were given information about life licence conditions – and the potential consequences for the offender of violating these conditions – they would be more satisfied with the sentence and less likely to rate it as being too lenient. We therefore assigned half the sample to read a brief summary of the way a life sentence works in practice while the remaining respondents simply read about the case without having been provided with any information about the life sentence.

All respondents were asked to read and impose sentence in the following summary of an actual case of murder:

Jack's elderly father, Charles, was very wealthy, but when Jack refused to get a job they had a major argument and Charles cut his son out of his will. Jack did then get a job but continued to claim unemployment benefit. When Charles reported his own son to the local social services department Jack became so angry that he punched his father several times and killed him. He was subsequently convicted of murder. The court imposed a life sentence with a tariff period of 15 years. This meant that the offender would serve 15 years in prison and then be released on licence.[1]

Before sentencing this case, half the sample was provided with a brief description of release on licence. This group may be considered the 'informed' group, although reading a very brief description of this kind must be regarded as a very modest information 'manipulation', and therefore a weak test of the Information-Opinion hypothesis. All respondents were asked whether this sentence was much too lenient; too lenient; about right; too harsh or much too harsh.

As you now know, all offenders convicted of murder are sentenced to imprisonment for life. Most offenders serve a substantial period in custody – on average around 13 to 15 years – before being released on licence to live in the community. Although they

[1] For the purposes of this scenario, respondents were asked to assume that Jack would be released on licence, although in practice he would only be released if he did not pose an unacceptable risk to the public.

are no longer in prison, these offenders will be living on licence for the rest of their natural life. They will have to report to the authorities as and when required to do so, and can be recalled to prison if they violate any of their conditions of release. In this way the criminal justice system is able to monitor the offender's behaviour in the community.

Even a very short communication of this kind changed respondents' attitudes to the sentence. Knowing just a little more about the life licence conditions significantly reduced the percentage of respondents who held the stereotypical view that the sentence imposed was too lenient ($X(2)\ (1) = 4.3$; $p < 0.05$). The obvious conclusion from this analysis is that some of the public criticism of lenient sentencing for murder (see previous chapter) would be attenuated if people had a more accurate idea of what a life sentence actually entails.

i. Focus Group Discussions

Similar findings emerged from the focus group discussions. When initially invited to comment on the fact that most prisoners serving life for murder are released on licence at some point, without being given any explanation of the life licence, participants in the focus groups responded rather hesitantly or slowly to identify any value or purpose in it. But after hearing an explanation about the function and nature of the life licence, many recognised the purpose of the life licence and the potential value it offers to the offenders. A few participants, for example, who had earlier suggested that those offenders (like Jim in scenario 5 (see the previous chapter) who commit the more serious murders should be sent to prison without the possibility of parole, then changed their minds and thought that release on licence might well be appropriate.

B. The Acceptability of Alternative Sanctions: Fixed Terms instead of Life

When most people are asked about sentencing, imprisonment is the sanction which first comes to mind; they seldom stop to consider the full range of sentencing options available to courts. Thus when asked to impose sentence in specific cases, people gravitate to custody, even if in fact an alternative community-based sentence may prove equally acceptable. One consequence of this is that surveys which asked respondents to sentence offenders and fail to provide an adequate range of alternatives may over-estimate the degree of public support for imprisonment as a sanction. Translated into the domain of murder, it is possible that public support for the mandatory life sentence reflects in part the fact that researchers have not made alternative disposals – such as determinate sentences of imprisonment – salient.

Researchers have asked respondents who have decided on a particular sentence whether they would find an alternative sentence acceptable. Sometimes this research involves asking people who have selected prison as the appropriate punishment to consider the acceptability of a high-level community penalty instead (eg, Roberts et al, 2008; Tufts and Roberts, 2001). For example, in one typical study participants were first asked to sentence an offender convicted of assault. Researchers then asked those respondents favouring custody whether they would find it acceptable for a court to substitute a community-based sentence involving supervision and a requirement of unpaid work for term of custody. Over half of those initially in favour of imprisoning the offender now endorsed the community-based alternative (Tufts and Roberts, 2002).

Respondents in our survey were randomly assigned to one of three conditions and were asked to sentence one of three cases of murder. After each case description the respondent was told the sentence imposed in the case (life imprisonment), but were then asked if they considered a particular alternative sentence acceptable. The proposed alternative involved a fixed period of custody, after which the offender would be released without conditions – a fixed-term sentence. This question therefore explored the limits on public support for a mandatory life sentence – one of the central objectives of our research. Once again, if the public is inflexibly wedded to the life sentence for all cases of murder it is unlikely that they will find alternative determinate sentences to be acceptable as a substitute for life imprisonment.

Since the three murders described in the scenarios varied in relative seriousness, it was necessary to provide different alternative sentences for the three cases. It is also important to note at this point that we were interested here in the question of whether a fixed-term alternative to a mandatory life sentence would prove acceptable to members of the public – the specific value of the alternatives provided is therefore relatively unimportant. Whether a 20 year fixed-term sentence is the 'appropriate' alternative to life imprisonment for murder is a separate question which raises other issues. For example, the role of parole or some form of early release would need to be clarified. Presumably, if the mandatory life sentence for murder were repealed, some authority – likely the Sentencing Council of England and Wales – would be tasked with determining what appropriate determinate sentence would replace, for example, a life sentence with a minimum term of 15 years. However, the point of the exercise in all three conditions was nevertheless the same: to determine whether a fixed sentence of custody would attract any support as an alternative to life imprisonment for the crime of murder.

The three case[2] descriptions along with the alternative sentences offered to respondents can be seen in Box 7.1.

[2] These three scenarios were fictitious but they reflect the variations in seriousness that are characteristic of murder convictions.

Box 7.1

Murder Cases used in Alternative Sanctions Component

Case 1: Margaret.

Please consider the following case. Margaret and her husband Richard were in financial difficulties. Richard told her he had just spent a lot of money on a new car and she became very angry. They had a furious row and Margaret picked up a very heavy ashtray and hit him over the head with it. Richard died shortly afterwards. Margaret was convicted of murder and sentenced to life imprisonment and required to serve 12 years in prison before being released on licence.

Question: How would you react if instead of imposing the life imprisonment sentence the court imposed a sentence of 20 years custody? After serving all 20 years Margaret would be released from prison without being on licence.

Case 2: Stephen

Please consider the following case. Sue[3] *was 12 years old and severely disabled. She had the mental age of a 4-month old baby and suffered frequent fits. She was in frequent pain and faced the prospect of further major surgery with no guarantee of any improvement. Her father Stephen testified that he could not bear to see her suffer any more. One day he decided it was in her best interests that she should die and he overdosed her medication so that she died peacefully. Stephen was convicted of murder and sentenced to life imprisonment and required to serve eight years in prison before being released on licence.*

Question: How would you react if instead of imposing the life imprisonment sentence the court imposed a sentence of 10 years custody? After serving all 10 years Stephen would be released from prison without any further conditions.

Case 3: Sarah

Please consider the following case. Sarah had been looking after her uncle Max for 10 years. He suffered severely from dementia, was also bad-tempered and regularly criticised her. One day Sarah decided she couldn't stand it any longer. While her uncle was asleep Sarah smothered him with a pillow, and he died. She was sentenced to life imprisonment and required to serve 10 years in prison before being released on licence.

Question: How would you react if instead of imposing the life imprisonment sentence the court imposed a sentence of 15 years custody? After serving all 15 years Sarah would be released from prison without any further conditions.

[3] This is a summary of a well-known Canadian case in which a man was convicted of murder having taken the life of his severely disabled daughter. A murder conviction carries a mandatory life sentence in Canada, and although the trial judge imposed a lesser sentence (having determined that this was an exceptional case), the mandatory life term was ultimately upheld by the Supreme Court of Canada (see *R v Latimer* [2001] 1 SCR 3).

After reading about the case, respondents were asked whether the substitute sanction would be definitely or possibly be an acceptable substitute sentence or whether it would be unacceptable.[4]

Table 7.1 summarises public responses to the alternative sentences in the three cases. As can be seen, respondents in all three conditions were more likely than not to find the alternative fixed-term sentence an acceptable substitute for life imprisonment. Thus for the case of Stephen, the father who had been convicted of murder for killing his severely disabled infant daughter, fully 70 per cent of the sample found the fixed-term sentence 'definitely' or 'probably' acceptable as an alternative to the life sentence. Over a third of the participants who considered this case responded that the alternative sentence would definitely be acceptable. There was less support for the alternative sentences in the other two cases – reflecting their higher perceived seriousness – but for both murders a majority of the respondents found the alternative sentence acceptable.

Table 7.1 Public Acceptance of Definite Term Alternative to Life Imprisonment

	Case 1 (Margaret): 20 year alternative	Case 2 (Stephen): 10 year alternative	Case 3 (Sarah): 15 year alternative
This sentence would definitely or probably be acceptable as a substitute sentence	55%	70%	56%
This sentence would definitely or probably *not* be acceptable as a substitute sentence	45%	30%	44%
Total	*100%*	*100%*	*100%*

Notes: n per condition, average = 342; Question: 'How would you react if instead of imposing the life imprisonment sentence the court imposed a sentence of 20/ 10/ 15 years custody? After serving all 20/10/15 years the offender would be released from prison without any further conditions'. For offence descriptions see text.

i. Focus Group Discussions

Further evidence that members of the public are not wedded to the idea of a mandatory life sentence comes from participants in the focus groups who, having been informed of the nature of the supervision that accompanies release on licence expressed the view that the licence should not necessarily be indefinite. They were of the view that if the offender has complied with the conditions in the licence and shown that he has truly been rehabilitated, then the licence should be terminated. These trends support those reported in the previous chapter and

[4] Respondents in all conditions were also allowed to respond 'don't know'.

further demonstrate that the public in this country is not rigidly wedded to a life sentence for murder.

B. Relationship between Knowledge and Attitude: Multivariate Analyses

We can illustrate the relationship between knowledge and opinion through bivariate and multivariate analyses. As will be seen, the relationship between knowledge and attitudes emerges both for general questions such as '*Is sentencing too harsh, too lenient or about right?*' and also questions in which respondents are asked to impose sentences in actual cases. The relationship between two variables – for example, levels of punitiveness and levels of knowledge – may be explained by the effects of other intervening factors. In order to rule out this possibility it is necessary to conduct multivariate analyses. We also explored whether misperceptions of trends in crime and punishment were associated with more punitive attitudes.

In the first analysis we created groups of respondents who might be classified as more or less well informed on the basis of their responses to our knowledge questions. We classified as 'less well informed' any respondent who provided an incorrect answer to at least two of the three knowledge questions described in Chapter five (murder trends; time served in prison; and licence recall rates). Respondents were classified as 'informed' if they provided a correct response to at least two of the three knowledge questions. Approximately half the respondents fell into one of these two categories. Perceptions of sentencing trends were clearly more negative in the 'misinformed' group: slightly over half (52 per cent) of this group perceived sentencing in general to be too lenient, compared to only one third of the informed respondents ($p < 0.001$[5]). Similarly, 52 per cent of the misinformed sample held the view that sentencing for murder was too lenient compared to only 33 per cent of the 'informed' subsample (X2(1) 16.9, $p < 0.001$).

Table 7.2 presents the findings of a logistic regression which uses responses to the general question about sentencing severity as the dependent variable. As can be seen, misperceptions predict a more critical attitude towards sentencing trends, independent of other predictors such as age and self-reported education. This is unsurprising; when asked about sentencing in general or for the category of murder respondents will draw upon their knowledge of sentencing patterns.

Misinformation is also predictive of punitiveness, however. This can be demonstrated by using the number of years recommended in response to the scenarios as the dependent variable. Respondents classified as 'informed' were significantly less punitive: the mean number of recommended years was 14.8, compared to 17.0 in the misinformed sub-sample (t (517) = 4.7, $p < 0.001$).

[5] The significance test at this level means that there is less than one chance in 100 that this effect could have occurred by chance. In other words, it is almost certainly a 'treatment' rather than a chance outcome; the difference between the two groups cannot therefore be explained by random variation.

Table 7.2 Predictors of General Punitiveness Scale

	Unstandardised Coefficient
Gender (Male)	–0.033 (–0.690)
Education: Gcse	–0.193 (–3.005)**
Education: Degree	–0.508 (–7.623)**
Age	0.004 (2.663)**
Misinformed	0.359 (7.103)**
Child	0.072 (1.335)
Constant	4.136 (36.958)**
R-squared	0.137
Adj. R-squared	0.132
Observations (n)	996

Notes: Absolute value of t-statistics in parentheses ** p *<.01*

Informed respondents were more likely to find the fixed sentence an acceptable alternative to a life term. Thus two thirds of the informed group found the alternative acceptable compared to only half of the 'misinformed' sample. Table 7.3 confirms this relationship using logistic regression analysis. The dependent variable is the respondents' assigned sentences in response to the scenarios.

Table 7.3 Predictors of Number of Assigned years

	Unstandardised Coefficient
Gender (Male)	–0.144 (–0.454)
Education: Gcse	–1.112 (–2.591) **
Education: Degree	–1.939 (–4.373) **
Age	–0.021 (–2.052) *
Misinformed	1.175 (3.458) **
Child	0.881 (2.448) *
Constant	17.592 (23.858) **
R-squared	0.040
Adj. R-squared	0.035
Observations (n)	1027

Notes: Absolute value of t-statistics in parentheses;
* p *<.05;* ** p *<.01*

This table confirms the predicted role of misperceptions about murder trends and statistics; misperceptions about murder trends was associated with harsher recommended sentences, independently of the influence of other predictors such as age and level of self-reported education.

II. CONCLUSION

This chapter has used two analytical approaches to demonstrate the link between attitudes to sentencing murder and respondents' level of knowledge about sentencing for murder. First, multivariate analysis revealed a significant relationship between levels of knowledge about the crime and punishment of murder and punitiveness: the more knowledgeable respondents were also less punitive. This relationship emerged even after controlling for other variables which might be related to attitudes. Secondly, the causal nature of the relationship between knowledge and opinion was demonstrated by the experimental component of the survey. Respondents who had been randomly assigned to read information about the life sentence were less punitive than the people who had not been provided with this information.

Perhaps the most significant aspect of the findings is the experimental outcome: even a brief communication, taking just a few seconds to read, had a demonstrable effect on public responses. In our view this has consequences for public legal education initiatives; it suggests that it may be possible to change public opinion with a communication that is brief enough to be used in a mass media initiative. Of course we do not know how long the effect of information on attitudes may last; we measured attitudes immediately after the respondents encountered the materials. Exploring the longer-term effects of information on attitude change is a priority for future research in this area.[6]

Finally, the questions in which people were given alternative sentences are also revelatory, and carry important methodological lessons for researchers. By demonstrating a high degree of acceptance of determinate alternatives to a life sentence we have shown the importance of providing a range of sentencing options.

This chapter completes our review of the law of murder and public attitudes towards sentencing for murder. In the next and final chapter we discuss the implications for law reform in this area.

[6] Very few studies have tested the impact of information interventions over a longer period of time; this reflects the fact that much of this research is conducted in social science laboratories or using a 'one shot' survey (see Hough and Park (2002), for one of the few such analyses).

8

Reforming the Sentence for Murder: the Way Forward

INTRODUCTION

We begin this final chapter by recapitulating the most important points made in the preceding chapters. After noting these we proceed to outline our proposals for reform of the sentencing arrangements for murder in England and Wales. Throughout this volume we have noted the important commonalities in the murder sentencing provisions around the world; our proposals therefore have relevance beyond this jurisdiction to all others which employ a mandatory life sentence for murder. To foreshadow our model, we will propose a new sentencing scheme containing three possible sentences for murder: life imprisonment without parole; life imprisonment with parole, and fixed terms of imprisonment, the last portion of which will be served on parole. Once this period of supervision in the community has ended, the sentence will be over. We propose clear criteria for use of the three sentences, and incorporate a limited degree of judicial discretion to override these criteria where it is deemed in the interests of justice to do so. In this way we hope to promote consistency of approach to sentencing for murder yet without restricting unduly the discretion of a court.

I. THE CASE AGAINST THE STATUS QUO

In general, we have argued that the current sentencing arrangements, whereby persons convicted of murder are automatically sentenced to life imprisonment regardless of the circumstances of their case, are far from satisfactory, on a number of grounds.

- First, despite popular conceptions, not all cases resulting in conviction for murder are uniquely serious. Some are not clearly (and always) distinguishable from conduct which gives rise to a conviction for manslaughter – an offence without a mandatory sentence. Some cases of manslaughter may in fact be more serious, due to the influence of the offender's level of culpability. Indeed, the variations in seriousness among cases are such that the differences between them cannot adequately be reflected in the length of the minimum term. There are some cases where, regardless of the term of imprisonment, an indeterminate sentence is inappropriate.

- Second, all mandatory sentences violate essential principles of sentencing found across the common law jurisdictions. These include: proportionality, restraint in the use of custody, and individualisation. Imposing the same sentence on all offenders prevents a court from reflecting the individual circumstances of each case – a violation of proportionality. Important mitigating factors which distinguish cases are of necessity overlooked. In addition, there will always be some offenders for whom a sentence less than life imprisonment is appropriate yet the MLS prevents a court from imposing any lesser sentence. This is a violation of the principle of restraint in the use of imprisonment.
- Third, while there may be an argument for these sentencing principles to be over-ridden if a mandatory sentence commands very strong public support, our research demonstrates no great public enthusiasm for the current arrangements. In our research conducted for this volume we demonstrated considerable public support for fixed-term alternatives to the mandatory life sentence.
- Fourth, there is no reason to believe that all (or even most) offenders convicted of murder remain a danger to society for the rest of their natural lives – yet that is the assumption underlying a sentence which expires only at the time of the offender's death. The argument in favour of deterrence is based far more on faith in prediction scales than on reliable objective evidence.
- Fifth, there are good reasons to suspect that the MLS *undermines* rather than bolsters public confidence in the criminal justice system. People hear about the offender receiving a sentence of life imprisonment, yet they later learn he will spend only a few years in prison. Finally, at least two other common law jurisdictions – viz New South Wales and Victoria – have abandoned the mandatory life sentence for murder without provoking widespread public criticism (see, for example, Yeo, 1987).

The hour for reform of the murder provisions is at hand. In this concluding chapter we outline a way forward which would replace the status quo with a more principled and rational sentencing system. Constraints of time and space prevent us from offering a detailed set of guidelines for sentencing murder – indeed, that would surely be the subject of a separate book in its own right. But we can at least suggest how the process of law reform should proceed.

II. OBJECTIVES OF THE SCHEME

In what follows we have attempted to construct a revised sentencing regime that satisfies a number of criteria. First – and foremost – it addresses a number of the structural weaknesses of the current regime which, we have argued, give rise to significant injustices. Secondly, we hope to reflect to a greater extent than at present, sound sentencing principles such as proportionality, restraint, and individualisation – to which we have already referred. Thirdly, we propose a scheme which is sufficiently close to the present regime to stand some chance of adoption by Parliament and acceptance by legal practitioners. A totally different set of arrangements – for example, some form of sentencing grid such as those which apply to all offences in some US jurisdictions – would be unlikely to be adopted here. Finally, this proposal is designed to more closely track community views – where we believe these views reflect a principled foundation rather than mere populism.

III. SOME ASSUMPTIONS UNDERLYING THE MODEL

For this purpose, and for the sake of avoiding any further complication, we make a number of assumptions about the environment in which sentencing reform is likely to take place. The first assumption is that the substantive law – ie, the recognition of separate crimes of murder and manslaughter, along with the currently recognised range of complete and partial defences, as presently defined[1] and interpreted – will remain unchanged for the foreseeable future. In Chapter one a number of criticisms were made of the current definition of murder, and in particular it was argued that some cases result in murder convictions – in accordance with the legal definition – that do not constitute the most serious forms of homicide.[2]

Secondly, we also assume therefore that there will continue to be some manslaughter cases that are more serious than these 'lesser' cases of murder, and that manslaughter will continue to attract a discretionary life sentence. Thirdly, we assume that (i) a sentence requiring an offender to spend the rest of his/her natural life in prison and (ii) a life sentence consisting of a period of imprisonment followed by release into the community on indefinite licence, will both remain as sentencing disposals for murder. These assumptions made, what considerations should determine the sentence imposed for this offence?

IV. TOWARDS A MORE PRINCIPLED SENTENCING REGIME

In broad terms, the sentence for any given case of murder should be determined by two major factors – the *seriousness* of the offence and the *culpability* of the offender for the offence. Despite the loss of human life – which is not remediable – murder is an offence like any other, with great variation in terms of seriousness and offender culpability. These two variables guide sentencers in almost all other sentencing decisions (see Ashworth, 2010; Roberts and Baker, 2007).

[1] Put succinctly, distinguishing the more serious from the lesser criminal homicides by reference to the presence of malice aforethought, coupled with the absence of any of the current limited range of mitigating circumstances, is inadequate.

[2] For the purposes of this chapter, we ignore the other criticisms outlined in chapter 1 where it was argued that some current cases of manslaughter should instead be treated as murder.

Some readers may part company with us at this point, arguing that the offender's ascribed level of dangerousness should also determine the appropriate sentence. However, we see little role for predictions of dangerousness in the determination of the *length* of sentence imposed, and for three reasons. First, for the sentences we are discussing the offender's release date is so far in the future that almost nothing can be reliably inferred regarding his likely risk level after possibly decades of confinement, and having taken many correctional programmes. Thus, in addition to aging – which will lower risk – the offender will (presumably) have benefitted from any number of correctional interventions that will have addressed his risk of re-offending. Secondly, dangerousness predictions are at best imprecise; predicting re-offending is notoriously difficult, particularly when the predicate conduct – serious crimes of violence – is so rare. Thirdly, research with life prisoners serving their sentences in the community on licence in this country and others suggests that they represent a relatively low risk of re-offending.

Consider a typical murder committed in 2013 – for example, an offender kills his drug-supplier following an argument over money. A crime of this seriousness will likely warrant a sentence in the range of 15–20 years' custody, whether as the minimum term of a life sentence under the current arrangements, or a fixed sentence under a revised sentencing regime. It makes little sense to speculate now about the offender's likely level of dangerousness in, say, 2033, with a view to determining whether he should be released in that year, 2035, or at some later point. The number of life prisoners serving their sentences in the community and who are recalled is low. In the most recent year (2009–10), of the approximately 1,800 life prisoners living in the community, five per cent were recalled to prison (Parole Board of England and Wales, 2012). When a life licence is revoked and the offender recalled to prison, it is generally for a violation of some technical requirement rather than following an allegation of fresh offending – and still less new offending of a violent nature. One reason for this is that life prisoners serving their sentences in the community are much older than when the offence took place, and in many cases have taken numerous courses to lower their risk of re-offending. In many important respects they often are – or have the potential to be – a different person from the person who committed the crime (see Appleton, 2010).[3]

All this is to say that the justification for a lengthy term of custody – and for whatever specific number of years of imprisonment should be imposed – is found in the seriousness of the offence (including harm and culpability), rather than ascriptions of dangerousness. Of course, some long-term prisoners will remain at risk to re-offend, even after years of confinement and much treatment. Prior to release these prisoners should be subject to a rigorous risk-needs analysis by prison authorities, and this analysis should be placed before the releasing authority (the Parole Board of England and Wales).

[3] In addition, a high proportion of murders involve people in a domestic relationship, the unique nature of which has given rise to the circumstances precipitating the crime.

To anticipate our recommended model of sentencing, we believe that even fixed-term sentences of custody should be subject to staged, or graduated release. The last portion of the sentence should be served in the community under strict conditions and with close supervision. The level of supervision and surveillance would, presumably, tail off as the final expiry of the sentence approaches.

The remainder of this chapter will therefore concentrate on evaluating the seriousness of murders for the purpose of determining the appropriate sentence.

V. THREE SENTENCE CATEGORIES: (I) LIFE WITHOUT PAROLE; (II) LIFE WITH PAROLE; (III) FIXED TERMS OF IMPRISONMENT

The current mandatory element of the life sentence for murder should be abolished. Courts would still be able to sentence offenders to life imprisonment for murder. The status quo would be replaced with what is essentially a *discretionary* life sentence, but the new structure should be sufficiently flexible to allow the judge to tailor the punishment much more specifically to the particular circumstances of the individual case. We suggest that the law should thus provide for three broad categories of cases, each with a distinct sentence:

1. those for whom a whole-life minimum term is appropriate – ie life imprisonment without the possibility of release into the community ('LWOP');
2. those for whom a life sentence with the possibility of release on licence is appropriate – ie, life imprisonment with the possibility of parole ('LWP'); and;
3. the remainder of cases in respect of which the sentence would be a fixed term of imprisonment ('fixed-term imprisonment') with the offender released without conditions at the end of the fixed term.

Since it is generally recognised around the world that 'flat time' sentences – where the offender serves, say, 15 years and is then released without supervision or conditions – are unwise,[4] the fixed terms found in category three would include a portion of the sentence served in the community on licence (on parole). Finally, in assessing the seriousness of each case, courts should continue to be influenced by section 143(1)[5] of the *Criminal Justice Act 2003*, which requires them to focus on the elements of harm and culpability (as earlier asserted by von Hirsch and Jareborg, 1991).

[4] Without graduated release, through diminishing levels of restraint, and without supervision immediately upon release ex-prisoners have great difficulty adjusting to life in open society. Moreover, the adjustment process is likely to be much more challenging for offenders who have been incarcerated for over a decade, as is the case for the lifer population.

[5] Section 143(1) states: 'In considering the seriousness of any offence, the court must consider the offender's culpability in committing the offence and any harm which the offence caused, was intended to cause or might foreseeably have caused'. Courts are assisted in determining seriousness by a definitive guideline issued by the Sentencing Guidelines Council (2004).

How would cases of murder fall into this revised set of sentencing options? At present all cases fall into the first two categories, with the vast majority falling into category two of our proposed scheme. It is hard to predict how cases will distribute themselves across the three new categories. Clearly, it is our intention that a significant number of cases will fall into the third category (which represents the principal departure from the status quo) – or there would be no point for the reforms we propose. We would also expect that only a very small number of cases will fall into the first and most serious category which attracts a life sentence without release.[6] For reasons which we discuss below, we regard LWOP as an exceptional sentence which should be reserved for exceptional cases. It seems likely that a small percentage – possibly one or two per cent – of cases will fall into category one, and the remainder may well, for the foreseeable future divide approximately equally into the second two categories.[7] An essential element of the reform is of course to achieve a greater degree of separation among cases of murder to reflect the variable degrees of harm and culpability; degrees which are insufficiently recognised under Schedule 21.

A. Category 1: Life Without Parole (LWOP)

We think it is important to state at the outset that we envisage LWOP cases as being very rare – a sentence of this nature should be confined to cases of truly exceptional seriousness. Imposing a life sentence on an individual in effect denies their human capacity for reform. We are mindful of the ongoing series of cases coming before the European Court of Human Rights that are effectively testing the legality of LWOP.[8] Our view is that whilst the Court, and the Grand Chamber, are very wary of it, for the present at least, it is unlikely that they will declare LWOP to be *automatically* illegal. The European Court has been critical of irreducible sentences – ie, cases in which there seems to be no possibility for a LWOP sentence to be subsequently reviewed – although it seems reluctant to treat irreducibility per se as a sufficient ground for declaring the sentence unlawful. Quite apart from that, however, the ultimate criterion seems to be whether a LWOP sentence is 'grossly disproportionate' – ie, whether the offence is serious enough to justify such a punishment. The obvious implication here is that there may be a very few cases where the offence really does merit LWOP.

Our proposed sentencing model therefore includes the option of imprisonment for the natural life of the offender – known in the United States as life with-

[6] Except for a small minority of this group who may benefit from our exceptional consideration provision – see text.

[7] Over time, and consistent with the long-term liberalisation of community attitudes and sentencing practices, we would anticipate a gradual shift of cases down from category two to the fixed sentences found in category three.

[8] See, for example, *Vinter and others*, Application Nos 66069/09 and 130/10 and 3896/10, 17 January 2012; and *Ahmad and others*, Application Nos 24027/07 and 11949/08 and 36742/08.

out parole. This sentence also exists in England and Wales[9] and seems a necessary evil in a contemporary sentencing regime for murder – at least in most western nations.[10] It is necessary, we believe, because some rare cases of murder involve levels of harm and moral turpitude which call for a uniquely punitive state response. This is certainly true of cases prosecuted in international criminal proceedings where defendants are convicted of mass violations of human rights including the murder of thousands of people. Yet some exceptional cases of murder appearing for sentence in domestic courts will also strike most members of the community as requiring a unique sentence. These cases presumably involve multiple victims[11] and/or murders in which the victim was particularly young or vulnerable, or was made to suffer greatly prior to death. For offenders convicted of these crimes, a sentence of a minimum term of custody followed by release on life licence may be insufficient to achieve the goals of denunciation and protection of the public.

On the other hand, the imposition of a sentence which calls for the close confinement of the offender and without any possibility of release raises concerns about the cruelty of the punishment.[12] There is a powerful argument – advanced by critics of natural life imprisonment – that this sentence is inhumane and potentially degrading.[13] Consider a 20-year-old individual sentenced to imprisonment for his natural life in 2020. In light of the progressive increases in human life expectancy,[14] it is easily conceivable that this person will live to see the next century and still be incarcerated. Is confinement for such a protracted period consistent with humane sentencing practices? Moreover, there are important questions which need to be addressed regarding the effect of decades of penal confinement and sequestration upon the mental state of the prisoner.

A great deal of correctional research has been conducted upon the impact of long-term imprisonment. That work has demonstrated significant deterioration of mental functioning and a variety of pathologies arising from spending years in prison (see, for example, Sykes (1958); Flanagan, 1995; Liebling and Maruna,

[9] As at 30 June 2012 there were 45 indeterminate sentence prisoners in England and Wales with a whole life minimum term (Ministry of Justice 2012, Table 1.4).

[10] Taking a broader approach to the issue of legal punishment, it is clear that community and judicial attitudes towards the appropriate punishment for all offences, murder included, evolve over time. The general trend is for attitudes to become more liberal over the years – witness the decline in support for capital and corporal punishment in this and other western democracies over the past century. In all likelihood, natural life will one day follow these sentences and be replaced by terms of imprisonment with release on licence at some point.

[11] It is important not to lose sight of the fact that even a single-victim murder inflicts permanent harm upon potentially dozens of victims, including relatives and friends of the deceased (see discussion in Rock, 1998).

[12] See Leigey (2010) for research demonstrating that prisoners sentenced to life without parole report much higher levels of psychological distress than long-term determinate prisoners.

[13] For documentation of the considerable volume of research which has demonstrated the adverse effects of long-term and indeterminate sentences of custody, see for example Sapsford (1983); Walker (1995); Flanagan (1995); Liebling and Maruna (2005).

[14] Life expectancy for a male born in England in 2008 was 78.3 years, an increase of six years in longevity over a male born JUST a decade earlier; see www.ons.gov.uk/ons/publications/re-reference-tables.html?edition=tcm%3A77-223356.

2005; Crawley and Sparks, 2006). Yet much of this research has focused on what may be termed 'conventional long-term confinement', meaning periods of imprisonment of around a decade. Less is known about the effects of confinement without release upon the mental health of prisoners who will never be released.[15] Many opponents of capital punishment have long argued that LWOP is an appropriate alternative to execution, and indeed, most US states which have abolished the death penalty have done so by substituting life without parole. While this alternative may not carry the barbarity of state-sanctioned killing, the concept of confinement until death will strike many people as uncivilised.

A natural life sentence also conveys a message which will be unacceptable to some members of the community, namely that certain offenders carry no potential for redemption. These offenders thus become defined by their conduct in a way that deprives them of their humanity; the capacity to change, to repent and reform is surely an essential element of what it means to be human. The message aside, the concept of irredeemability is also empirically unsafe. Many examples may be cited of individuals who at an early age commit horrific acts and who nevertheless ultimately reform themselves and become law-abiding and productive citizens. Indeed, the experience with life prisoners released on parole after many years in prison sustains this position.[16]

i. *Justifying Exceptional Punishment: Dangerousness and Denunciation*

If a natural life sentence is necessary for some cases, it is important, we believe, to incorporate a mechanism to offer even these offenders some hope of release. Let us return to the two-fold justifications for lifelong confinement. First, it may be argued that a natural life sentence is necessary because the offender will always remain a threat to the community. This view assumes that the nature of the offence demonstrates that the offender will always be dangerous. In our view, such generalisations are inherently implausible. As we have already argued, predicting whether Offender *X* will be a threat to society 25 years hence is a notoriously difficult decision to make. If it is hard to predict with any certainty that an offender admitted to custody in 2020 will still constitute a threat to society in 2040, how much harder is it to predict the prisoner's likely level of threat in 2090, after the prisoner has been confined for, say 70 years?

The second justification for lifelong detention is at once more plausible and yet more controversial. Certain acts are so heinous – so the argument runs – that they call for an extreme level of public condemnation, namely imprisonment for the

[15] There is of course a substantial research literature on discretionary life prisoners.

[16] Many memoirs by ex-prisoners serving life sentences for murder may be cited; see for example, Sauve (2012); James (2003) amongst others. Sauve was convicted of murder, sentenced to life imprisonment and served almost 20 years before being released on parole. During his lengthy term of custody he initiated several programmes to assist prisoners and upon his release on parole became a leading figure in prisoner rehabilitation programming. Yet his sentence of life imprisonment remains in force and will never expire.

offender's natural life.[17] This claim raises again the concept of community values. Expressed in a different way, the argument is that anything short of natural life – release after many years for example – would demoralise the community, undermine perceptions of legitimacy, and possibly have adverse consequential effects to which we have already referred.[18]

Basing normal release decisions on whether, and to what extent, the public will be scandalised by the prisoner's release runs counter to sound correctional principles and indeed the rule of law. Under conventional parole procedures, a prisoner's release decision should be determined by a careful and comprehensive review of his risk level, and the evidence for continued detention should be subject to adversarial scrutiny – the prisoner should be able to rebut assertions relating to his risk level. Yet in the case of offenders convicted of the most serious crimes, and in conditions of great aggravation, the argument for some form of community input is stronger. There are several ways in which community input into the releasing decision may be accomplished. One possibility is to use lay persons – members of the public – effectively as members of the parole board. As discussed below, we favour a model which creates a separate 'community filter' through which the prisoner must pass before he may apply for release.

To recap, the assumption is made that release of a prisoner serving a life sentence for a heinous case of murder will threaten public safety and undermine public confidence in the criminal justice system. Absent a mechanism to consider release, however, we can never know what the consequences of release might be. In the case of Myra Hindley, for example, we will never know whether, if she had been released, she would have threatened the lives of other children. Similarly, we cannot know whether the British public could have tolerated her release to serve the remainder of her life sentence under licence. No systematic research of which we are aware ever explored the nature of community reaction to the prospect of her release.

This analysis suggests that there are grounds – both humanitarian and penological – to permit at least consideration of release for prisoners serving natural life imprisonment. Such a position is also consistent with EU jurisprudence which suggests that natural life imprisonment without any possibility of release is contrary to the European Convention on Human Rights. What mechanism might be appropriate? One possibility which would satisfy a legal requirement for some possibility of release would be to permit the natural life prisoner to make an application to the Home Secretary. He or she would then have the power to authorise a subsequent application to the Parole Board. This approach may well violate

[17] This justification – rather than one based on dangerousness – must surely apply to cases such as Myra Hindley, convicted in 1966 of the 'Moors murders' involving several young children. Over the years, many people opposed releasing Hindley on licence, but the opposition was surely not based on a reasonable apprehension that after 40 years of confinement the prisoner constituted a risk to commit further murders. In the event, Hindley died while still incarcerated in 2002, aged 60.

[18] For example, public demoralisation or a decline in perceived legitimacy may result in public disengagement from the criminal justice system, lower crime reporting rates and possibly private retaliation against the offender (see discussion in Chapter 5).

earlier European law, in that it permits political interference in the determination of sentence, a judicial role. Regardless of whether it is compliant with European law, we see no merit in such a position. Few politicians are likely to take on the responsibility of facilitating release of a notorious prisoner – even if ultimate release remains within the jurisdiction of the parole board. In our view (and experience) politicians are likely to be responsive to what they perceive to be the tenor of public opinion – based on polls. The result will be that no application from this category of prisoner is likely to proceed beyond the desk of the Home Secretary.

ii. Two-stage Review: Jury and Parole Board

There is an alternative, arguably better way of permitting some cases to benefit from release on parole, and we can turn to the experience in another jurisdiction for a model. For 20 years, Canada employed a mechanism to permit the accelerated release of prisoners convicted of the most serious murders. As noted earlier in this volume, murder in Canada carries a mandatory sentence of life imprisonment, regardless of whether the offence is first- or second-degree murder (see Roberts and Cole, 1999; Roberts, 2002; 2009). These two categories of murder are distinguished with respect to the number of years of imprisonment that must be served prior to eligibility to apply for parole – the equivalent of the minimum term in England and Wales. Offenders convicted of second-degree murder must spend at least 10 years in prison before becoming eligible to apply for parole, while offenders convicted of the more serious offence[19] of first-degree murder must serve 25 years prior to consideration for parole.

When these sentencing arrangements were introduced in 1976 at the time of abolition of the death penalty in Canada, the legislature inserted a provision[20] into the Criminal Code which allowed prisoners who had served at least 15 years to apply for a jury review of their parole eligibility date. Thus a prisoner serving life for first-degree murder and who was required to serve 25 years before becoming eligible for parole would be able to apply for a jury review of his parole eligibility date after serving 15 years in prison.[21] We would propose a provision of this kind to enable exceptional cases to discharge the last portion of their life sentence in the community – provided (a) they received the approval of the jury to make an application to the Parole Board and (b) that they were successful in convincing the Board that they no longer constituted a threat to the community.

[19] See Appendix A for the definition of first-degree murder in Canada.

[20] Section 745. In 2011, the federal government legislated the prospective repeal of the provision for all murder convictions recorded after December 2011. The decision to repeal was made without any evidence that the provision was malfunctioning or generating adverse consequences in terms of public safety or public confidence. In fact, a government research report had demonstrated the effectiveness of the release provision. Life prisoners granted released through this provision were less likely to re-offend than other life prisoners released on parole (Zhang and Ha, 2010). This report was only made public once the legislation repealing the provision had been passed, and then only following an access to information (freedom of information) request.

[21] We consider the timing of the application for parole later in the chapter.

Such a feature could be inserted into the statutory definition of the whole life sentence in England and Wales. This would make it clear to offenders, the public, and relatives of deceased victims that there is an opportunity, albeit a challenging one, for the prisoner to be released at some point. One of the weaknesses of the Canadian legislation was that although the review mechanism was codified, it was not part of the murder provisions and attracted little attention from the media, criminal justice professionals or politicians. When applications began to be reviewed by juries, the provision was criticised as being an offender-friendly 'loophole for lifers', when in fact it had existed as an integral element of the new murder sentencing arrangements since their creation (see Roberts and Cole, 1999).

Experience with the exceptional case release provision in Canada suggests that it was successful. Had it been the case that no prisoners ever received the approval of the jury to make an application for parole, it might have been tempting to conclude that the provision was a waste of court time and judicial resources. Similarly, had all applications routinely been approved this would suggest a level of public opposition to the existing sentencing arrangements. In the event, however, there was significant variability in juries' responses. In this respect they mirrored the decision of judges, modulating the response to the individual characteristics of prisoners applying for relief under the provision (see Roberts, 2002; 2009). In some cases juries refused any reduction in the number of years that the applicant must serve; in others the jury made the applicant immediately eligible for parole at the 15-year point – potentially reducing the number of years in prison before parole from 25 to 15. In other cases the jury reduced the number of years that had to be served in prison by some lesser number than 10. Most telling for the present purposes is the finding that in 80 per cent of cases the applicant received some relief from the jury.[22] This further reinforces our point that members of the public – in this case serving as jurors – do not always respond to murder with maximal punitiveness.

Perhaps the main objection to a proposal to introduce a late-term review of this kind is that it amounts to a re-sentencing exercise; the offender is first sentenced at the end of the trial, but may then be effectively re-sentenced at a later date. We reject this criticism. No re-sentencing would be involved because it would be made clear to the offender when the sentence is passed that there will be an opportunity to seek review of his natural life imprisonment – ie it is an integral feature of the court-imposed sentence. Moreover, the indeterminacy and unique severity of natural life imprisonment are such that we should create an opportunity to reconsider its justification in each case. The review should be seen as an exceptional element[23] of an exceptional sentence.

This then raises the question of *when* natural life prisoners should become eligible to make an application under a mechanism of this kind. Establishing a

[22] See Table 1 in Roberts (2002) for a breakdown of jury decisions.

[23] Exceptional in the sense that only the most meritorious cases serving natural life would ultimately benefit from release.

specific number of years creates another 'minimum term' or starting-point sentence, albeit at a much higher level to reflect the enhanced seriousness of the conduct giving rise to a natural life sentence. We have no clear answer to this question. One way of determining the appropriate level would be in relation to the average number of years that discretionary life prisoners serve before becoming eligible for release. If this figure is 15, then possibly the jury review of the natural life sentence should not occur until the natural life prisoner has served at least 30 years in custody.

There are several advantages to a two-stage review mechanism of this nature. First, the community – represented by a panel of sworn jurors[24] – serves as the gatekeeper to the application.[25] This feature protects a decision to release a life prisoner from the charge that it was made by a politician soft on offenders or an offender-friendly Parole Board. It also simultaneously addresses the concern about community reaction to releasing the most heinous offenders into open society. A public backlash against the release of a prisoner serving life for an aggravated murder is far less likely if the decision is taken, or as in this case, facilitated by members of the public serving as jurors.[26] Secondly, it also addresses the twin justifications for detention – community reaction and dangerousness – in separate stages. The determination of whether sufficient time has been spent in prison is decoupled from the adjudication with respect to the prisoner's level of dangerousness. Thirdly, by placing the review on a statutory footing the provision protects the regime from the potential of litigation regarding the irreducible nature of the natural life sentence, since there is the possibility of release at some point.

To recap, for the most serious cases of murder, tightly defined in statute, we envisage a natural life sentence which nevertheless contains a relief provision which offers the hope of release, albeit by means of a two-stage review, involving community input and a releasing authority such as the Parole Board of England and Wales.

[24] Under the Canadian legislation, the jury is empanelled in the jurisdiction in which the murder was committed. This means that a prisoner serving a life sentence in Quebec for a murder committed in British Columbia will be transferred back to BC to face a jury composed of residents of that province. This further strengthens the community's role by defining the relevant community as the one directly affected.

[25] The Canadian scheme incorporated an additional step in the process. Before applying for a jury review, the prisoner had to apply to a court for permission. The decision confronting the court was whether, on the balance of probabilities, the applicant had a reasonable prospect of success with a jury. This additional step was added after the original legislation was passed and was intended to screen out applications where the prisoner had made no progress and where therefore the hearing before a jury would be a waste of time and might cause additional suffering to the victim's relatives. Some similar judicial screening provision may be useful in the scheme we have proposed here.

[26] In a similar way, public evaluations of sentencing decisions tend to be less negative when people informed that the sentence was composed of lay magistrates representing the community, rather than professional judges (see Roberts et al, 2011). One explanation for this is that professional judges are often perceived to be out of touch with 'what the ordinary person thinks' and this results in their decisions been seen in a more negative light (see Hough and Roberts, 1998). We believe that public acceptance of releasing some natural life cases would be more likely if the community had played a role in allowing their release.

iii. Characteristics of LWOP Murders

What kinds of cases would be sentenced to life without parole? Category one cases should be characterised by an *intent to kill* together with *multiple primary aggravating factors*. In Chapter one we set out some of the major arguments relating to the current law whereby an intent merely to cause serious injury (which may not even be life-threatening) suffices for murder. In our view the criticisms are significant, certainly to the extent that such an intent is inconsistent with treating a case as warranting LWOP. What a person intends has a fundamental and crucial bearing on his moral culpability for the consequences that follow from his actions. A killer who intended to kill carries greater ownership and moral responsibility for the victim's death than one who intended no more than serious injury.[27] It is therefore surely uncontroversial that offenders who intend only serious bodily harm (rather than death) are less blameworthy than offenders who intend to kill, even if the outcome is ultimately the same.

Yet further evidence, if any were needed, of the inadequacy of an intent to seriously injure as a constituent of the most serious homicides was provided by the Law Commission. In its consultation paper the Commission stated that such an intent is an unsatisfactory alternative to intent to kill (Law Commission, 2005, para 3.39), and it went on to recommend that killers who intended to seriously injure should be guilty of murder in the *second* degree, which would attract a discretionary life sentence (Law Commission, 2006: para 9.6 and Appendix A, para A.5 respectively). In other words, intent-to-seriously-injure homicides should be regarded as 'second-tier' homicides. Further, various other jurisdictions do not regard an intent to cause serious injury per se, as implying sufficient moral culpability to justify conviction for the most serious form of criminal homicide – there has to be some additional aggravating factor. This is true of, for example, Canada,[28] certain Australian States (such as Australian Capital Territory,[29] and Western Australia[30]) and New Zealand.[31] It is also worth noting the law in some civil systems; both the French and German Codes require an intent to kill for their basic homicide offences. In both systems there is an aggravated form of the basic offence that also requires an intent to kill.

iv. Primary Aggravating Factors

We take the view that, for the purpose of determining the appropriate sentencing category for murder, some aggravating factors should be given more potential

[27] In order to avoid complication we ignore the possibility that the current law relating to the defendant's state of mind may be amended, but we accept that there are good reasons to consider reform on this issue.

[28] See sections 222–229 *Criminal Code.*

[29] See section 12 *Crimes Act 1900.*

[30] Western Australian *Criminal Code* 1913.

[31] The only instance of murder where the offender does not intend to kill arises in section 168 *Crimes Act 1961.* This requires and intent to seriously in jure to facilitate one of a list of (other) serious crimes or to avoid detection or resist apprehension etc.

influence than others. We suggest, therefore, a distinction be made between *primary* and *secondary* aggravating factors.[32] In the scheme that follows we make a distinction between primary and secondary aggravating factors. This two level approach corresponds to a number of guideline schemes which make comparable distinctions. The guidelines issued by the Sentencing Council of England and Wales for example distinguish between factors which comprise 'the principal factual elements of the offence' and other, less important factors which provide the context of the offence or which relate to the offender. The factors we identify as primary are in our view, central to the offence or to the determination of the offender's level of culpability for the offence. The other factors, which we describe later as 'secondary', are relevant but less important as determinants of seriousness or culpability. The distinction – like those found in established guideline schemes – is not of course airtight; we would anticipate that any guidelines authority devising a guideline for murder would conduct a careful analysis of the factors to ensure that they are appropriately located at each level. This analysis would presumably draw upon a careful review of relevant case law, scholarship on sentencing factors and possibly public opinion research. No such review appears to have guided the architects of Schedule 21.Whilst both primary and secondary factors relate to the harm or culpability of the offence, we feel that in order to restrict LWOP to cases of truly exceptional seriousness only the following exhaustive list of characteristics should be taken into account:

- the murder of two or more victims;
- planning or premeditation;
- sexual or sadistic conduct;
- the murder of a child or other vulnerable victim such as a disabled or institutionalised individual; or
- murder committed by a person previously convicted of murder.

Our proposal is that in addition to an intent to kill, the court should be satisfied there are at least two factors from this list, though we would add that this requirement would be met either where there are two or more victims or where the offender has previously been convicted of murder. In other words, these two factors should be given double weighting.

v. Multiple-victim Murders

An exception ought to be made in cases of multiple victims[33] – ie, where defendants are sentenced for multiple murders (a series of single victims) or multiple-

[32] Although there is no such distinction in English sentencing law, some other countries employ two levels of sentencing factors, with certain factors having a greater impact on the severity of sentence imposed (see discussion in Roberts, 2008).

[33] We are clearly referring here to primary victims – ie those who are killed – but we fully accept there are usually other, 'secondary' victims (the family and friends of the deceased), who also suffer as a result of the homicide.

victim murders. One of us has previously argued elsewhere that such cases should be regarded as automatically more serious than single-victim murders (Mitchell, 2011). This is not the place to repeat the arguments in full, but suffice it to say that both the harm and moral culpability elements, even where there are two (rather than any more) victims, are significantly greater than is true of any other aggravating factor. A murder involving two victims is, by definition, distinctly more serious because it is not simply an 'aggravated murder' but two counts of murder.[34] We therefore, propose that the presence of two or more victims should carry twice the weight of most other primary aggravating factors. Thus, an intent-to-kill murder either of two or more victims should be a candidate for a LWOP sentence.

vi. Previous Murder Convictions

There should be a clear justification offered for 'double weighting' any aggravating factor, or, in the other direction for discounting a mitigating factor which in lesser crimes can have an important effect in reducing the severity of sentence. We shall discuss the justification for reducing the impact of mitigation later in this chapter. Here we address the question of why the existence of a prior conviction should carry additional weight.

The role of previous convictions at sentencing is a controversial topic which has generated much scholarship in recent years (eg, Tamburrini and Ryberg, 2012; Roberts and von Hirsch, 2010). From a utilitarian perspective the justification for enhancing the sentence when a previous conviction exists is relatively straightforward: offenders with prior convictions carry an elevated risk of re-offending. When the previous conviction is for exactly the same predicate conduct – as is the case here – the justification seems even more compelling, particularly since the act is not one that is generally easily committed. Some forms of homicide – gross negligence manslaughter or perhaps even causing death by dangerous driving for example – can be committed through careless inattention. Intentional killing however, does not fall into this category. The act is more likely to be predictive of future behaviour than acts which can be committed more easily. One consequence of this is that it is more reflective of the will of the actor – and hence his personal dispositions. We hold such an offender to be more culpable than someone convicted of causing the death of another, but without this element. Utilitarian sentencers would therefore easily justify double weighting a prior conviction for murder: it is predictive of future offending and required by the extreme seriousness of the conduct – which enhances the need to deter and hence prevent future murders.

Retributive theorists, however, are divided on the role of prior convictions. Some regard a prior conviction as unrelated to culpability for the current offence, and therefore irrelevant to sentencing the offender for the new crime (eg, Fletcher,

[34] This is why in some countries consecutive sentences are imposed for such cases.

2000). Others perceive a limited role for prior convictions. For example, von Hirsch (2010) argues that previous offending should disentitle an offender to mitigation but should not aggravate the sentence for a new offence. Finally, other scholars argue that an offender may reasonably be regarded as more culpable by virtue of the fact that he has previously offended (eg, Lee, 2010; Roberts, 2008; 2010).

We cannot resolve this debate here. Some retributive theorists aside, the law on the role of prior convictions – including convictions for murder – is clear. At sentencing in England and Wales,

> the court must treat each previous conviction as an aggravating factor if (in the case of that conviction) the court considers that it can reasonably be so treated having regard, in particular, to –
>
> (a) the nature of the offence to which the conviction relates and its relevance to the current offence, and
>
> (b) the time that has elapsed since the conviction.[35]

However, there are several reasons relating to retributivism why we believe that a previous conviction for murder should carry extra weight at sentencing.

First, and related to the previous point about intentionality, the arguments against a recidivist premium for sentencing murder seem less compelling when the conduct which is repeated is so extreme in its consequences for the victim and the wider community. It is hard to take the view that a person who has previously intended to kill – and succeeded in killing another person – should be treated in the same way as someone without any criminal antecedents. Similarly, the aggravating power of having previously been convicted of murder seems much stronger than most other aggravating circumstances such as planning or premeditation.[36] Finally, we return to the issue of community reaction. A great deal of research has demonstrated that the public sees prior convictions as a powerful aggravating circumstance,[37] and that this is particularly true for the more serious crimes and for previous convictions which are similar to the current offence of conviction (see Roberts, 2008, for a review). A previous conviction for the most serious offence in the criminal calendar will be deemed by most members of the public to be a very significant aggravating circumstance.[38] For this reason, imposing a fixed

[35] *Criminal Justice Act 2003*, s 143(2). Under the definitive sentencing guidelines issued by the Sentencing Council, previous convictions are located as a factor relating to crime seriousness at Step Two of the guidelines methodology (see Sentencing Council, 2011).

[36] As noted earlier in this volume, planning may be relatively perfunctory and may last only a few minutes. If this is the case, it is not clear that an offender who plans to kill is demonstrably much more culpable than one who, for example, spontaneously but intentionally pushes his victim off a bridge, thereby causing his death.

[37] It is also worth noting that in most jurisdictions a previous conviction for murder places an offender in a higher sentencing category. For example, in jurisdictions with a tiered structure for murder, one definition of first degree murder is any murder convicted by a person with a prior conviction for murder. These recidivist murder provisions reflect the enhanced culpability and community reaction arguments we have advanced here.

[38] If the previous offence is exactly the same as the current conviction, both public opinion and sentencing law would deem the prior conviction to be particularly relevant to sentencing.

term of imprisonment for murder when the offender has a previous conviction for murder[39] is likely to outrage the public and bring the sentencing regime into disrepute.[40] For all these reasons we would assign double weight to a prior murder conviction.

It is worth noting that the number of cases affected by this feature of the proposed regime would be small. Over the decade 2000–01 to 2010–11, thirteen offenders who were convicted of murder had a prior conviction for murder (see Smith et al, 2012: Table 1.14). A further 16 cases of murder involve an offender with a prior conviction for manslaughter.

vii. Judicial Discretion

Having described the essential architecture of the revised sentencing framework – the three categories – we turn to discuss the difficult question of the role of judicial discretion. What we have proposed here is a broad framework for sentencing in murder, but we are very conscious that a structure that provides no flexibility is likely to lead to injustice. Indeed, this observation is the foundation of our inquiry. The identification of offence characteristics for the purpose of sentencing categorisation is undoubtedly necessary but should not ultimately be relied on by itself. We therefore recommend that in addition to our basic proposition that there should be an intent to kill coupled with two or more primary aggravating factors, judges should be given some discretion to impose LWOP in other cases if they are satisfied that the case is of sufficient seriousness.

There are two distinct ways in which this discretion might be exercised: (1) to impose LWOP even though the case does not meet the general requirement of an intent to kill plus at least two primary aggravating factors; and (2) to impose a lesser sentence if, for example, although there is an intent to kill together with two primary aggravating factors, there is also significant mitigation. In due course, we would look to the Sentencing Council of England and Wales to draft some guidelines for the exercise of such discretion, and we would also expect the Court of Appeal to do likewise. Naturally, we feel that on the rare occasions when the discretion is exercised the judge should give a full explanation in open court of the reasons for so doing.

We now turn to our second murder sentencing category.

[39] We are divided on the question of whether the previous conviction which triggers a double weighted factor should be for murder only or any homicide offence. In light of the thin and permeable line between murder and manslaughter some may argue that any prior killing should trigger a double weighted aggravating factor. The public are unlikely to see any merit in restricting the double weighting to a prior murder conviction, and would undoubtedly favour the more broadly defined trigger for a double weighted factor.

[40] There is also the point that for the foreseeable future, any offender convicted of murder and who has a prior conviction for murder will have been on life licence for the previous killing; committing an offence while on bail or parole is itself a recognised and powerful aggravating circumstance.

B. Category 2: Life With the Possibility of Parole (LWP)

For murders characterised by an intent to kill we suggest that, provided they are not also characterised by (1) two primary aggravating factors that would warrant a LWOP sentence, or (2) significant mitigating factors – see *Category 3* below – they should generally attract a sentence of life imprisonment with the possibility of parole. Since our third category (fixed-term sentences – described below) also involves the potential for release on parole, we postpone discussion of releasing arrangements until we have outlined this third category.

C. Category 3: Fixed-Term Imprisonment

Assuming the offender is not regarded as posing an unacceptable risk to public safety, then as a general rule, we suggest that two groups of murders should be met with a fixed-term sentence of imprisonment. These are (1) murders in which the offender intended to cause serious injury falling short of death; and (2) intent-to-kill murders in which there is also significant mitigation.

With regard to this latter group of cases a high-level of moral culpability for causing death does not automatically suggest that a life sentence even with release on licence is necessary. An obvious example of this is mercy or mitigated killing. We have referred earlier (for example, in Chapters one and six) to cases such as *Inglis* and *Cocker* as homicides that do not deserve to be regarded as characteristic of murder. A call from the Law Commission for a public consultation on how the law should regard and respond to such cases (Law Commission, 2006, para 9.25) has been met by both the previous and the current government with indifference and inaction. The prospects of any change in the substantive law in this respect appear remote, and so we must assume there will continue to be cases – however few – of mercy or greatly mitigated killings that result in conviction for murder.

Research evidence (for example, Mitchell, 1998) indicates that the majority of the public shares our view that a life sentence is unjustified in these cases – at most, a modest term of imprisonment would be more appropriate.[41] In addition, during the course of this book we have offered evidence from our survey that members of the British public support fixed-term sentences rather than life imprisonment for a range of forms of murder, and in particular those where there is a strong element of mitigation (see Chapters six and seven).

[41] It will be recalled that in the case of Robert Latimer – the father who killed his severely disabled daughter – the jury which convicted him of murder recommended a sentence of only one year in prison. Public opinion research involving this case suggested that most members of the public shared the jury's view.

i. Role of Conditional Release from Prison

We believe that it would be appropriate for offenders sentenced to a fixed term of imprisonment to have the possibility of release on parole before the expiry of the full term. Our suggestion is that offenders should be able to formally apply for parole after they have served a minimum of 75 per cent of the sentence in custody. The percentage of sentence served in the community should thus be relatively modest (no more than one-quarter of the total term). If the prisoner was allowed to serve, say, 10 years of a 30-year sentence in the community this would undermine proportionality – as some offenders would be released much earlier than others on grounds related to differential levels of ascribed risk.

Such an arrangement would also keep alive the public criticism of longer term sentences with a liberal conditional release process. Similarly, for life sentences – namely that they are a fiction in that the offender does not serve anything like the remainder of his life in prison. As the gap between the sentence imposed in court – life or, say, 25 years – and the sentence as served in prison – say 10 years – grows, public criticism is likely to become even stronger. Part of the public objection to life sentences turns upon the fact that it is not consistent with a colloquial definition of life imprisonment. Release on parole would be determined by the Parole Board, and the sole criterion would be public safety.

ii. Role of Suspended Sentences

Suspended sentences of imprisonment have long played an important role in sentencing homicide – albeit in a small number of cases.[42] Manslaughter and also murder are sometimes committed in circumstances of extreme mitigation, to the point that any custodial sentence seems hard to justify on the ground of desert or dangerousness. For example, in *Wilson*[43] a 13-year-old boy was so terrified by his father that he helped him to kill a woman, but since the defence of duress was (and is) unavailable, he was convicted of murder. In an unreported case, a young man stabbed his brother to death in self-defence. Members of the family stated that the deceased had been bad-tempered, aggressive and paranoid and had attacked them on previous occasions. Charged with murder, the defendant's plea to manslaughter on the basis of provocation was accepted and he was sentenced to two years' imprisonment suspended for two years. The imposition of a term of custody accompanied by its immediate suspension is a way of avoiding injustice in such cases. Since, in our view, the sentencing court should be able to exercise some discretion when determining the precise details of the sentence, and bearing in mind the current interpretation of what constitutes a custodial sentence, it should be possible for the court to suspend the sentence, although we envisage that this would only be on very rare occasions.

[42] During the last decade up to 2.6% of those convicted of manslaughter other than by diminished responsibility received a suspended sentence of imprisonment (Smith et al, 2012, Table 1.12).

[43] *Wilson v R* [2007] EWCA Crim 1251.

VI. JUDICIAL DISCRETION

Although at first sight we regard intent-to-kill murders as likely to be more serious than intent-to-seriously-injure cases, we recognise that some instances of this latter group may contain a number of aggravating factors. Thus, for example, the defendant may only have intended serious injury but he may have planned the offence, his victim may have been a child (or other vulnerable person) and it may have been sexually or sadistically motivated. Similarly, intent-to-cause-serious-injury cases might involve multiple victims. In our view there must come a point at which the presence of a number of aggravating factors, reflecting much higher levels of harm and culpability, pushes an intent-to-seriously-injure case up from category 3 (fixed-term imprisonment) into category 2 (LWP). In cases such as these we think this should be made possible through the exercise of judicial discretion (see earlier sections of this chapter).

A. Secondary Aggravation

Apart from the primary aggravating factors listed above for the purposes of characterising a LWOP sentence, other aggravating factors that are likely to influence a judge in deciding what sentence to impose include:

- abduction of the victim;
- the murder of a police officer or prison officer who was acting in the course of his/her duty, or of any person who was providing or performing a public duty;
- murder committed for gain (such as in the course or furtherance of robbery or burglary, or for payment or in the expectation of gain resulting from the death);
- murder that is racially or religiously aggravated or aggravated by sexual orientation; or
- the use of duress or threats against another person to facilitate the commission of the murder.

B. Starting-points and Lengths of Imprisonment

The approach taken under the current law when determining the minimum term, of identifying a starting-point indicated by the presence of specific factors and then taking account of other aggravating and/or mitigating factors, could be retained in relation to category 2 (LWP) cases. The identification of a starting-point sentence provides a kind of 'steer' or 'ball park' figure, from which the judge can then add and/or subtract years according to the other factors that characterise the case appearing for sentencing.[44] This, of course, encourages the judge to analyse the

[44] There will, nonetheless, be cases where taking account of the other aggravating and/or mitigating factors will have a significant influence on the length of the minimum term that is finally determined.

offence in a systematic fashion, although there will inevitably be a degree to which the minimum term that is ultimately arrived at will be subjective and somewhat arbitrary. It is impossible to produce a universal series of guidelines that quantify, in an objective or scientific manner, the impact of aggravating or mitigating factors. But we would hope that the Sentencing Council and/or the Court of Appeal would produce some guidance as to the appropriate starting-points in category 2 cases. Similarly, we would anticipate that they would issue a definitive guideline regarding the lengths of fixed-term sentences in category 3 cases.

When imposing a LWP sentence the judge should, as under the existing scheme, state in open court the length of the minimum term and identify both what he or she regarded as the appropriate starting-point and all the aggravating and/or mitigating factors that have influenced his decision. Again, as under the current system, judges should also identify the factors they have taken into account when imposing a fixed-term sentence.

C. The Need for Greater Guidance

Following the enactment of the *Coroners and Justice Act 2009* the Sentencing Council of England and Wales was created in 2010. Aside from the Court of Appeal, this is the only statutory body responsible for issuing sentencing guidelines. The Council devises guidelines for specific offences and then conducts a comprehensive consultation exercise on a draft guideline, before issuing what is described as a definitive guideline.[45] Under the *Coroners and Justice Act 2009*, courts are obliged to 'follow' any relevant guideline at sentencing, unless it would be contrary to the interests of justice to do so.

To date (March 2012) the Council has issued a definitive guideline for the assault offences, burglary and drug offences. The Council's offence-specific guidelines follow a specific formula. For each offence for which a definitive guideline is available, the guideline contains a series of eight or nine steps which courts must follow, unless they elect to depart from the guideline, having invoked the interests of justice (see above, and discussion in Ashworth, 2012; Roberts, 2011). At present there is no guideline for murder, and there appear to be no plans to develop such a guideline. However, there is a clear utility to having a sentencing guideline for murder. The Council is best placed to devise a guideline which would flesh out the rather skeletal statutory regime found in Schedule 21 or some revised set of arrangements such as that which we have proposed here. Only the Council has the necessary resources and expertise to generate a sentencing guideline, one which would reflect extensive public and professional consultation as well as empirical research.[46] One of the goals of any guidelines authority is to ensure a degree of

[45] See www.sentencingcouncil.org.uk.

[46] Public opinion and sentencing is another of the Sentencing Council's areas of research. Before it issues a definitive guideline the Council usually conducts (or commissions) research into public attitudes to the sentencing of the offence which is the subject of the guideline. See, for example,

coherence within the sentencing process. Within a system such as that found in England and Wales this means ensuring that ordinal proportionality exists – namely that the more serious offences are punished more severely.

D. Overview

An overview of our proposed sentencing framework for murder is set out in Box 8.1.

Box 8.1
Sentencing Framework for Punishing Murder

Sentence Category	Offence Characteristics
1. Life Without Parole	Intent to Kill + Multiple Primary Aggravating Factors*
2. Life With Parole with **minimum term**	Intent to Kill *or* Intent to Cause Serious Injury + Significant Aggravation*
3. Fixed Term Imprisonment	Intent to Cause Serious Injury or Intent to Kill + Significant Mitigation*

* Subject to judicial discretion.

VII. A NECESSARY PROCEDURAL ADJUSTMENT

It follows from what has been proposed here that a procedural amendment would be necessary where the defendant is convicted of murder. In cases where there was a trial the jury would have to state, through their spokesperson, whether they had convicted on the basis of an intent to kill or an intent to cause serious injury. It might be objected that this would add to the already weighty burden on juries, and that it would either lead to more hung juries or at the very least increase the length of murder trials. In reply we would note that effectively the same decision is made by juries in other jurisdictions (such as Canada) where conclusions about the object of the defendant's intent are crucial for determining the nature of the crime. In addition, the defendant surely has a right to know the factual basis on which the jury reached their verdict, particularly when the consequences in terms of time in prison are so significant.

There is no evidence that this requirement is unduly difficult or problematic for juries. Moreover, not long ago the Law Commission recommended a restruc-

research on public attitudes to sentencing sexual offences or to the reduction in sentence for a guilty plea (available at www.sentencingcouncil.org.uk).

turing of the substantive law so that, inter alia, the jury would have to be able to distinguish intent-to-kill cases – which would constitute murder in the first degree – from intent-to-cause-serious-injury cases, which would constitute murder in the second degree under the Commission's proposals (Law Commission, 2006). Naturally, in cases in which there was a guilty plea to murder, the defendant would have to formally indicate the basis of the plea – whether he intended to kill or seriously injure.

VIII. MITIGATING FACTORS

We have previously argued that the factors which influence the sentence should be those which are related to the offence, and we therefore advocate that personal mitigation should be given less weight when deciding the length of the term of imprisonment. There is a general argument that mitigation plays a lesser role as the offence becomes more serious. One reason for this is that many claims in mitigation relate to a lack of awareness of the full gravity of the offence, or possibly the ease with which some offences – such as causing death or injury though careless driving – can occur. Appeals along these lines lose their plausibility for a crime such as intending to kill another person.

The mitigating factors[47] that we believe should have most bearing on the sentence therefore include:

- the fact that the assault on the victim was spontaneous or impulsive, including cases where the defendant had been provoked (but the facts did not fall within a plea of loss of control;
- the fact that the offender was suffering from a mental disorder or disability which, although not falling within section 2(1) of the *Homicide Act 1957*, lowered the degree of his culpability;
- the fact that the offender acted to some extent in self-defence, in order to prevent crime or while under duress;
- an honest belief by the offender that the murder was an act of mercy;
- the fact that the victim was a grievously ill or permanently and severely disabled family member;
- the fact that there was an element of misfortune in the victim's death – eg the injuries inflicted by the offender would not normally cause the death of a victim;
- the fact that the offender made a serious attempt to save the victim's life.

Although mitigating factors play a more modest role in the sentencing of people convicted of the most serious crimes this should not result in mitigating factors – or factors which reduce the appropriate sentence[48] – being overlooked.

[47] Some of the factors listed here clearly resemble those in paragraph 11 of Schedule 21 to the *Criminal Justice Act 2003*.

[48] Strictly speaking the guilty plea does not constitute a mitigating factor per se; an offender is no less culpable for the offence because he pleads guilty to a criminal charge, and nor is the seriousness of

One the general arguments we have made during the course of this volume is that murder is an offence like any other – with the one obvious distinction that the harm is irreparable. That aside, there is great variation in seriousness and culpability as there is for all other crimes. This implies that factors which mitigate should do so across the entire spectrum of offending, although there may be reasons for moderating their influence at the top of the range. In addition to the mitigating factors identified here, a court sentencing an offender for murder should consider all relevant arguments put in mitigation by the defence advocate.[49]

IX. SENTENCE REDUCTION FOR A GUILTY PLEA

This potential mitigating factor requires some additional commentary. Offenders sentenced in England and Wales and who plead guilty generally receive a reduction in their sentence. A definitive guideline is in effect, issued by the Sentencing Guidelines Council in 2007.[50] According to that guideline, an offender who pleads guilty at the earliest opportunity is likely to receive a reduction of one-third off the custodial sentence.[51] Should offenders convicted of murder benefit from this same reduction? If no plea-based reduction in severity were offered to defendants charged with murder, there would be no incentive to plead, and the consequence would undoubtedly be more contested trials. One of the strongest arguments against the use of a mandatory sentence is that it removes the incentive to plea – the offender will receive the same sentence regardless of his plea.[52] The justification for a reduction in sentence for a guilty plea turns upon the need to save court costs and time as well as the inconvenience and possibly suffering of relatives of the victim – themselves victims – and witnesses.

The definitive guideline makes it clear that the reduction is not offered in recognition of the offender's remorse; this factor is found in the sentencing guidelines as a mitigating circumstance at Step Two of the guidelines methodology. Since the cost savings associated with avoiding a murder trial, and the inconvenience and psychological distress occasioned to witnesses who testify in a murder

the offence affected by the nature of the perpetrator's plea. The sentence reduction is offered to defendants to save court time (and costs) and to spare victims and witnesses from having to testify. This is one reason why the guilty plea is a separate step in the English guidelines, rather than being listed as a mitigating factor at Step Two of the guideline methodology, where it would otherwise appear if it were considered a mitigating factor (see Sentencing Guidelines Council, 2007).

[49] We further assume that if the Sentencing Council were to issue a definitive guideline for murder, as we propose, this would include a non-exhaustive list of mitigating factors to be considered at Stage Two of the guidelines methodology.

[50] The *Coroners and Justice Act 2009* creates a statutory duty on the current guidelines authority (the Sentencing Council) to produce a guideline for the guilty plea reduction. Although the Council's work on this guideline has been on hold due to government proposals in the area, issuing a guideline on this matter is on the Council's workplan for 2012–13 (see www.sentencingcouncil.org).

[51] Sentencing Guidelines Council (2007).

[52] This helps to explain the high rate of contested trials for offences carrying a mandatory sentence.

trial are very significant, there is an argument that defendants charged with murder should receive the maximum[53] one-third reduction noted by the guideline if they plead guilty at the first available opportunity. Accordingly, we believe that the definitive guideline relating to a guilty plea should apply equally to offenders who plead guilty to murder.[54]

X. PUBLIC LEGAL EDUCATION

In the course of this volume we have advocated reconciling the law of murder with the views of informed members of the public. We have argued that there are benefits to ensuring a better correspondence between the two. One of the strengths, as we see it, of our proposed sentencing scheme is that it is closer to the views of the community. Reconciling courts and community, however, is a two-way exercise. In addition to aligning sentencing arrangements more closely with informed community opinion, it is equally important to promote public understanding of the reality of the crime and punishment of murder in this country.

Public views of sentencing are informed by media coverage of specific decisions. This coverage is often erratic, misinformed and incomplete. It is small wonder then that most people have negative views of sentencing and sentencers (see Roberts and Hough, 2005a). Most people believe that the criminal justice system in general is tilted towards the interests of offenders, and deaf to the interests of crime victims. Any reform of the law and punishment of murder would have to be accompanied by a significant public legal education initiative. The regime we have proposed in this volume could (and would) easily be misrepresented as a movement towards softer treatment of offenders convicted of murder when, as we have noted, the impact on sentence lengths for many offenders would remain the same. At the heart of the reform is an attempt to rationalise sentencing for murder and to make it more proportionate and more closely reflecting the levels of harm and culpability.

XI. CODA

Criminal law reform is never easy or uncontroversial. It is particularly challenging when the reforms involve offenders convicted of the most heinous offence on the criminal menu. Defendants convicted of murder are the offender category for

[53] The one-third reduction statistic is a guideline maximum; courts have the discretion to award a greater reduction and sometimes exercise their discretion to do just that.

[54] This is the position taken by the SGC in its definitive guideline. The only complication is that offenders sentenced for murder receive a maximum reduction of one-sixth rather than one third. The reason for this is that a one-third discount would have double the effect of a one third discount on a determinate sentence of imprisonment, since only 50% of the determinate sentence is served (see Sentencing Guidelines Council, 2007).

whom the public has least sympathy and whom politicians are least likely to consider worthy of legislative attention. Yet we should not shrink from the task of addressing the problems created by the mandatory life sentence for murder. Calls for repeal of the mandatory element have been made for years by a diverse constituency of scholars and practitioners, without success. A revision of the law of murder is long overdue; we can only hope that our volume has made such a review somewhat more likely.

Appendix A

Comparative Approaches to the Definition and Sentencing of Murder

This appendix outlines the way in which a small sample of jurisdictions (other than England and Wales) identify what are regarded as the most serious forms of criminal homicide, and how they punish offenders.

Australia

In many respects, Australian criminal law seems to define the mental element in murder very similarly to England and Wales law, but there are important differences between them.[1] There are also important distinctions between the different States.[2] All States accept that intending to kill is sufficient, and most States agree that either an intent to cause serious injury or being reckless as to causing death is enough for murder. Most States do not think that being reckless as to causing serious injury is sufficient for murder. However, the concepts of intention and recklessness are not construed in the same way as in England and Wales. Intent in Australian law is usually confined to its most natural meaning – a person intends to kill only if it is his purpose or desire to do so. Recklessness, on the other hand, encompasses a variety of situations in which the defendant foresees a consequence, stretching from envisaging the possibility of it arising to thinking that it certainly will arise. So whereas in England and Wales the defendant may be said to have intended to cause death if he foresaw death as inevitable even though he did not desire it, in Australia such a defendant would be regarded as having been reckless as to causing death.

Murder arises in Australian law where the defendant believes that death or serious harm is probable or likely,[3] provided the risk of death or serious harm is an

[1] Valuable expositions of Australian criminal law relating to homicide can be found in Ian Leader-Elliott, 'Recklessness and Moral Denunciation in the Australian Law of Murder' in Jeremy Horder (ed), *Homicide Law in Comparative Perspectives* (Oxford, Hart Publishing, 2007) 143–85; and Stanley Yeo, *Fault in Homicide* (Sydney, The Federation Press, 1997).

[2] See Leader-Elliott, ibid, at 149.

[3] Foresight of death or serious harm as *possible* is not enough for a murder charge; ibid.

unjustifiable[4] one. Thus, murder is given a slightly wider definition in Australia than it is in England and Wales. Those who foresee that death or serious harm is a probable consequence of their action would only be guilty of (reckless) manslaughter in this country.

In addition, some Australian States also recognise a form of what is commonly called 'constructive murder'. Essentially, this arises where the defendant kills in the course of pursuing a separate form of illegal activity and liability for murder is 'constructed' therefrom. More precisely, in this instance, liability may arise for what is sometimes called 'escape-murder' or 'felony-murder'. The former variety of murder occurs where the defendant kills whilst using violence in trying to resist, prevent or escape from lawful arrest or custody. It is important to note here that the only elements of moral blame are that (1) the defendant must know that the deceased was some sort of officer in the justice system who was acting in the course of his duties as such; and (2) the defendant must have intended to resist, prevent or escape etc. Thus, this is a very different kind of murder from that described in the previous paragraph, and the fact that the defendant need not have intentionally or recklessly caused death or serious harm has led to calls for the law to be changed.[5]

Unfortunately, those States that recognise 'felony-murder' vary in the way they define it. Sometimes the felony must contain an element of violence, but at other times it need not. Similarly, the seriousness of the felony varies between States, often because the range of felonies that suffice for this purpose is determined by reference to the sentences they attract, rather than the extent to which they necessarily involve the endangerment of life. Like 'escape-murder', the recognition of 'felony-murder' has been criticised for its lack of sufficient moral blame for killing. In both instances, this criticism does not ignore the significance of the context in which the deceased is killed; rather it seeks to emphasise that such cases do not deserve to be included amongst the most heinous homicides.

Only four States punish murder with a mandatory life sentence – Northern Territory, Queensland, South Australia and Western Australia. In the remaining States the life sentence is discretionary. Throughout Australia though, the courts can set a non-parole period, the effect of which usually means that the offender will be released before s/he dies. Ian Leader-Elliott explains that where the courts have discretion it is rare for them to impose a life sentence, and where the sentence is mandatory it is even more unusual for the courts not to set a non-parole period (Leader-Elliott, 2007: 150).

In other words, imprisonment for the rest of the offender's natural life is exceptional. In some States, such as New South Wales, legislative guidelines regarding the length of non-parole periods based on offence characteristics have been set. Thus, despite some basic differences between the two, it is possible to identify

[4] ie, there is no social utility in taking the risk. This, of course, is necessary in order not to convict the surgeon who bona fide performs an operation on a patient. The surgeon is aware of the inevitable risks in such a procedure but acts with the genuine intention of improving the patient's health.

[5] See Yeo, n 1 above, at 91, 92.

some very general similarities in the punishment of murder in Australia on the one hand and in England and Wales on the other.

Canada

In Canada, the death penalty was abolished in 1976 and those convicted of murder in the first or second degree face a mandatory sentence of life imprisonment.[6] Murder in the first degree is regarded as reflecting the most heinous homicides and offenders convicted of this offence are automatically ineligible for parole until they have served 25 years in prison.[7] Such murders may include any of the following characteristics

(a) planning or premeditation; or
(b) by way of an example of a planned or premeditated murder, where the killing is carried out in pursuance of an arrangement whereby money or anything of value is obtained (or promised); or
(c) regardless of any planning or premeditation, where the victim is (i) a police officer, police constable, constable, sheriff, deputy sheriff, sheriff's officer or other person employed to preserve and maintain the public peace, acting in the course of his duties; or (ii) a warden, deputy warden, instructor, keeper, jailer, guard or other officer or permanent employee of a prison, acting in the course of his duties; or (iii) a person working in a prison with permission from the prison authorities and acting in the course of his work there;[8] or
(d) regardless of any planning or premeditation, where death is caused whilst the killer is committing or attempting to commit one of a list of crimes – hijacking an aircraft, sexual assault, sexual assault with a weapon, threats to a third party or causing bodily harm, aggravated sexual assault, kidnapping and forcible confinement, or hostage-taking; or
(e) regardless of any planning or premeditation, where death is caused whilst the killer was committing or attempting to commit criminal harassment and s/he intended to cause the deceased to fear for their safety or that of someone else known to the deceased; or
(f) regardless of any planning or premeditation, where death is caused whilst the killer was committing or attempting to commit an indictable offence[9] involving 'terrorist activity'; or

[6] Section 235 (1) Canadian *Criminal Code.*

[7] ibid, s 745(a).

[8] The prosecution must show that the killer was aware of the victim's status; see *R v Collins* (1989) 32 OAC 296 (Ont CA).

[9] The term 'indictable' offences refers to a category of crimes which are regarded as generally more serious.

(g) regardless of any planning or premeditation, where death is caused for the benefit of, or at the direction of or in association with a criminal organisation;[10] or
(h) regardless of any planning or premeditation, where death is caused whilst the killer was committing or attempting to commit the offence of intimidation of a justice system participant or a journalist.

All other murders that do not fall within any of the above descriptions constitute murder in the second degree, and those convicted of this lesser form of murder are ineligible for release on parole until they have served between 10 and 25 years in prison.[11]

As is the case in England and Wales, an application for parole carries no guarantee of success, and the overriding consideration of the National Parole Board will be the risk to the public if the offender is released. If parole is granted the offender's release will probably proceed in stages. S/he will initially be released for short periods and will then graduate towards full release.

France

The French Code pénal (Penal Code) creates a basic offence of 'meutre' that consists of intentional killing (Article 221-1) and is punishable with 30 years' imprisonment. Meutre is thus more narrowly construed than murder (in England and Wales) because an intent to cause anything less than death will not suffice.

In addition, there are various aggravated forms of meutre. Under Article 221-2, murder that 'precedes, accompanies or follows' another serious crime is punishable with a maximum of life imprisonment. (This might be regarded as a form of 'felony-murder'.) So too is murder that 'is intended either to prepare or to facilitate' a lesser crime, or to 'assist an escape or to ensure the impunity of the author or accomplice'.

Another aggravated form of meutre, attracting a life sentence – 'assassination' – is created under Article 221-3, and involves killing with premeditation.

Finally, Article 221-4, recognises several additional aggravated varieties of meutre, viz:

- where the victim is under 15 years of age;
- where the victim is a natural or legitimate ascendant or the adoptive parent;
- where the victim is vulnerable due to age, sickness or infirmity, or to any physical or psychological disability or to pregnancy, and the defendant was aware of the vulnerability;

[10] A 'criminal organisation' is defined as 'a group of three or more persons which has as its main purpose or main activity the facilitation or commission of one or more serious offences that if committed would likely result in receipt of a material benefit by the group or individuals in the group'; see s 467(1).

[11] ibid, s 745(b).

- where the victim is a judge or prosecutor, or juror, advocate, legal professional officer or public officer, a member of the gendarmerie, a civil servant of the national police, customs, or prison administration, or any other person who holds public authority or discharges a public service mission – including a fireman – or one of various other public officials (including public transport works and health professionals), and the victim's capacity is known or apparent to the defendant;
- where the victim is the spouse or ascendant or direct descendant of those mentioned in the previous list;
- where the victim is a witness, victim or civil party, to prevent him/her from denouncing the action, filing a complaint or making a statement to the court;
- on account of the victim's actual or supposed membership or non-membership of a particular ethnic group, nation, race or religion;
- on account of the victim's sexual orientation;
- where the crime was committed by several people acting as an organised gang.

Germany

The German Strafgesetzbuch (Penal Code) creates a basic homicide offence, 'totschlag', that is described as being characterised by an intent to kill which is not murder (see § 212). The more (or most) serious forms of criminal homicide, 'mord' (see § 211), arise where the defendant intended to kill and there was some additional aggravating factor, namely:

- the defendant killed for pleasure,[12] or for sexual gratification,[13] or greed,[14] or some other base motive;[15] or
- the killing was by stealth[16] or cruel,[17] or it was committed by means that posed a danger to the public;[18] or
- the killing was in order to facilitate or conceal the commission of another crime.[19]

The German Penal Code also recognises a third type of intentional killings that are generally less serious than totschlag. These constitute a form of mitigated murder and arise (under § 213) where the murderer was provoked to rage by

[12] ie the defendant killed for the sake of doing so and demonstrated a contempt for human life.

[13] What matters is that the defendant desired sexual gratification; it is irrelevant that he did not achieve it.

[14] The defendant must benefit economically or materially from the killing (at least in his mind).

[15] The killing must show the deepest moral depravity according to society's values – Bohlander suggests, by way of example, the victim refused to have sexual intercourse with the defendant, or the defendant killed his spouse in order to pursue an adulterous relationship (Bohlander, *Principles of German Criminal Law* (Oxford, Hart Publishing, 2009) 190).

[16] ie the defendant exploited the victim's unpreparedness or defencelessness.

[17] ie the victim was made to suffer more pain than was necessary to kill him or her.

[18] An obvious example would be the detonation of explosives in a public place.

[19] The other crime need not be especially serious in its own right.

maltreatment inflicted on him or a relative, or was seriously insulted by the victim and immediately lost self-control and committed the offence, or (under § 216) where the killing was at the request of the victim ('mercy killing').

As Antje Du Bois-Pedain explains, if the facts of the case bring it within the definition of mord, the court has no power or authority to impose a lesser sentence even if it is thought that there are factors which prevent it from truly reflecting a particularly serious homicide.[20] The presence of what we might regard as a significant mitigating factor ought not be used to justify the imposition of a lesser sentence. Thus,

> if an abused wife kills her husband in his sleep after drugging him with liquor, this counts as a 'devious' killing. If her mental state was not sufficiently deranged to draw her into the fold of diminished responsibility, she would have to be given a life sentence for murder, despite the fact that she also (as an abused wife) responded to provocation and, were it not for the *manner* (deviously) in which she killed her husband, would have . . . faced a maximum sentence of 10 years' (and a minimum sentence of one year's) imprisonment.[21]

Yet in practice, it seems that the courts have very occasionally disregarded such attempts to statutorily constrain their sentencing powers and have imposed lesser punishments. As Du Bois-Pedain comments, it is especially interesting that even where murder (mord) is defined relatively narrowly, in a deliberate attempt to make sure that only truly deserving offenders are convicted of it, the mandatory life sentence can bring about injustice in unusual cases.[22]

Mord carries a mandatory life sentence (§ 211). In practice, there is a general policy that offenders will be imprisoned for 15 years and can then apply to a court consisting of three judges for release. It is theoretically possible for such offenders to be detained for the rest of their natural lives, but the need for their continued detention must be regularly reviewed. Release on probation will only be sanctioned if (a) the offence does not require continued detention, (b) s/he is regarded as not posing an unacceptable risk to public security, and (c) s/he consents. The court that determines parole must have expert evidence relating to the offender's perceived dangerousness, and predictably it must consider public security. Bohlander comments that it should be comparatively rare that a case is regarded as sufficiently serious to warrant a particularly lengthy stay in prison beyond the 15 years, though he adds that 'if one compares what the elements are that are routinely accepted by the courts, there is a large overlap with those used in England and Wales for making a whole life order or an increased minimum tariff'.[23]

[20] Antje Du Bois-Pedain, 'Intentional Killings: The German Law' in Jeremy Horder (ed), *Homicide Law in Comparative Perspective* (Oxford, Hart Publishing, 2007) 69.

[21] ibid.

[22] ibid, 70.

[23] Michael Bohlander, 'The Remains of the Day – Whole Life Sentences after *Bieber*' (2009) 73 *Journal of Criminal Law* 30, 46.

Ireland

Although the legal definition of murder in the Irish Republic superficially appears to be the same as in England and Wales, there may in fact be some slight differences. By section 4(1) of the *Criminal Justice Act 1964* murder is defined as unlawfully killing a person with the intent to kill or to cause serious injury. Section 4(2) then states that the defendant will be presumed to have intended the 'natural and probable consequences of his conduct', but that presumption may be rebutted. So ultimately the intent is defined in a subjective sense – the question is what the defendant actually intended (rather than what some hypothetical person would have intended in the circumstances). However, in contrast to the situation in England and Wales, there has been relatively little case law on the meaning of 'intent' in Ireland and, as the Irish Law Reform Commission recently acknowledged, the precise meaning of 'intent' is not absolutely clear (Law Reform Commission of Ireland, 2008: 2.06). 'As well as conscious object or purpose, "intention" may extend to foresight of a probability of death, or it may be confined to foresight of a virtual certainty'. In other words, we are not sure whether, in the context of the mental element in murder, 'intent' is interpreted in the same way as in England and Wales, or whether it is broader and encompasses some cases that are treated in England and Wales as manslaughter.

The Irish Law Reform Commission felt that there are some cases of what might broadly be described as 'reckless (rather than intentional) killing' that deserve to be treated as murder because they essentially reflect equivalent levels of moral culpability. In its 2008 report the Commission thus recommended that the law be amended so as to include 'reckless killing manifesting an extreme indifference to human life' (LRC of Ireland, 2008: 3.40). This is clearly based on the provision in the American Law Institute's Model Penal Code (§ 202.2(b)). The Commission rejected the criticism that the law would become more complicated and felt that such an amendment would be practicable.

The *Criminal Justice Act 1964* abolished the death penalty in Ireland for all offences except treason, 'capital' murder and certain other crimes subject to military law. 'Capital' murder included murder of a member of the *garda* acting in the course of his/her duty; murder of a prison officer acting in the course of his/her duty; certain murders in the course or furtherance of activities of unlawful organisations; and murder committed for a political motive of a head of a foreign state or of a member of the government or diplomatic officer of a foreign state. Non-capital murder was punished by penal servitude for life. But the abolition of the death penalty in Ireland was completed by section 2 of the *Criminal Justice Act 1990.* All convicted murderers receive a mandatory life sentence. Section 3 of the *Criminal Justice Act 1990* provides that a person convicted of capital murder must serve a minimum term of 40 years in prison (or 20 years for attempted murder).

The MLS is broadly similar to that in England and Wales in that offenders are unlikely to spend the rest of their natural lives in prison. According to a recent consultation paper by the Irish Law Reform Commission, the average time spent in custody between 2004 and 2010 was 17 years and, as in England and Wales, the period of time spent in prison by lifers has steadily increased over the last few decades (Law Reform Commission of Ireland, 2011: 2.07). Theoretically, life sentence prisoners are eligible for two forms of early release, that may be granted by the Executive. 'Special remission' is an approximate equivalent to the royal prerogative of mercy and, if granted, effectively terminates the sentence. It is more likely though, that a lifer would benefit from what is called 'temporary release'. This suspends the sentence. Prisoners are released for a specified number of years and, provided they commit no further crimes and do not breach their release conditions, they will remain in the community.

In addition, 'non-capital' murderers may be given temporary release if the Minister for Justice, Equality and Law Reform refers their case to the Parole Board. In deciding whether to grant release the Board should take into account:

- the nature and seriousness of the offence;
- the sentence and any recommendations made by the trial judge;
- the amount of time already served and the prisoner's conduct whilst in prison;
- the apparent threat that would be caused to the public and the risk of re-offending if the prisoner were released;
- the apparent risk that the offender would not return to prison after any period of temporary release; and
- the extent to which the offender engaged in therapeutic services and the likelihood that temporary release would enhance his prospects of reintegration.

These factors are generally similar to the issues that the Minister for Justice should take into account when considering temporary release.

New Zealand

The criminal justice system in New Zealand is based on the common law, but the mandatory sentence of life imprisonment has been replaced and there is now a *presumption* in favour of life imprisonment for murder, which can be rebutted if an indefinite period of incarceration would be 'manifestly unjust'.[24] Where the presumption is rebutted the court can impose a sentence of less than 10 years. Conversely, where the presumption is not rebutted the court must order that the offender should serve at least 10 years in prison. In deciding the actual length of the minimum term of the offender's imprisonment the court should take into account the need for 'accountability, denunciation, deterrence and protection of

[24] Section 102 of the *Sentencing Act 2002*.

the community'.[25] In what are regarded as the most serious cases, the court can impose a minimum period of at least 17 years' imprisonment.[26] This may arise where the murder was committed:

- in an attempt to avoid detection, prosecution or conviction or in any way to attempt to subvert the course of justice;
- if it involved calculated or lengthy planning, including making an arrangement whereby money or something of value is gained;
- if it involved unlawful entry into or presence in a dwelling-place;
- if it was committed in the course of another serious crime;
- if it was committed with a high level of brutality, cruelty, depravity or callousness;
- if it was part of a terrorist act;
- if the deceased was a constable or prison officer acting in the course of his or her duty;
- if the deceased was particularly vulnerable through age or health or through any other factor;
- if the offender has been convicted of two or more murders (whether or not arising from the same circumstances); or
- in any other exceptional circumstances.

Having served the minimum length of time in prison, lifers are eligible to apply to the Parole Board for release on parole. The paramount consideration in the Board's decision should always be the safety of the community.[27] If release is granted, it is subject to standard conditions that are broadly similar to those in England and Wales.[28] Again, as in this country, special conditions may be attached to a lifer's release on parole, either to reduce the risk of re-offending or to facilitate or promote his/her rehabilitation and re-integration into the community, or to address any reasonable concerns of the victim's next of kin.[29] As might be expected, lifers in New Zealand are subject to being recalled for the remainder of their natural lives. The possible grounds for this resemble those that obtain in England and Wales. They are set out in section 61 of the *Parole Act 2002:*

- the offender poses an undue risk to the safety of the community or to any individual or class of individuals;
- the offender has breached his or her release conditions;
- the offender has committed an offence punishable by imprisonment, whether or not this has resulted in a conviction;
- where the offender's parole is subject to residential restrictions, the offender is endangering the safety of any person at his or her residence, or a suitable

[25] ibid, s 103.
[26] ibid, s 104.
[27] Section 7 of the *Parole Act 2002*.
[28] See s 14.
[29] ibid, s 15.

residence ceases to be available, or the offender no longer wishes to be subject to residential restrictions; or

- where there is a special condition requiring attendance at a residential programme, the offender is endangering the safety of any person at the residence or the order or security of the residence, or the offender failed to remain at the residence for the duration of the programme, or the programme ceased to operate, or the offender's participation in it was terminated for any reason.

Appendix B

Comparison of Schedule 21 with the Practice Direction

Schedule 21	Practice Direction
Para 4(2): Whole life – 'exceptionally high' seriousness:– 1. Two or more victims each involving (a) substantial planning or premeditation, or (b) abduction of victim, or (c) sexual or sadistic conduct; or 2. Murder of child involving abduction of child, or sexual or sadistic conduct; or 3. Murder to advance political, religious, racial or ideological cause; or 4. Murder by offender previously convicted of murder	Whole life – 'not expressly recommended, but (in cases of exceptional gravity, the judge, rather than setting a whole life minimum term, can state that there is no minimum period which could properly be set in that particular case'. (para 49.19)
Para 5(2): 30 years – 'particularly high' seriousness:– 1. Murder of police or prison officer in course of his duty; or 2. Use of firearm or explosive; or 3. Murder for gain (e.g. in furtherance of robbery or burglary, or for payment); or 4. Murder intended to obstruct or interfere with the course of justice; or 5. Murder involving sexual or sadistic conduct; or 6. Two or more victims; or 7. Murder that is racially or religiously aggravated or aggravated by sexual orientation; or 8. Murder under para 4(2) by offender under 21 at date of offence	30 years – 'in the most serious cases, for example, those involving a substantial number of murders, of if there are several factors identified as attracting a higher starting-point present'. (para 49.19)
Para 5A: 25 years:– Offender is aged at least 18 at date of offence, and took a knife or other weapon to scene intending to (a) commit any offence, or (b) have it available to use as a weapon, and used that knife or other weapon to commit murder.	

Para 6: 15 years:– Offender is aged at least 18 at date of offence and case falls outside paras 4(2), 5(2) and 5A.	15 or 16 years – offender's culpability was exceptionally high or the victim was in a particularly vulnerable position – likely characteristics include:– • Killing was 'professional' or contract killing; • Killing was politically motivated; • Killing for gain (robbery or burglary etc); • Killing intended to defeat the ends of justice; • Victim was providing a public service; • Killing was racially aggravated; • Victim was deliberately targeted because of his religion or sexual orientation; • Evidence of sadism, gratuitous violence or sexual maltreatment, humiliation, or degradation of victim; • Extensive and/or multiple injuries inflicted on victim before death; or • Offender committed multiple murders (para 49.13)
Para 7: 12 years:– Offender is aged under 18 at date of offence.	Normal starting-point of 12 years – normally involve killing of adult victim, arising from quarrel or loss of temper between two people known to each other – will not have characteristics in para 49.13 (para 49.10)
	Less than 12 years (perhaps to 8 or 9 years) – where offender's culpability is significantly reduced because, eg • Case was close to borderline between murder and manslaughter; • Offender suffered from mental disorder, or mental disability that lowered his criminal responsibility for killing, though not amounting to diminished responsibility; • Offender was provoked (in non-technical sense) eg by prolonged and eventually unsupportable stress; • Case involved over-reaction in self-defence; or • Offence was mercy killing (paras 49.11 and 49.12)

Appendix C

Survey Instrument

PUBLIC OPINION AND SENTENCING FOR MURDER

We are conducting a survey about the crime of murder and we are keen to avoid upsetting people who are the next of kin or close friend of someone who was unlawfully killed.

Could you please tell me whether you would prefer not to answer our questions for this reason. I am going to ask you a series of questions about sentencing offenders. We will begin with some general questions, then I will ask you to imagine that you are a judge and I will ask you to impose sentence in some actual cases.

Q.A1 SHOWCARD A
Looking at this card what do you think is the MOST important purpose of sentencing offenders?

CODE ONE ONLY

1. *Punish an offender*
2. *Restrict an offender's opportunities to re-offend*
3. *Change behaviour/attitudes of an offender to prevent them re-offending (rehabilitation)*
4. *Deter others from committing the same crime (general deterrence)*
5. *Make amends to the victims for harm done*
6. *Express society's disapproval*
7. *Scare the offender so that he/she won't do it again (individual deterrence)*
8. *Don't know*

Q.A2 SHOWCARD A
And what do you think is the MOST important purpose of sentencing when the offender has been convicted of murder?

CODE ONE ONLY

1. *Punish an offender*
2. *Restrict an offender's opportunities to re-offend*
3. *Change behaviour/attitudes of an offender to prevent them re-offending (rehabilitation)*
4. *Deter others from committing the same crime (general deterrence)*

5. *Make amends to the victims for harm done*
6. *Express society's disapproval*
7. *Scare the offender so that he/she won't do it again (individual deterrence)*
8. *Don't know*

Ask 1A or 1B

1A. Q: In your view is sentencing in cases of murder in this country much too lenient, too lenient, about right, too harsh or much too harsh? PROBE AS NECESSARY

Sentencing in cases of murder in this country is generally much too lenient
Sentencing in cases of murder in this country is generally too lenient
Sentencing in cases of murder in this country is about right
Sentencing in cases of murder in this country is generally too harsh
Sentencing in cases of murder in this country is generally much too harsh
Don't know

1B. Q: In your view is sentencing in this country much too lenient, too lenient, about right, too harsh or much too harsh? PROBE AS NECESSARY

Sentencing in this country is generally much too lenient
Sentencing in this country is generally too lenient
Sentencing in this country is generally about right
Sentencing in this country is generally too harsh
Sentencing in this country is generally much too harsh
Don't know

Ask 2A or 2B

2A. Q: Over the past decade, has the number of murders in this country READ OUT

Increased greatly
Increased somewhat
Stayed about the same
Declined somewhat
Declined greatly
Don't know

2B. Q: Do you think the murder rate in this country is higher, lower or about the same as in other western European nations? PROBE AS NECESSARY

The murder rate is much higher in this country
The murder rate is somewhat higher in this country
The murder rate is about the same in this country
The murder rate is somewhat lower in this country
The murder rate is much lower in this country
Don't know

Ask 3A or 3B

3A. Q: All people convicted of murder are sentenced to life imprisonment. Most will eventually be released from prison on licence to be supervised in the community.

Compared to other western European nations, do you think offenders convicted of murder in England spend more time in prison than those from other Western nations, about the same length of time in prison or less time in prison?

Offenders convicted of murder in England spend more time in prison than murderers in other countries
Offenders convicted of murder in England spend about the same amount of time in prison as murderers in other countries
Offenders convicted of murder in England spend less time in prison than murderers in other countries
Don't know

3B. Q: All people convicted of murder are sentenced to life imprisonment. Most will eventually be released from prison on licence to be supervised in the community. On average, how many years do offenders convicted of murder and sentenced to life imprisonment actually spend in prison?

4. Q: What percentage of offenders convicted of murder and who have been released on licence to live in the community are recalled to prison for committing another criminal offence? Would you say it is closest to? PROMPT FOR BEST GUESS

1 %
5 %
10 %
15 %
Or 20 %
No idea

Q. 5
Half sample receive A

5A. As you now know, all offenders convicted of murder are sentenced to imprisonment for life. Most offenders serve a substantial period in custody – on average around 13 to 15 years – before being released on licence to live in the community. Although they are no longer in prison, these offenders will be living on licence for the rest of their natural life. They must report to the authorities as and when required to do so, and can be recalled to prison if they violate any of their conditions of release. In this way the criminal justice system monitors offenders' behaviour in the community.

Now please consider the following case.

Jack's elderly father, Charles, was very wealthy, but when Jack refused to get a job they had a major argument and Charles cut his son out of his will. Jack did then get a job but continued to claim unemployment benefit. When Charles reported his own son to the local social services department Jack became so angry that he punched his father several times and killed him. He was subsequently convicted of murder.

The court imposed a life sentence with a tariff period of 15 years. This meant that Jack would serve 15 years in prison and then be released on licence for the rest of his life.

Do you think this sentence was:–

Much too lenient
Too lenient
About right
Too harsh
Much too harsh
Don't know

5B. Please consider the following case:

Jack's elderly father, Charles, was very wealthy, but when Jack refused to get a job they had a major argument and Charles cut his son out of his will. Jack did then get a job but continued to claim unemployment benefit. When Charles reported his own son to the local social services department Jack became so angry that he punched his father several times and killed him. He was subsequently convicted of murder.

The court imposed a life sentence with a tariff period of 15 years. This meant that Jack would serve 15 years in prison and then be released on licence for the rest of his life.

Do you think this sentence was:–

Much too lenient
Too lenient
About right
Too harsh
Much too harsh
Don't know

Q. 6

For the purposes of this question the overall sample of respondents is divided into three sub-groups – A, B and C. Respondents in each sub-group will be asked to read three cases.

Each respondent reads three cases at random.

Now I am going to ask you to imagine you are a judge sentencing people convicted of murder. Please decide which of the sentences on this card is most appropriate. I would like you to tell me, in each case, how long the offender should spend in prison:

SHOWCARD B
Up to 4 years in prison;
Between 5 and 9 years in prison;
Between 10 and 14 years in prison;
Between 15 and 19 years in prison;
Between 20 and 24 years in prison;
Between 25 and 29 years in prison;
At least 30 years in prison, but released at some time;
Imprisonment for the rest of his/her natural life – that is s/he will never be released.

Sub-group A:–

1. *Frank, aged 18, burgled the home of Alex who was a 64-year-old widower. Alex disturbed Frank during the burglary, and Frank hit him several times over the head with a hammer, killing him. Frank said he just reacted without thinking.*
2. *Jess had recently ended her relationship with Mark, but he went to her house to try to persuade her to take him back. When she told him she did not love him anymore, he became upset and stabbed her to death with a kitchen knife.*
3. *Nick and Oliver ran rival minicab businesses. Nick thought that Oliver had sabotaged his radio system preventing him from contacting his drivers. Knowing he had a knife in his pocket, Nick went to Oliver's offices and confronted him about this. They argued and that led to a scuffle, in the course of which Nick fatally stabbed Oliver in the chest.*

Sub-group B:–

4. *One evening Terry accused his partner Peter of having an affair with another man. They argued and Peter, who denied the allegation, called Terry a 'bastard'. Terry then picked up an ashtray and hit Peter over the head with it, killing him.*
5. *Jim decided to rob a bank. He bought a shotgun and was prepared to kill anyone who tried to prevent him. He entered the bank, pointed the gun at the cashier and demanded money. When the cashier pushed the alarm bell Jim shot him dead and fled.*
6. *Pete and Bert had an argument and Pete punched Bert in the face. Pete then left to walk home. Meanwhile Bert got into his car and set off after Pete. He approached Pete from behind and drove the car straight at Pete, tossing him high into the air. Bert then drove off leaving Pete lying dead on the pavement.*

Sub-group C:–

7. *Gary and Jane had an argument at a party at their house. When Max intervened to try to calm things down, Gary picked up a knife and stabbed him with it.*
8. *Graham was six years old and suffered from a series of untreatable extremely serious mental and physical disabilities. His mother Jane testified that she could not bear to see him suffer any more. One day she walked into a side ward in a hospital and disconnected the life-support machinery from Graham.*

9. *Brian was 18 years old and he broke into the house of Fred who was 68. Brian was just about to pick up the TV set when Fred confronted him. Fred kept shouting out 'Help! Help!' and Brian picked up a cushion and suffocated him with it.*

Q.7 Ask respondent scenario A, B or C

Consider the following case:

7A. Margaret and her husband Richard were in financial difficulties. Richard told her he had just spent a lot of money on a new car and she became very angry. They had a furious row and Margaret picked up a very heavy ashtray and hit him over the head with it. Richard died shortly afterwards. Margaret was convicted of murder and sentenced to life imprisonment and required to serve 12 years in prison before being released on licence.

How would you react if instead of imposing the life imprisonment sentence the court imposed a sentence of 20 years' custody? After serving all 20 years Margaret would be released from prison without being on licence.

SHOWCARD C
This would definitely be an acceptable substitute sentence
This would possibly be an acceptable substitute sentence
This would possibly be an unacceptable substitute sentence
This would definitely be an unacceptable substitute sentence
Don't know

7B. Sue was 12 years old and severely disabled. She had the mental age of a 4-month old baby and suffered frequent fits. She was in frequent pain and faced the prospect of further major surgery with no guarantee of any improvement. Her father Stephen testified that he could not bear to see her suffer any more. One day he decided it was in her best interests that she should die and he overdosed her medication so that she died peacefully.

Stephen was convicted of murder and sentenced to life imprisonment and required to serve eight years in prison before being released on licence.

How would you react if instead of imposing the life imprisonment sentence the court imposed a sentence of 10 years' custody? After serving all 10 years Stephen would be released from prison without any further conditions.

SHOWCARD C
This would definitely be an acceptable substitute sentence
This would possibly be an acceptable substitute sentence
This would possibly be an unacceptable substitute sentence
This would definitely be an unacceptable substitute sentence
Don't know

7C. Sarah had been looking after her uncle Max for 10 years. He suffered severely from dementia, was also bad-tempered and regularly criticised her. One day Sarah decided she couldn't stand it any longer. While her uncle was asleep Sarah smothered him with a pillow, and he died. She was sentenced to life imprisonment and required to serve 10 years in prison before being released on licence.

How would you react if instead of imposing the life imprisonment sentence the court imposed a sentence of 15 years' custody? After serving all 15 years Sarah would be released from prison without being on licence.

SHOWCARD C
This would definitely be an acceptable substitute sentence
This would possibly be an acceptable substitute sentence
This would possibly be an unacceptable sentence
This would definitely not be an unacceptable sentence
Don't know

Q.8

Ask Respondents 8A or 8B

8A. Jim and Pete, two 16-year-old schoolboys, were walking home when they met Steve, also 16. Jim didn't like Steve, and they argued. A fight began during which Jim pulled out a knife and stabbed Steve to death. Pete shouted to Jim 'Go on mate', but otherwise simply stood and watched, making no attempt to intervene. Jim was subsequently convicted of the murder of Steve.

I would like to ask you about Pete who simply stood and watched, making no attempt to intervene. Do you think he should be:

Guilty of murder – just like Jim because he let Jim kill Steve
Guilty of manslaughter – a less serious offence than murder which carries a lighter sentence
Not guilty of murder or manslaughter – since he did not attack Steve.
Don't know

8B. Bob and Mike decided to rob a bank. Bob drove them to the bank and waited outside in the car. Mike went in, waved a gun and demanded that the cashier hand over money. The cashier pressed the alarm bell. Mike shot her dead and ran out of the bank. He jumped into the car and was driven away by Bob. Bob knew that Mike had a loaded gun with him. Mike was subsequently convicted of the murder of the cashier and robbing the bank.

I would like to ask you about Bob who drove the car but who did not enter the bank. Do you think he should be:

Guilty of murder – just like Mike he participated in the robbery even though he didn't shoot the cashier
Guilty of manslaughter – a less serious offence than murder which carries a lighter sentence
Guilty of robbery but not murder or manslaughter – since he did not shoot the cashier.
Don't know

BIBLIOGRAPHY

Appleton, C (2010) *Life after Life Imprisonment* (Oxford: Oxford University Press)

Appleton, C and Roberts, C (2005) *The Resettlement of Discretionary Life Sentence Offenders.* Home Office Practice Report 44 (London: Home Office)

Ashworth, A (2007) 'Principles, Pragmatism and the Law Commission's Recommendations in Homicide Law Reform' *Criminal Law Review* 333

—— (2009) *Principles of Criminal Law,* 6th edn (Oxford: Oxford University Press)

—— (2010) *Sentencing and Criminal Justice,* 5th edn (Cambridge: Cambridge University Press)

—— (2012) 'Departures from the Sentencing Guidelines' 2 *Criminal Law Review* 81

Ashworth, A and Mitchell, B (eds), (2000) *Rethinking English Homicide Law* (Oxford: Oxford University Press)

Blom-Cooper, L and Morris, T (1996) 'The Penalty for Murder: A myth exploded' *Criminal Law Review* 707

—— (2004) *With Malice Aforethought: A Study of the Crime and Punishment for Homicide* (Oxford: Hart Publishing)

Bohlander, M, (2009a) *Principles of German Criminal Law* (Oxford: Hart Publishing)

—— (2009b) 'The Remains of the Day – Whole Life Sentences after *Bieber*' 73 *Journal of Criminal Law* 30

Bluglass, R (1980) *Psychiatry, the Law and the Offender: present dilemmas and future prospects* (London: Institute for the Study and Treatment of Delinquency)

California Assembly Committee on Criminal Procedure (1975) 'Public Knowledge of Criminal Penalties' in R Henshel and R Silverman (eds), *Perception in Criminology* (Toronto: Methuen)

Chapman, B, Mirrlees-Black, C and Brawn, C (2002), *Improving public attitudes to the Criminal Justice System: The impact of information* (London: Home Office)

Committee on the Penalty for Homicide (1993) *Report* (London: Prison Reform Trust)

Crawley, E and Sparks, R (2006) 'Is there Life after Imprisonment? How elderly men talk about imprisonment and release' 6 *Criminology and Criminal Justice* 63–82.

Creighton, S and Arnott, H (2009) *Prisoners: Law and Practice* (London: LAG Education and Service Trust Ltd)

Criminal Law Revision Committee (1980) *Offences Against the Person* (London: HMSO)

Dawes, W, Harvey, P, McIntosh, B, Nunney, F and Phillips, A (2011), *Attitudes to Guilty Plea Sentence Reductions.* Sentencing Council Research Series, 02/11. (London: Sentencing Council of England and Wales)

De Keijser, J, van Koppen, P, and Ellfers, H (2007), Bridging the gap between judges and the public? 3 *Journal of Experimental Criminology* 131–61

Doble, J (1987) *Crime and Punishment: The Public's View* (New York: the Public Agenda Foundation)

Doob, A and Roberts, JV (1982) *Crime and official response to crime: The view of the Canadian Public* (Ottawa: Department of Justice Canada)

Doob, A and Roberts, JV (1983) *Sentencing: An Analysis of the Public's View* (Ottawa: Department of Justice Canada)

Doob, AN and Roberts, JV (1988) 'Public Punitiveness and Public Knowledge of the Facts: Some Canadian Surveys' in N Walker and M Hough (eds), *Public Attitudes to Sentencing.* Cambridge Studies in Criminology. LIX (Aldershot: Gower)

Doob, AN, Sprott, J, Marinos, V and Varma, K (1998) *An exploration of Ontario residents' views of crime and the criminal justice system* (Toronto: University of Toronto, Center of Criminology)

Dowds, L (1995) *The Long-eyed view of law and order. A Decade of British Social Attitudes Survey Results* (London: Home Office)

Du Bois-Pedain, A (2007)'Intentional Killings: The German Law' in J Horder (ed), *Homicide Law in Comparative Perspective* (Oxford, Hart Publishing) 69

Duff, RA (1990) *Intention, Agency and Criminal Liability* (Oxford: Basil Blackwell)

Ewing, AC (1929) *The Morality of Punishment* (London: K Paul Trench)

Finkel, N and Duff, K (1991) 'Felony murder and community sentiment: testing the Supreme Court's assertions' 15 *Law and Human Behavior* 405–23

Flanagan, T (1995) *Long-Term Imprisonment. Policy, Science and Correctional Practice* (London: Sage)

Fletcher, GP (2000) *Rethinking Criminal Law* (Oxford: Oxford University Press)

Florida Department of Corrections (1997) *What the Public Thinks: Results of a Survey of Floridians* (Miami: Florida Department of Corrections)

Focus Canada (1987) *Attitudes Toward Capital Punishment* (Toronto: Focus Canada)

Gainey, R and Payne, B (2003), 'Changing Attitudes Toward House Arrest with Electronic Monitoring: The Impact of a Single Presentation' 47 *International Journal of offender Therapy and Comparative Criminology* 196–209

Golash, D and Lynch, J (1995) 'Public Opinion, Crime Seriousness, and Sentencing Policy' 22 *American Journal of Criminal Law* 703–32

Green, D (2006) 'Public Opinion versus Public Judgment about Crime: Correcting the Comedy of Errors' 46 *British Journal of Criminology* 131–54

Hancock, R (1963) *Ruth Ellis: The Last Woman to be Hanged* (London: Orion)

Hart, HLA (1968), *Punishment and Responsibility* (Oxford: Oxford University Press)

Holland, WH (2007) 'Murder and Related Issues: An Analysis of the law in Canada' in J Horder (ed), *Homicide Law in Comparative Perspectives* (Oxford: Hart Publishing)

Hollis, C (1964) *The Homicide Act 1957* (London: Victor Gollancz Ltd)

Home Office (2001) *Prison Statistics, England and Wales 2000* (London: HMSO)

HOMRAG (2011) *Public opinion and the penalty for murder: Report of the Homicide Review Advisory Group on the mandatory sentence of life imprisonment for murder* (London: HOMRAG)

Hood, R and Seemungal, F (2011) *Public Opinion on the Mandatory Death Penalty in Trinidad* (London: The Death Penalty Project)

Horder, J (1997) 'Two Histories and Four Hidden Principles of *Mens Rea*' 113 *Law Quarterly Review* 95

—— (ed), (2007) *Homicide Law in Comparative Perspective* (Oxford: Hart Publishing)

Hough, M (1996) 'People Talking about Punishment' 35 *The Howard Journal* 191–214

—— (2010) Unpublished analysis of 2008/09 British Crime Survey. (Details available on request from author)

Hough, M and Park, A (2002) 'How Malleable are Public Attitudes to Crime and Punishment?' in J Roberts and M Hough (eds), *Changing Attitudes to Punishment: Public opinion around the Globe* (Cullompton: Willan Publishing)

Hough, M and Roberts, JV (1998) *Attitudes to punishment: findings from the British Crime Survey*. Home Office Research Study No 179 (London: Home Office)

—— (1999) 'Sentencing Trends in Britain: Public Knowledge and Public Opinion' 1 *Punishment and Society. The International Journal of Penology* 7–22

—— (2004) *Youth Crime and Youth Justice: Public Opinion in England and Wales* (Bristol: Policy Press)

—— (2012) 'Public Opinion, Crime, and Criminal Justice' in R Morgan, M Maguire and R Reiner (eds), *Oxford Handbook of Criminology*, 5th edn (Oxford: Oxford University Press)

Hough, M, Roberts, JV, Jacobson, J, Bredee, A and Moon, N (2008) *Attitudes to the sentencing of offenders convicted of offences involving death by driving* (London: Sentencing Advisory Panel)

House of Lords Select Committee (1989) *Murder and Life Imprisonment*, 3 vols HL Paper 78 (London: HMSO)

ICM Research (2005) *Prison Sentences*. ICM Omnibus. Available from ICM or the authors.

—— (2006) *Crime and Punishment*. Available from ICM or the authors.

Indermaur, D (1987) 'Public Perception of Sentencing in Perth, Western Australia' 20 *Australia and New Zealand Journal of Criminology* 163–83

Inns of Court Conservative and Unionist Society (1956) *Murder: Some Suggestions for the Reform of the Law Relating to Murder in England*

Ipsos MORI (1978) British Public Opinion, June 1978 (London: Ipsos MORI)

—— (2000) *Attitudes to Capital Punishment* (London: Ipsos MORI)

—— (2007) *Attitudes to the Death Penalty* (London: Ipsos MORI)

James, E (2003) *A Life Inside. A Prisoner's Notebook* (London: Atlantic Books)

Jeremy, D (2010) 'Sentencing Policy or Short-term Expediency?' 12 *Criminal Law Review* 593–607

Justice Centre (2007) *Kansas Criminal Justice Public Opinion Survey*. Available at: www.justicecenter.csg.org.

Justice 1 Committee (2002) *Public attitudes towards sentencing and alternatives to imprisonment*. Available at: www.scottish.parliament.uk/official_report/cttee/just1-02/j1ro2-pats-02.htm

Kadish, S (1976) 'Respect for Life and Regard for Rights in the Common Law' 64 *California Law Review* 871

Kennedy, L (1961) *Ten Rillington Place* (London: Victor Gollancz Ltd)

Kury, H, Obergfell-Fuchs, J and Smartt, U (2002) 'The evolution of public attitudes to punishment in Western and Eastern Europe' in JV Roberts and M Hough (eds), (2002) *Changing Attitudes to Punishment* (Cullompton: Willan Publishing)

Law Commission of England and Wales (2004) *Partial Defences to Murder*. Law Commission Report No 290 (London: TSO)

—— (2005) Consultation Paper No 177, A *New Homicide Act for England and Wales? A Consultation Paper* (London: TSO)

—— (2006) Law Com No 304, *Murder, Manslaughter and Infanticide* (London: TSO)

Law Reform Commission of Ireland (2008) *Homicide: Murder and Involuntary Manslaughter* (LRC 87 – 2008)

—— (2011) *Consultation Paper: Mandatory Sentences* (LRC CP66 – 2011)
Law Reform Commission of Victoria (1988) *Homicide* (Melbourne: The Commission)
Leader-Elliott, I (2007) Recklessness and Moral Denunciation in the Australian Law of Murder in J Horder (ed), *Homicide Law in Comparative Perspectives* (Oxford: Hart Publishing)
Lee, Y (2010) 'Repeat Offenders and the Question of Desert' in JV Roberts and A von Hirsch (eds) *Previous Convictions at Sentencing* (Oxford: Hart Publishing)
Leigey, M (2010) 'For the longest time: The adjustment of inmates to a sentence of life without parole' 90 *The Prison Journal* 247–52
Liebling, A and Maruna, S (2005) *The effects of imprisonment* (Collumpton: Willan)
Lord, C, Ross, L and Lepper, M (1979) 'Biased Assimilation and Attitude Polarization: The effects of prior theories on subsequently considered evidence' 37 *Journal of Personality and Social Psychology* 2095–109
Mackay, RD (1995) *Mental Condition Defences in the Criminal Law* (Oxford: Clarendon Press)
Mark, L and Van Den Bergh, T (1990) *Ruth Ellis: A Case of Diminished Responsibility?* (Harmondsworth: Penguin)
Mattinson, J and Mirlees-Black, C (2000) *Attitudes to Crime and Criminal Justice: Findings from the 1998 British Crime Survey* Home Office Research Study No 200 (London: Home Office, Research, Development and Statistics Directorate)
Ministry of Justice (2006) *Serving the Indeterminate Sentence* (London: TSO)
—— (2010) *Offender Management Caseload Statistics 2010* (London: TSO)
—— (2012) *Offender management Caseload Statistics Quarterly Bulletin* (London: TSO)
Mitchell, BJ (1990) *Murder and Penal Policy* (Basingstoke: MacMillan Press)
—— (1998) 'Public Perceptions of Homicide and Criminal Justice' 38(3) *British Journal of Criminology* 453
—— (2000) 'Further Evidence of the Relationship Between Legal and Public Opinion on the law of Homicide' *Crim LR* 814
Mitchell, B (2007) 'Distinguishing between Murder and Manslaughter in Practice' 71(4) *Journal of Criminal Law* 318–41
Mitchell, B (2011) Multiple-victim Murder, Multiple Murders and Schedule 21 to the Criminal Justice Act 2003 75(2) *Journal of Criminal Law* 122
Mitchell, BJ and Mackay RD (2011) 'Investigating Involuntary Manslaughter: An Empirical Study of 127 Cases' 31(1) *Oxford Journal of Legal Studies* 165
Morris, T and Blom-Cooper, L (2011) *Fine Lines and Distinctions: Murder, Manslaughter and the Unlawful Taking of Human Life* (Hook: Waterside Press)
Nuttall, C, Eversley, D, Rudder, I, and Ramsay, J (2003) *Views and Beliefs about Crime and Criminal Justice* (Bridgetown, Barbados: Barbados Statistical Department)
Parmentier, S, Vervaeke, G, Doutrelepont, R, and Kellens, G (eds), (2004) *Popular Perceptions and their implications for policy-making in western countries* (Brussels: Politeia Press)
Parole Board of England and Wales (2012) *Annual Report, 2011* (London: Parole Board of England and Wales.)
Paulin, J, Searle, W and Knaggs, T (2003) *Attitudes to Crime and Punishment: A New Zealand Study* (Wellington: Ministry of Justice)
Public Safety Canada (2000) *Comparative Murder Provisions.* Unpublished manuscript. Ottawa: Public Safety Canada
Redondo, S, Luque, E and Funes, J (1996) 'Social Beliefs about Recidivism in Crime' in G Davies, S Lloyd-Bostock, M McMurran and C Wilson (eds), *Psychology, Law, and*

Criminal Justice. International Developments in Research and Practice (New York: Walter de Gruyter)

Roberts, JV (1988) *Public Opinion and Sentencing: Surveys by the Canadian Sentencing Commission.* Research Reports of the Canadian Sentencing Commission. (Ottawa: Department of Justice Canada)

—— (2001) *Public Evaluations of Criminal Justice Professionals: The Effects of Information on Attitudes.* Manuscript available from author at: Julian.roberts@crim.ox.ac.uk

—— (2002) 'Determining parole eligibility dates for life prisoners: lessons from jury hearings in Canada' 4 *Punishment and Society: The International Journal of Penology* 103–14

—— (2003) 'Public Opinion and Mandatory Sentences of Imprisonment: A Review of International Findings' 20 *Criminal Justice and Behavior* 1–26

—— (2008) *Punishing Persistent Offenders. Community and Offender Perspectives on the Recidivist Sentencing Premium* (Oxford: Oxford University Press)

—— (2009) '"Faint Hope" in the Firing Line: Repeal of S. 745.6?' 51 *Canadian Journal of Criminology and Criminal Justice* 537–46

—— (2011) 'Community Views of Sentencing: Intuitive and Principled Responses to Offending' in M Tonry (ed), *Punishment Futures. Studies in Penal Theory and Philosophy* (Oxford: Oxford University Press)

Roberts, JV and Baker, E (2007) 'Sentencing in Common Law Jurisdictions in S Shoham, O Beck, and M Kett (eds), *International Handbook of Penology and Criminal Justice* (New York: Routledge)

Roberts, JV and Cole, D (1999) 'Sentencing and Parole arrangements for cases of Murder' in *Making Sense of Sentencing* (Toronto: University of Toronto Press)

Roberts, JV, Crutcher, N, and Verbrugge, P (2007) 'Public Attitudes to Sentencing in Canada: Exploring Recent Findings' 49 *Canadian Journal of Criminology and Criminal Justice* 75–107

Roberts, JV and Doob, AN (1990) 'News Media Influences on Public Views of Sentencing' 14 *Law and Human Behavior* 451–68

Roberts, JV, Feilzer, M and Hough, M (2011) 'Measuring Public Attitudes to Criminal Justice' in D Gadd, S Karstedt and S Messner (eds), *Handbook of Criminological Research Methods* (London: Sage Publications)

Roberts, JV and Gebotys, R (1989) 'The Purposes of Sentencing: Public Support for Competing Aims' 7 *Behavioral Sciences and the Law* 387–402

Roberts, JV and Hough, M (eds), (2002) *Changing Attitudes to Punishment* (Cullompton: Willan Publishing)

—— (2005a) *Understanding Public Attitudes to Criminal Justice* (Maidenhead: Open University Press)

—— (2005b) 'Sentencing Young Offenders: Public Opinion in England and Wales' 5 *Criminal Justice* 211–32

Roberts, JV, Hough, M, Jacobson, J, Bredee, A and Moon, N (2008) 'Public attitudes to sentencing offenders convicted of offences involving death by driving' *Criminal Law Review* 525–40

Roberts, JV, Hough, M, Jacobson, J, and Moon, N (2009) 'Public Attitudes to Sentencing Purposes and Sentencing Factors: An Empirical Analysis' *Criminal Law Review* 771–82

Roberts, JV, Nuffield, J, and Hann, R (2000) 'Parole and the Public: Attitudinal and Behavioural Responses' 1 *Empirical and Applied Criminal Justice Research* 1–29

Roberts, JV and Rafferty, A (2011) 'Sentencing Guidelines in England and Wales: Exploring the New Format' 9 *Crim LR* 680

Roberts, JV and Stalans, L (2000) *Public Opinion, Crime, and Criminal Justice* (Boulder: Westview Press)

Roberts, JV, Stalans, LS, Indermaur, D, and Hough, M (2003) *Penal Populism and Public Opinion. Lessons from Five Countries* (Oxford: Oxford University Press)

Roberts JV and Tufts, J (2002) 'Sentencing Juvenile Offenders: Public Preferences and Judicial Practice' 13 *Criminal Justice Policy Review* 46–64

Roberts, JV and von Hirsch, A (eds), (2010) *The Role of Previous Convictions at at Sentencing: Theoretical and Applied Perspectives.* Studies in Penal Theory and Ethics (Oxford: Hart Publishing)

Roberts, JV and White, N (1986) 'Public Estimates of Recidivism Rates: Consequences of a criminal stereotype' 28 *Canadian Journal of Criminology* 229, 241

Roberts, L and Indermaur, D (2009) *What Australians think about crime and justice* (Canberra: Australian Institute of Criminology)

Robinson, P (2007) *How Psychology is Changing the Punishment Theory Debate.* Public Law and Legal Theory Research Paper Series (Philadelphia: University of Pennsylvania Law School)

—— (2008) *Distributive Principles of Criminal Law* (Oxford: Oxford University Press).

—— (2009) 'Empirical Desert' in P Robinson, S Garvey and K Ferzan (eds), *Criminal Law Conversations* (Oxford: Oxford University Press)

Rock, P (1998) *After Homicide: Practical and Political Responses to Bereavement* (Oxford: Clarendon Press)

Roy Morgan Research (2010) *Australians Say penalty for murder should be Imprisonment rather than the death penalty.* Finding Number 4411. Available at: www.roymorgan.com/news/polls/2009/4411/index.cfm?printversion=yes

Royal College of Physicians Working Group (1995) 'Criteria for the Diagnosis of Brain Stem Death' 29 *Journal of the Royal College of Physicians* 381

Royal Commission on Capital Punishment 1949–1953, (1953) *Report*, Cmnd 8932 (London: HMSO)

Ryberg, J (2011) 'Punishment and Public Opinion' in J Ryberg and A Corlett (eds), *Punishment and Ethics: New Perspective* (London: Palgrave Macmillan)

Ryberg, J and Peterson, T (2012) 'Punishment, Criminal Record, and the Recidivist Premium' in C Tamburrini and J Ryberg (eds), *Recidivist Punishments. The Philosopher's View* (New York: Lexington Books)

Salisbury, H (2004) *Public attitudes to the criminal justice system: the impact of providing information to the British Crime Survey respondents.* Home Office Online Report 64/ 04.

Sanders, A (2001) *Community Justice. Modernising the Magistracy in England and Wales* (London: IPPR)

Sanders, T and Roberts, JV (2000) 'Public Attitudes toward Conditional Sentencing: Results of a National Survey' 32 *Canadian Journal of Behavioural Science* 199–207

Sapsford, R (1983) *Life Sentence Prisoners. Reaction, Response, and Change,* (Milton Keynes: Open University Press)

Sauve, R (2012) 'Release from Prison: Rick Sauve's Story' in JV Roberts and M Grossman (eds), *Criminal Justice in Canada. A Reader*, 4th edn (Toronto: Thomson Nelson)

Schonteich, M (1999) *Sentencing in South Africa. Public Perception and Judicial Practice.* Occasional Paper No 43 Institute for Security Studies

Sentencing Guidelines Council (2004) *Overarching Principles. Seriousness: Definitive Guideline* (London: Sentencing Guidelines Council)

—— (2007) *Reduction for a Guilty Plea. Definitive Guideline* (London: Sentencing Guidelines Council)

Singer, L and Cooper, S (2008) *Inform, persuade and remind. An evaluation of a project to improve public confidence in the criminal justice system.* London: Ministry of Justice.

Simpson, K (1978) *Forty Years of Murder: An Autobiography* (London: Harrap)

Smith, K (ed), Osborne, S, Lau, I and Britton, A (2012) *Homicides, Firearms Offences and Intimate Violence 2010/11: Supplementary Volume 2 to Crime in England and Wales 2010/11* 02/12, January 2012 (London: TSO)

Sourcebook of Criminal Justice Statistics (2011). Available at: www.albany.edu/sourcebook/.

Stalans, L (2002) 'Measuring Attitudes to Sentencing' in JV Roberts and M Hough (eds), (2002) *Changing Attitudes to Punishment* (Cullompton: Willan Publishing)

St Amand, M and Zamble, E (2001) 'Impact of Information About Sentencing Decisions on Public Attitudes to the Criminal Justice System' 25 *Law and Human Behavior* 515–28

Sykes (1958) *The Society of Captives. A study of a maximum security prison* (Princeton: Princeton University Press)

Tufts, J and Roberts, JV (2002) 'Sentencing Juvenile Offenders: Public Preferences and Judicial Practice' 13 *Criminal Justice Policy Review* 46–64

Tyler, T (2006) *Why People Obey the Law* (Princeton: Princeton University Press)

US Bureau of Justice Statistics (2011) *Criminal Victimization 2010* (Washington, US Bureau of Justice Statistics)

Vandiver, M and Giacopassi, D (1997) 'One Million and Counting: Students' Estimates of the Annual Number of Homicides in the U.S.' 8 *Journal of Criminal Justice Education* 135–43

Viki and Bohner (2009) 'Achieving accurate assessement of attitudes toward the criminal justice system: methodological issues' in J Wood and T Gannon (eds), *Public Opinion and Criminal Justice* (Cullompton: Willan)

von Hirsch, A (1976) *Doing Justice. The Choice of Punishments* (Boston: Northeastern University Press)

—— (1993) *Censure and Sanctions* (Oxford: Clarendon Press)

—— (2010) 'Proportionality and the Progressive Loss of Mitigation: Some Further Reflections' in JV Roberts and A von Hirsch (eds), *Previous Convictions at Sentencing* (Oxford: Hart Publications)

von Hirsch, A and Ashworth, A (2005) *Proportionate Sentencing* (Oxford: Oxford University Press)

von Hirsch, A and Jareborg, N (1991) 'Gauging criminal harm: A Living Standard Analysis' 11 *Oxford Journal of Legal Studies* 1–38

Walker, N (1995) 'The Unintended Consequences of Life Imprisonment' in T Flanagan (ed), *Long-Term Imprisonment. Policy, Science and Correctional Practice* (London: Sage)

Walker, J, Hough, M and Lewis, H (1988) 'How the Public sees sentencing: an Australian survey' in N Walker and M Hough (eds), *Public Attitudes to Sentencing.* LIX Cambridge Studies in Criminology (Aldershot: Gower)

Weatherburn, D and Indermaur, D (2004) *Public Perceptions of Crime Trends in New South Wales* (Sydney, NSW: New South Wales Bureau of Crime Statistics)

Williams, K, Gibbs, J and Erickson, M (1980) 'Public Knowledge of Statutory Penalties: The Extent and Basis of Accurate Perceptions' 23 *Pacific Sociological Review* 105–28

Wilson, W (2000) 'Murder and the Structure of Homicide' in A Ashworth and B Mitchell (eds), *Rethinking English Homicide Law* (Oxford: Oxford University Press)
Wilson, W (2006) 'The Structure of Criminal Homicide' *Criminal Law Review* 471
—— (2007) 'What's wrong with murder?' 1 *Criminal Law and Philosophy* 157
Windlesham, Lord (1993) *Responses to Crime; Volume 2: Penal Policy in the Making* (Oxford: Oxford University Press)
Yallop, D (1990) *To Encourage the Others* (London: Corgi)
Yeo, S (1987) 'Sentencing Murderers: A New South Wales Innovation' *Criminal Law Review* 23
—— (1997) *Fault in Homicide* (Sydney: Federation Press)
Zhang, T and Ha, L (2010) *An Analysis of the Faint Hope Clause* (Ottawa: Department of Justice Canada)

INDEX